An Introduction to Torrance Theology

An Introduction to Torrance Theology

Discovering the Incarnate Saviour

Edited by

GERRIT SCOTT DAWSON

t&t clark

Published by T&T Clark
A Continuum imprint
The Tower Building, 11 York Road, London SE1 7NX
80 Maiden Lane, Suite 704, New York, NY 10038

www.continuumbooks.com

All rights reserved. No part of this publication may be reproduced or transmitted in any form or by any means, electronic or mechanical, including photocopying, recording or any information storage or retrieval system, without permission in writing from the publishers.

Copyright © Gerrit Scott Dawson and contributors, 2007

Gerrit Scott Dawson and contributors have asserted their right under the Copyright, Designs and Patents Act, 1988, to be identified as the Authors of this work.

First published 2007

British Library Cataloguing-in-Publication Data
A catalogue record for this book is available from the British Library

ISBN-10: HB: 0-567-03180-2
PB: 0-567-03181-0
ISBN-13: HB: 978-0-567-03180-8
PB: 978-0-567-03181-5

Typeset by Kenneth Burnley, Wirral, Cheshire
Printed and bound in Great Britain by Cromwell Press Ltd, Trowbridge, Wilts

CONTENTS

	Editor's Preface	vii
	Permissions	ix
	Introduction: Discovering the Incarnate Saviour of the World *David W. Torrance*	1
1	Who *is* the Incarnate Saviour of the World? *Andrew Purves*	23
2	The Incarnate Saviour: T. F. Torrance on the Atonement *Elmer M. Colyer*	33
3	Far as the Curse is Found: The Significance of Christ's Assuming a *Fallen* Human Nature in the Torrance Theology *Gerrit Scott Dawson*	55
4	The Realist Epistemology of Thomas F. Torrance *Douglas F. Kelly*	75
5	The Bible as Testimony to our Belonging: The Theological Vision of James B. Torrance *Alan J. Torrance*	103
6	Calvin and the Café Church: Reflections at the Interface Between Reformed Theology and Current Trends in Worship *Graham Redding*	121
7	The Christian Life and Our Participation in Christ's Continuing Ministry *Gary W. Deddo*	135
8	The Hermeneutical Nightmare and the Reconciling Work of Jesus Christ *C. Baxter Kruger*	157
	About the Authors	175
	Index	177

With our Heartfelt Gratitude to the Triune God of Grace

For Tom, James, David and their Families

EDITOR'S PREFACE

For three remarkable days, 16–18 March 2006, we gathered to focus upon the person of Jesus Christ. We each looked through the theological lens of the work of Thomas, James and David Torrance. The conference was called 'Discovering the Incarnate Saviour: The Theological Vision of the Torrance Tradition'. It was the largest-ever gathering of scholars specifically speaking about the theological distinctives of the Torrance brothers. More than 200 participants – pastors, academic theologians and lay people of all ages – joined us at the First Presbyterian Church of Baton Rouge, Louisiana. Given our subject, it is not surprising that the weekend of theological presentations was wrapped in song, prayer, discussion and the celebration of the Lord's Supper.

As we collected the papers presented at the symposium, we realized that we actually had an engaging, interactive introduction to the Christology advanced by the Torrances. Not every one of us would agree with every point the others have made. We each come from various places along the span of Reformed Theology, and have particular, sometimes conflicting, emphases in our theology. Yet there is a wonderful resonance between these essays. Each writer is passionate about Christ. Each rejoices in the way the work of the Torrances directs us to centre on the God who came to us as the man Jesus in order to save us as we are united to him by the Holy Spirit. As you read, you will see the Torrances' key theological emphases develop as the essays enhance, nuance and interrelate with each other.

I am grateful that David Torrance agreed to write an introduction which sets up the whole collection. We were also able to add two more essays from Torrance scholars who did not attend the symposium. Together, we have a book that is welcoming and accessible for those just testing the Torrance theological waters, yet intellectually rigorous enough for serious engagement by fellow scholars.

I am also grateful to the session and staff of the First Presbyterian Church of Baton Rouge for the vision, generosity, hospitality and hard work required for such a conference. In particular, we recognize Tee Gatewood and Donna Munson for their organizing, Jaci Gaspard for assistance in manuscript preparation and the Don Phillips Fund for additional support. The contributors are also very pleased that T&T Clark, the premier publisher of T. F. Torrance's major work, has agreed to produce this edition.

As students of the Torrances, we often make reference to a 'Torrance Theology'. Of course the Torrances themselves, as David notes in his introduction, declare they are merely pointing to Jesus Christ as faithfully as possible. That, we realize, is why we love them so.

PERMISSIONS

All Scripture quotations are, unless noted, from *The Holy Bible, English Standard Version* (Wheaton, IL: Crossway Bibles, 2000).

Excerpts from Thomas F. Torrance, *The School of Faith, Theology in Reconstruction, Theological Science* and *The Ground and Grammar of Theology* are reprinted by the kind permission of Wipf and Stock Publishers, Eugene, Oregon.

INTRODUCTION: DISCOVERING THE INCARNATE SAVIOUR OF THE WORLD

David W. Torrance

It is a privilege to be invited to write an introduction to a book on the important subject of 'Discovering the Incarnate Saviour of the World'. The Torrance family is grateful to the First Presbyterian Church of Baton Rouge for organizing the symposium and assembling so many scholars and participants to engage this topic. By introducing their essays, I hope to illuminate the theological themes that are both central to the Christian faith and dear to my heart. Though we are deeply honoured by the consideration given to our work, we would wish to resist any suggestion of a 'Torrancian theology'! Just like Karl Barth when people mentioned 'Barthian theology', my brothers Tom and James would wish to say, 'We have given our understanding of the Word of God. We encourage members of the Church to read the Bible and discover for themselves what God is saying and discover whether what we have said helps towards a deeper understanding of the gospel once committed to the saints and treasured by the evangelical church through the centuries.' In the Acts of the Apostles, we read that 'The Bereans were of more noble character than the Thessalonians, for they received the message with great eagerness and examined the Scriptures every day to see if what Paul said was true' (Acts 17:11). We would hope that the same would be true of those who read and study anything that Tom and James or myself have written or said.

MINISTRY AND FAMILY BACKGROUND

After some years in parish ministry, both Tom and James entered the academic world while I continued in parish ministry. For both of them, as for me, true biblical theology is not just a matter of academic study and research. It is not just something to be grasped by the mind. It involves the whole of life and must be lived out in practical Christian living and service, worship and prayer within the Church. Throughout their teaching careers both had a continuing and deep concern for the spiritual welfare of the Church and each exercised in their own way a pastoral ministry. Both saw their ministry as pastors and teachers within the worldwide Church, and before and after my own entering the ministry I enjoyed and profited from many theological conversations and discussions with them. With our shared love for God's Word and varied experiences of Christ, we learned from each other, although both advanced far ahead of me in their theological research and understanding.

Our love for the Scriptures and our theological education in fact started from a very early age with our parents' teaching, and my brothers and sisters (of whom three have already passed over to be with the Lord) and myself have always been grateful to God to have been born into a Christian family. Our parents had a steadfast faith in God, a love for the Word of God and a firm belief in the power of prayer. Every day we met for family worship which was led by one or other of our parents. This continued from our earliest years of infancy until one by one we left home. It has continued since on occasions when we have met together. As children, our parents expounded to us the Scriptures. They inspired us with a love for the Lord and a love for God's Word. From our earliest years they encouraged us to read the Bible every day for ourselves and to read it through each year, which we have continued to do. They were concerned that each of us should hear for ourselves God speaking through Scripture. They encouraged us always before reading from the Bible to pray and ask God to speak to us and make himself known. Mother often said when we were still quite young, 'When you grow up you will meet people who will criticize or deny what is said in the Bible. When you hear God speaking then you will know that the Bible is God's Word and will never doubt it.' They encouraged us to memorize fairly large portions of Scripture, particularly the Psalms, which we have always appreciated. None of us, however, ever managed to emulate our father who, until the end of his life, could repeat from memory the entire book of Psalms along with the Epistle to the Romans! Our parents also guided us in our Christian reading, introduced us to various commentaries like Luther's *Galatians*, and encouraged us to read such books as Robert Bruce on the Sacraments,[1] which was a favourite of our mother, and Luther's *Bondage of the Will*. While still at high school we were introduced to Calvin's *Institutes*.

I thus owe to my parents, and to both brothers, a deep spiritual and theological debt. As brothers, sharing the same parents, growing up in

---

1 Robert Bruce, 'The Mystery of the Lord's Supper' (1589), in *The Mystery of the Lord's Supper: Sermons on the Sacrament Preached in the Kirk of Edinburgh in A.D. 1589 by Robert Bruce*, ed. and trans. Thomas F. Torrance (London: James Clarke, 1958). See also Bruce's 'Sixth Sermon on Isaiah 38', published in 1591.

the same family and having shared together so much, it is perhaps not surprising that we have the same basic theology, and though we each have our own favourite ways of expressing things we have never differed theologically.

THE CENTRALITY OF CHRIST

Karl Barth would sometimes say to his students, 'I know no God but the man Christ Jesus.' In this, Barth was affirming the importance of the incarnation and the centrality of the man Jesus Christ, in all our Christian and theological understanding. Only in Christ do we encounter God and come to know him (Jn 14:6; see also Acts 4:12). Barth rejected all the many theologies where Christ was not the pivotal figure and source of all our understanding of God. True theology begins with the incarnation. Equally, he was affirming with Paul (Col. 1:19) that all the fullness of God was present in the man Jesus Christ, the incarnate saviour of the world. Jesus was and is fully God and fully man although one person. It is in and through the man Jesus, and through the Holy Spirit who is himself God, coequal with the Father and the Son, that God forgives, reconciles and unites us to himself. In this, Barth was affirming the message not only of the New Testament but of all Scripture. As John Calvin used to say, Christ is the scope (*scopus*) or goal of the Bible. All Scripture is fulfilled in him. He is the content of the biblical witness.

THE SYMPOSIUM

The contributors to this symposium are well-known biblical scholars, theologians, ministers and authors. Each agrees with Barth and with Calvin on the importance of the incarnation and of the central place that the incarnate saviour of the world occupies in the gospel message and on the importance of union with Christ. In their respective, illuminating, thought-provoking essays, each draws out the implications of this for theology and for our living the Christian life. In what they write there is not only a natural overlap but also a wonderful spiritual and theological harmony. I have allowed introducing their papers to be the springboard for adding my own reflection on the important theological themes each raises.

ANDREW PURVES: 'WHO *IS* THE INCARNATE SAVIOUR OF THE WORLD?'

Purves examines the all-important question, 'Who is Jesus Christ?' and its priority in the matter of salvation over the 'How' question. In Christ, we are confronted with the stupendous, breathtaking fact that God the creator of all things has himself entered into his creation and become a creature. He became a man, fully human, bone of our bone, flesh of our flesh, while at the same time remaining God. Jesus Christ is at once man and at the same time God. In Jesus God became a particular man and at the same time he became a representative man who represents all humankind and all creation. In Jesus God united himself to all humankind and to all creation, so that we and the world are forever bound together in the same bundle of life with God in Christ.

The incarnate saviour entered into our weak, fallen, sinful humanity. He penetrated to its very heart in its alienation and rebellion against God in order to redeem humanity and all creation. As man he became completely one with us. He altogether identified himself with us in our sinfulness, although he himself remained holy and without sin (2 Cor. 5:21). He identified himself with us, although remaining himself, both God and man. In and through his own person, by what he was and did in our place, vicariously, he made atonement for us and reconciled us to God, so that we may for ever live in fellowship and communion with the Triune God of love in a renewed creation. From the incarnation to his ascension Christ lived and continues to live for us a vicarious life. Such was and is his incredible, all-embracing love for the world, and in that love all are redeemed in Christ.

This does not mean that all will forever enjoy his salvation. Our salvation is entirely of God. He took the initiative. He did it all. We contribute nothing towards our salvation. All we can do is to thank him and enjoy his salvation. Despite all that in his love he has done in Christ, however, we are still confronted with the mystery of sin. God gives us freedom to accept or reject his love and salvation in Christ. If we do reject Christ, we cut ourselves off from our redemption in him, denying the Lord who bought us (2 Pet. 2:1), and do not share in the joy of his salvation.[2]

---

[2] For further reading on this issue, Thomas F. Torrance, 'The Atonement: The Singularity of Christ and the Finality of the Cross – The Atonement and the Moral Order', in *Universalism and the Doctrine of Hell*, ed. Nigel M. de S. Cameron (Carlisle: Paternoster Press and Grand Rapids: Baker Book House, 1991). Also see Thomas F. Torrance, *Preaching Christ Today* (Edinburgh: The Handsel Press, 1993), 20–3; Thomas F. Torrance, 'Preaching Christ Today', in Thomas F. Torrance, James B. Torrance and David Torrance, *A Passion for Christ: The Vision That Ignites Ministry*, ed. Gerrit Dawson and Jock Stein (Edinburgh: The Handsel Press, and Lenoir, NC: PLC Publications, 1999), 31; and Thomas F. Torrance, *The Apocalypse Today* (Grand Rapids: Wm. B. Eerdmans Publishing Company), 1959, 101–9. Both Tom and James have frequently been criticized by evangelicals with the mistaken belief that because they believe in the all-embracing love of God and his offer of love and salvation to all people, they believe in universal salvation. This is emphatically not the case. Both have made their position clear in their lectures, preaching and writing.

The vicarious humanity of Christ. Both Tom and James emphasized 'the vicarious humanity of Christ', a phrase used to sum up the Pauline teaching that when Christ died we died, when he rose we rose, and when he ascended to heaven we ascended in him. So we read in 2 Cor. 5:14, 'one has died for all, therefore all have died,' and in Eph. 2:4–6, 'God . . . made us alive together with Christ . . . and raised us up with him.' Christ so identified himself with us that he took our humanity on himself. He took our sin on himself and died in our place, but in our place he also offered up to God the perfect human life that we could not offer. Thus his humanity became our new humanity, and in union with him his human faith and righteousness becomes our faith and righteousness. What is important here is that the whole life of Christ, from birth to ascension, was a life which Christ offered up to God in our place and on our behalf, so that his birth from above was our new birth, his life of righteousness our righteousness, his death our death, and his ascension our ascension. Through the Spirit we are united to Christ so that we may begin to participate in all that he has done for us and live out of his righteousness and his risen humanity.[3]

Emphasis upon the vicarious humanity of Christ and the fact that we are saved through his life as well as his death, has troubled many evangelicals. They mistakenly believe that speaking of Christ's vicarious humanity detracts from what took place on the cross. The very reverse is the case. By speaking of Jesus's vicarious humanity we are actually magnifying what Christ did in reconciling us to God. Christ's birth, life, death, resurrection and ascension belong intimately and inextricably together in the unity of his person and work. Christ's reconciling and atoning work began at Bethlehem in his becoming man for us, continued throughout his life and was brought to its great climax on the cross and in his resurrection and ascension.

Elmer M. Colyer: 'The Incarnate Saviour: T. F. Torrance on the Atonement'

Christ's atoning reconciliation was worked out in his own person. As Colyer and others rightly stress, 'None of what the incarnate saviour accomplished for us in atoning reconciliation, including the cross, takes place *outside* of Christ as something external to who he *is*, external to the incarnate reality of Christ's person as mediator and saviour of the world.'

Christ worked out his atoning reconciliation in his own person and through what he did and said from his incarnation right through to his death on the cross, his resurrection and ascension. We cannot separate

---

3 See Thomas F. Torrance, *The School of Faith* (London: James Clarke & Co., 1959), lxxx–lxxxii.

what he said and did from the person of Christ. We are healed and redeemed in and through our union with Christ.

If we fail to recognize the all-embracing nature of the vicarious humanity of Christ and fail to stress union with Christ, as so many do, we are in danger of separating the death of Christ from the ministry of Christ. We will almost inevitably interpret the atoning death of Christ solely in a juridical way. We will regard the event of Christ's atoning sacrifice as God's remedy for our sin – but a remedy that is external to the person of Christ.

As both my brothers Tom and James used to say, God does not act like a human physician, who comes, diagnoses our illness or disease, gives us a prescription and goes away, leaving us on our own to follow his advice and take what he has prescribed. God does not act like that! The atonement is not God's prescription which we are given and asked to accept, even with God's help, in order that we might be saved and inherit the kingdom. God having acted in Christ does not throw us back on ourselves, making our salvation to some extent dependent on ourselves. Christ has worked out his salvation for us in his own vicarious person, in the depths of our humanity. From first to last, salvation is an act of God through grace – although, as we said above, he gives us the freedom to accept or reject his salvation.

The blessings of Christ are not separate from the person of Christ. Again, by failing to recognize the vicarious humanity of Christ, we will inevitably become more interested in the blessings of the gospel than in Christ himself. Quite subtly we will separate the blessings of Christ from Christ, the work of Christ from his person. We can even regard 'the incarnation as just one optional way among others of accounting for the experience of salvation'.[4] This is true of theologians like Rudolph Bultmann, and it is true of many liberal theologians, but I believe that it is also true of evangelicals who reject the vicarious humanity of Christ and seek to interpret Christ's atonement as an event apart from union with Christ. For they are regarding the event of Christ's atoning sacrifice simply as God's remedy for our sin, and a remedy that is external to the person of Christ.

Christ's atoning sacrifice must not be understood in a purely juridical way.[5] As Colyer says, if we understand Christ's atoning sacrifice outside of the person of Christ and regard it in a purely juridical way, we are failing adequately to understand Christ's deliverance of us from the power of sin in our inner being. As Colyer further says, 'this juridical theory of the

---

4 See James B. Torrance, '*Christ in our Place*', in *A Passion for Christ*, 41.
5 i.e., in purely legal or judicial categories, as though Christ's death on the cross was to be interpreted purely in terms of Christ's suffering the penalty prescribed by the law of God.

atonement frees us from the penalty for sin, but the actual root of our alienation and sin in the ontological depths of our corrupt and fallen humanity is left untouched by Christ's atoning sacrifice'. We are delivered from the *guilt* of sin but not from the *power* of sin. Christ, however, came to deliver us both from the guilt of sin and from the power of sin in its lodgement in the human soul. He came to take away our old sinful nature, in order to give us a new nature, his own new life of righteousness.

We only receive the fruits of the cross and all the blessings of the gospel as we are inextricably united to the actual person of Jesus Christ. In redeeming us, as Calvin has said, God in Christ transacted a wondrous exchange. In taking away our old sinful rebellious life he gives us in exchange his own human life of righteous obedience to the Father and restores us to fellowship with God. In Christ we are made to rise and to ascend. As we are clothed with Christ's new life of righteousness, which becomes ours by grace through the Holy Spirit, we are in Christ welcomed into the presence of the Father. In Christ the Father treats us as if we were and are his only beloved Son. He says, 'Come inherit the kingdom prepared for you.' Only a son inherits. In Christ God treats us as he treats his only Son and, incredibly, we are embraced within the fellowship and love of the Triune God.

Union with Christ. The importance of our union with Christ in his life, death, resurrection and ascension is enshrined in the New Testament phrase 'in Christ'. According to Professor William Barclay, 'in Paul's letters the phrase "in Christ Jesus" occurs 48 times, "in Christ" occurs 34 times and "in the Lord" 50 times. That is to say the words "in Christ" and their equivalent occur 134 times.'[6] Clearly, for Paul union with Christ belongs to the heart of the gospel. Moreover, the word 'grace' occurs some 132 times and over 90 times in his writings. Hence, my brother Tom would sometimes say to a class of his students, 'You can sum up the theology of St Paul in the two sentences, "Union with Christ" and "Salvation by Grace".' It is never simply 'Salvation by Grace'. It is 'Salvation by Grace' and 'Union with Christ'. It is always the two together. He would also say that these two sentences could equally sum up Calvin's theology as expressed in his *Institutes*. These two words, 'in Christ', focus our attention on the actual person of Christ and reveal the important emphasis in the New Testament of Christ's union with us for the accomplishment of our salvation.

We are saved by Christ's faith and obedience to the Father, not ours. My brother Tom often quoted Gal. 2:20, a verse which our mother loved:

---

6 William Barclay, *The Daily Study Bible: The Letter to Philippians, Colossians, Thessalonians* (Edinburgh: Saint Andrew Press, 1959), 14.

'I am crucified with Christ: nevertheless I live; yet not I, but Christ liveth in me: and the life which I now live in the flesh I live *by the faith of the Son of God*, who loved me, and gave himself for me.' Such is the wording of the Authorized Version (AV), which I believe is a correct translation of the Greek, which reads '*en pistei zo te tou viou tou theou*' ('by the faith *of* the Son of God'). Other translators, like those of the New International Version (NIV) apparently because they found it so difficult to believe that we can live by Christ's faith rather than our faith, have altered the text to make it read, 'I live by faith in the Son of God'! – something altogether different.[7] That translation takes away from the vicarious nature of Christ's life of faith. It is by *his faith* (not ours) that we are saved and live! Our faith is a thankful response to his faith. When we look back along our lives and ponder how disobedient we at times have been and continue to be, it is marvellously comforting to know that Christ gives us his life of obedience to the Father and that it is Christ's obedience which counts. We are saved by his obedience not ours.

GERRIT SCOTT DAWSON: 'FAR AS THE CURSE IS FOUND: THE SIGNIFICANCE OF CHRIST'S ASSUMING A *FALLEN* HUMAN NATURE IN THE TORRANCE THEOLOGY'

In becoming man and entering our sinful humanity, Christ remained, as man and God, holy and without sin. Being holy he did not as man live a special and unique life distinct and separate from the rest of humanity. He entered into our sinful, rebellious, warped, estranged humanity. He altogether identified himself with it. He became one with it, taking on himself all the sin of the world. As Paul said, God 'for our sake, made him to be sin who knew no sin, so that in him we might become the righteousness of God' (2 Cor. 5:21).

Christ had the power not to sin: his struggle against temptation was real. Being holy does not mean, as so many have said through the years, that Christ as man was not able to sin. Rather, he had the power not to sin. Jesus's struggle on our behalf against temptation and sin, from the temptation in the wilderness, through Peter's attempt to dissuade him from taking

---

7 In Mk 11:22, Jesus said, '*echete pistin theou*', which the AV this time translates 'Have faith in God'. Yet the Greek says, 'Have the faith *of* God'. In Rev. 2:13, the Greek reads, *kai ouk erneso ten pistin mou*, 'you did not deny *my faith*'. The AV translates it, 'hadst not denied *my faith*'. The NIV translates it, 'You did not renounce your faith in me.' In Rev. 14:12, we have the words, '*ten pistin Jesou*', which the AV translates, '*the faith of Jesus*', and the NIV translates, 'faithful to Jesus'. These passages indicate the difficulty which translators have found over the reality of the vicarious humanity of Christ. In each case I believe that we should accept the original text as expressed in Greek and not seek to alter it according to our theological misconceptions!

the way of the cross, to Gethsemane, was in every sense a real struggle. On our behalf he battled against sin and temptation, against the sins and temptations which confront us, and for us he overcame them, giving us in his own person the victory. Such was both his power and his love that he so freely lavishes upon us (Heb. 2:18)!

Christ's atoning sacrifice commenced with his incarnation and extended to the cross and to his resurrection and ascension. Throughout his ministry on earth, his holy presence increasingly challenged and provoked sin, bringing it to light. Such was his love and determination to save, he did not draw back when his loving presence and invitation to save provoked sin to ever greater violence, and because of their sin aroused in people ever greater fury and hatred towards him. Because of his love and determination to save he lovingly and increasingly, throughout the course of his earthly ministry, pressed home his invitation of love and progressively entered ever more deeply into the heart of our sinful humanity. As sin was increasingly aroused and exposed so increasingly he took it upon himself, until he was fully clothed with the sin of the world, and became, in the language of St Paul, 'sin for us', although he himself remained without sin (2 Cor. 5:21). Fully clothed and identified with the sin of the world, he took on himself his own divine condemnation of sin and died. In his cry of dereliction on the cross, 'My God, my God, why have you forsaken me?' (Mt 27:46), we see the horror of sin as utter separation from God. We are given a glimpse of hell. But at the point of furthest separation from God, we are reconciled to God. Jesus said, 'Father, into your hands I commit my spirit' (Lk. 23:46).

Atonement and reconciliation wrought out in our humanity and in Christ's person. By identifying himself with humanity and with us in our sin he wrought out from within our humanity, in his own person, atonement and reconciliation between humanity and God. He did not do it, as we have said already, externally to himself or externally to humanity, which would never have accomplished what he desired. As the writer of the Epistle to the Hebrews says, 'Therefore he had to be made like his brothers in every respect, so that he might become a merciful high priest in service to God, to make propitiation for the sins of the people' (Heb. 2:17). Such was his amazing love! As our high priest he made atonement and reconciled us to God internally in himself and internally in our humanity.

Christ arose in the body. In his resurrection, he rose in the body as man, still united to and identified with humanity so that humanity is made to rise with him. Because he died so all died (2 Cor. 5:14) and because he rose so all are resurrected in him. Here, as we said above, comes the mystery of sin! Those who reject Christ and 'have done evil will rise to be condemned'. But those who welcome Christ and 'have done good will rise to live' (Jn 5:29, NIV). In rising to life, the righteous in Christ are made to ascend in Christ to the throne of the Father and are made to sit and reign with him in heavenly places, sharing in the intimate fellowship, joy and love of the Triune God.

Christ ascended in the body. As my brother Tom remarks, 'John Knox laid unusually strong emphasis on the ascension of Jesus Christ in the selfsame body which was born of the virgin Mary, and was crucified, dead and buried and which rose again, and very rightly. It is one of the most neglected doctrines of the faith.'[8] Without the ascension our salvation would not be complete. By his ascension in the body Jesus carried us up in newness of life through the Holy Spirit to the presence of the Father and 'seated us with him in the heavenly places in Christ Jesus, so that in the coming ages he might show the immeasurable riches of his grace in kindness toward us in Christ Jesus' (Eph. 2:6–7). Christ ascended as man in our name 'to take possession of his kingdom, to inaugurate it and enlarge it'.[9] In his ascension, the crucified Christ, as man and God, forever lives to make intercession for us (Heb. 7:25), bearing forever in himself the reality and fruits of our eternal salvation. In his ascension, Christ and the Father send down upon us the Holy Spirit to guide, counsel, comfort and unite us to Christ. Pentecost is the last act of atonement and the pledge that Jesus Christ will come again visibly to this earth in the same way that the disciples saw him go into heaven (Acts 1:11). The Holy Spirit of Pentecost is the pledge and assurance that all the promises of God will be fulfilled. His people will be made perfect and will live with him seeing him face to face in a new, or renewed, creation.

DOUGLAS F. KELLY: 'THE REALIST EPISTEMOLOGY OF THOMAS F. TORRANCE'

Douglas Kelly examines 'the supreme importance for revelation and reconciliation of the two natures of Christ' as both God and man in the one person – what is called the hypostatic union, the union of God and man in the one *hypostasis,* or person, of the eternal Son.

The hypostatic union is important for revelation. As finite creatures living in space and time we could not grasp or understand the eternal Word of God, who is God. We can only understand one who is man like ourselves, living in our space and time. Accordingly, the eternal Word, without ceasing to be the eternal Word, entered into our space and time. God, without ceasing to be God, assumed our human nature and in Christ became a man. For in no other way could we meet and apprehend God.

---

8 Thomas F. Torrance, *Scottish Theology: From John Knox to John McLeod Campbell* (Edinburgh: T&T Clark, 1996), 21.
9 Ibid.

His becoming man constitutes the act of revelation. Kelly quotes Tom in saying, 'Because the eternal has become temporal, man can know the eternal Truth in creaturely form.'

The hypostatic union is equally important for reconciliation. The fact that Christ is not only man but also God means that all that Christ did for our forgiveness and reconciliation, is not just the work of a good man. It is equally the work of God. It has 'final and ultimate validity'. All that Christ did is 'the eternal action of God, eternally real in the Godhead'. The deity of Christ is the ground of our assurance and our comfort in the Christian life, and therefore denial of his deity cuts away the ground of our assurance and cuts out the heart of the gospel.

The doctrine of the hypostatic union leads us to the doctrine of the Trinity, which is the reality and foundation of Christian theology. It is what Tom has called 'the ground and grammar of a realist theology'.[10] In their great love, God the Father gave his only begotten Son who redeemed us. God the Father and the Son gave us the Holy Spirit to unite us to Christ and in Christ to draw us into the loving fellowship and communion of the Triune God.

Only God can reveal God. We have no a priori (by reason or first principles) knowledge of God, We can only know him as he reveals himself in the incarnate saviour (Lk. 10:22). Jesus Christ cannot be known in terms of any other person. He is altogether unique. What he has done in his atoning reconciling sacrifice, and which he accomplished in his person, cannot be compared with any other event or thing in this world. From first to last, our knowledge of God and what he has done in Christ is given to us by revelation through the Holy Spirit. To know him and what he has done demands of us openness of mind and heart and humility.

Our attitude and our knowing the truth about objective reality in theological science, as my brother Tom has long argued and Douglas Kelly elaborates, is parallel with the attitude and approach used by scientists today as they seek to understand the mysteries of the universe. Tom has supported his arguments from the writings of scientists such as James Clerk Maxwell and Albert Einstein, and also the writings of Michael Polanyi. As Tom has said, Christians today have nothing to fear from science. Realist theology and realist science can rightly be regarded as complementary and supportive of one of another in their respective approaches to objective reality. Tom's teaching here has been published in quite a number of books, and these are helpfully listed in Kelly's essay.

---

10 Thomas F. Torrance, *The Ground and Grammar of Theology* (Charlottesville, VA: The University of Virginia Press and Belfast: Christian Journals, 1980), xi.

Alan J. Torrance: 'The Bible as Testimony to our Belonging: The Theological Vision of James B. Torrance'

Alan Torrance raises for us the all-embracing unconditional love and forgiveness of God. He develops and elucidates a number of important biblical issues which were dear to his father James in his teaching, preaching and pastoral ministry.

God's love in Christ is a covenant love. In Christ God gives himself unreservedly, totally to the people of the world. In covenant love he unites, binds, all the peoples of the world to himself in a love in which there are no limits, no restraints, no conditions. All the people of the world belong to God. They are his children. He for ever is their God and they for ever are his people.

A covenant is altogether different from a contract. A contract is between two parties where there are conditions. Both parties agree to certain conditions and obligations in entering the contract. God's covenant with the people of the world is not like that. There are no conditions.

There are, however, two kinds of covenant, both of which are mentioned in the Bible. On the one hand, there is a mutual, two-sided covenant such as between a man and wife or between two friends who pledge to be faithful in love to each other.

But, on the other hand, God's covenant is a unilateral covenant. As Alan stresses, God's covenant with his people is emphatically not a contract, and it is not a bilateral, two-sided covenant. It was a unilateral covenant. In his unilateral covenant with his people God pledged himself to be forever their God and Father and bound them forever to himself as his children.

God's love for his people is all embracing. All people, all over the world, of every generation, are his children. He does not love some and not others. He loved the world in Christ (Jn 3:16). He does not love only those who love him. He loves also those who hate him. They are all his children and he sorrows, weeps over those of his children who reject his love (Hos. 11:1–8; Lk. 19:41) and by their rejection become lost to him.

Arising out of his understanding of God's all-embracing love in Christ for everyone, James was always deeply opposed to the doctrine of limited atonement and deeply opposed to apartheid in South Africa. His strong social conscience and deep compassion for the disadvantaged were created and undergirded by this awareness of God's love.

God's love imposes 'obligations', but not conditions to love and obey him. Because he loves us we are called to love and obey him. His love is prior to our love for him. His love carries no conditions. Our love for him is a response through the Holy Spirit to his prior unconditional love for us.

Equally God's forgiveness is unconditional. That is to say, God does not forgive us only *if* we repent and obey him. In Christ Jesus God has forever forgiven and redeemed the world. There are no limitations and no restraints to his forgiveness. He forgives those who hate him and reject him. On the cross Jesus said, 'Father, forgive them, for they know not what they do' (Lk. 23:34). Our repentance is a response through the Holy Spirit to God's prior forgiveness of us. It is totally unbiblical to regard God's forgiveness of us as conditional on our repentance and therefore to make our repentance a form of work so that we rely for salvation both on God's forgiveness and on our repentance and faith.

Sadly, the doctrine of 'conditional grace', the doctrine that God will forgive you only *if* you repent, has greatly influenced large areas of the Church and particularly the evangelical wing of the Church. It has penetrated my own Church, the Church of Scotland. In our *Ordinal and Service Book*, there is a sentence in *The Form and Ordination of a Minister*, which reads, 'He [God] freely offers to all men, upon repentance and faith, the forgiveness of sins, renewal by the Holy Spirit, and eternal life . . .' The same sentence occurs in *The Form and Order for the Induction of a Minister already Ordained*. Those who hold to a doctrine of 'conditional grace', particularly evangelicals, generally do so in the mistaken belief that they are safeguarding the gospel! They are wishing to make clear that the gospel does not say that all people will ultimately be saved and that there is no need for repentance. In their misguided attempt to safeguard the gospel they are in fact misinterpreting and misrepresenting the gospel!

As a young soldier during the Second World War, I was stationed for some months in England before going abroad. While there I met regularly for fellowship, Bible study and prayer with about 12 other young Christian soldiers from various units. The teaching, which I encountered, was of 'conditional grace' or 'conditional repentance'. Despite my Reformed upbringing I was temporarily influenced and deeply troubled by it. Because of it I became much concerned in prayer to confess all my sins. According to this teaching unless I repented God would not forgive me. In my concern to receive God's forgiveness, my prayers grew longer and longer as I tried to confess all the sins which I could remember – even also imaginary sins! Then came the question, 'What about the sins of which I was ignorant and therefore did not confess?' I endeavoured to meet this problem by ending my lengthy prayers of confession by saying, 'Lord, have mercy upon me a sinner.' Then came the disturbing question (was it the loving prompting of the Holy Spirit trying to lead me in a different direction?), 'How do you know whether you are repenting? And if you don't repent you will not be forgiven.' This deeply disturbed me for to that question I had no answer.

Then some time later in reading Romans 6 in Greek the truth broke home to me like a light from heaven. I was deeply moved by the use of the aorist (past) tense of the verbs in verses 2 to 4. When Christ died, something momentous happened to Christ and also to myself. It was something decisive and it happened long ago, before I was born. Through the Holy Spirit my old sinful self died with Christ and was buried with Christ. Equally decisively I was raised with Christ through the Holy Spirit. I had become in Christ a new person. It was all God's doing. I was certainly very aware of the truth of what Paul says in Rom. 7:14–25. The 'old sinful nature' still makes its wretched presence felt. At times I was and am, to borrow a phrase from Professor Barclay of Glasgow, 'a walking civil war!'. But, I was redeemed. I was and am forgiven by grace alone. As a member of the Reformed Church, baptism took on a new meaning. It became for me a marvellous sign and proclamation of Christ and what he had done. Before I had sinned and before I was born, God in Christ had cleansed and forgiven me from all sin! With that marvellous light from heaven, there came a flood of relief and joy. I returned to the biblical and Reformed understanding and faith of my parents. Never again was I tempted towards a doctrine of 'conditional grace'. I discovered more and more that the entire Bible teaches that God's love is prior to ours and that God's forgiveness is prior to our repentance and totally unconditional. I never again doubted it. To doubt this great truth and to preach accordingly is to teach something utterly untrue. It is to dishonour God, to belittle his love and grace and to sow doubt and uncertainty among God's children.

How do we know the incarnate Saviour? All that we know of God, of Christ the incarnate saviour, is through revelation. What we know and understand is given to us by God through the Holy Spirit. Hence all our theology requires to be conducted with prayer.

We know the Lord in a way that is different from the way that we know a stone or plant or animal. The Lord is a living person and can only be known in a personal way which involves not only our minds but also, as John MacMurray, a former professor of moral philosophy in Edinburgh, would say, our emotions, our wills and indeed the whole of our being.[11]

Such knowledge involves humility. It involves listening to what the Lord is saying. Jesus said, 'Why is my language *(lalian)* not clear to you? Because you are unable to hear what I say *(logon)*' (Jn 8:43, NIV). Jesus's hearers could not understand what he was saying as man, his human speech *(lalia)*, because their ears were not open to hear what God is saying

---

[11] He was greatly influenced by Martin Buber the Jewish philosopher, and his book *I and Thou*. James and I studied under MacMurray, but all three of us were considerably indebted to him for his philosophy of persons, and found that and his understanding of the nature of reason very helpful as a background to theology.

(*logos*). Only as and when they heard God speaking would they hear and understand what he was saying as man. To hear what God is saying they had to allow God to strip away all earthly preconceptions of God, all human structures of thought. They had to allow God continually to renew their minds and hearts (Rom. 12:2) and open their ears to hear what God is saying. This is the work of the Holy Spirit. It involves on our part humility, repentance, commitment and obedience. Equally, unless they understand his humanity and hear and understand his human speech, they cannot hear nor understand what God is saying. Jesus is at once both God and man – fully God and fully man. We cannot separate the two natures of Christ and we cannot understand the one without the other. Yet how often have Bible scholars attempted to do precisely that![12]

Jesus said, 'If anyone chooses to do God's will, he will find out whether my teaching comes from God' (Jn 7:17, NIV). Jesus used two verbs, 'chooses' or 'desires' (*thele*), and 'to do' or 'practise' (*poein*). In order to know him, we must desire to practise obedience. The Lord is holy. He is God our redeemer. To know him we must submit to him, surrender our lives to him, surrender our minds to him, surrender our bodies to him, obey him. We must allow God through his Holy Spirit continually to change our behaviour, to change our lives, to give us the new life of Christ. Only so will we truly know him. Jesus said, 'Unless one is born again, he cannot see the kingdom of God' (Jn 3:3).

Graham Redding: 'Calvin and the Café Church: Reflections at the Interface Between Reformed Theology and Current Trends in Worship'

We are called to worship and glorify the Lord. For many years following the Reformation, there was little change in the form of worship. For the most part worship remained uniform. In recent years however there has been considerable experimentation and many new forms of worship have been introduced. Hence the need to ask, 'What is worship?' Graham Redding raises this question which is one my brother James

---

12 Consider the vast amount of research to try and find what has been called 'the Jesus of history'. Many theological attempts have been made to strip away what is claimed to be the theological interpretations of the early church, to demythologize the gospel in order to discover who Jesus the man is. We need, so it is claimed, to get behind history that we may discover the real Jesus, Jesus the man. But all such attempts, far from presenting us with a real human figure, have presented an anaemic figure far removed from the Jesus of the New Testament, the Mighty Redeemer of the world, and the Redeemer of us all, the one of whom Paul speaks in Col. 1:15–16, 'He is the image of the invisible God, the firstborn of all creation. For by him all things were created, in heaven and on earth . . . all things were created through him and for him.'

frequently raised. When there is so much focus on 'experimental and experiential worship, what is the right way to worship God?'

Worship is a Trinitarian event. As James often said, not all that we call worship, when we gather together in church, hear a sermon about God or even share in the administration of the sacraments, can rightly be called worship, in accordance with the teaching of Scripture or the writings of the Reformers. For Calvin, Knox and their fellow Reformers, worship is essentially a Trinitarian event. We can only worship the Father in and through the Son our great high priest and in the Spirit. As James would say, worship has too often become what we do. We come to church, we sing, we give thanks, we listen, we partake of the sacraments, and depart. The focus is not on Christ and what he does but on what we do. Often there is no mention of Jesus Christ the mediator between God and man, no mention of our high priest in and through whom alone we are able to approach the Father. As such, much of our worship today is really Unitarian![13]

True worship involves our actual meeting with God in Jesus Christ, our hearing him speak, our receiving a fresh insight into his revelation, our seeing his glory afresh. Moses said, 'Please show me your glory' (Exod. 33:18). Jesus prayed for his disciples, 'that they might see his glory' (Jn 17:24). True worship can only take place in and through our union with Jesus Christ. Only in Christ, in union with him, can we see God's glory.

Christ has a dual role in worship. On the one hand he is God whom we worship. We pray, 'Come, Lord Jesus' (Rev. 22:20). On the other hand, he worships vicariously on our behalf so that we may in him worship the Father, the Son and the Holy Spirit. As the Epistle to the Hebrews makes clear, Christ our high priest ascended on our behalf and entered through the veil, into the presence of the Father (Heb. 6:19–20). Only Christ could enter and live in the presence of the Father. Only in Christ can we enter and live in the Father's presence. Only in union with Christ can we worship. In true worship in the Holy Spirit, the focus is not on what we do but on what Christ does. The focus is on Christ and on the action of Christ.

Worship involves the whole of life. Worship is not simply what takes place when we gather in church on the Lord's day. It involves the whole of our life. We cannot rightly worship God and go out and deliberately sin. To worship aright, our whole life must be lived in union with Christ and in harmony with God. Paul said, 'I appeal to you therefore brothers by the mercies of God, to present your bodies as a living sacrifice, holy and acceptable to God, which is your spiritual worship' (Rom. 12:1–2). Jesus

---

13 James B. Torrance, *Worship, Community and the Triune God of Grace* (Carlisle: The Paternoster Press, 1996), 7.

lived a holy life of intimate fellowship with the Father, in harmony with the Father, through the Holy Spirit. He gives his perfect life to us through the Holy Spirit. Clothed with Christ we also are made to live a life of fellowship with God and are able to worship God. In worship we are altogether dependent on Jesus Christ, our high priest and leader in worship.

GARY W. DEDDO: 'THE CHRISTIAN LIFE AND OUR PARTICIPATION IN CHRIST'S CONTINUING MINISTRY'

Gary Deddo raises the question, 'What does a life of service involve?' Being called to worship we are called to serve God. Paul said, 'For we are his workmanship, created in Christ Jesus to do good works, which God prepared beforehand that we should walk in them' (Eph. 2:10). In the Epistle of James we read, 'Faith by itself, if it does not have works is dead' (Jas 2:17). As Christians we believe that we are called to be active and to serve God. Although some ministers are lazy, many ministers (and perhaps most) are workaholics. They find it difficult to stop working. The more that they do the more they realize how much there is yet to do and the more they imagine what they ought to be doing! As a result, most ministers deep down have a sense of guilt. A sense of duty and guilt drives them on and if they are honest they would say that they lack the joy that God wants them to have in serving him.

People in the church pews are little better. Probably the great majority of sermons preached are telling people what to do. We live in a desperately needy world, where many lack the knowledge of the gospel, where there is greed, oppression, violence, injustice, and where the majority in the world are poor and where many die of hunger. Sermon after sermon is preached exhorting Christians to do something about it. It is right that Christians should be active in seeking to help and redeem the world. The problem is, as Gary Deddo says, most Christians know 'that the Christian Church ought to be more involved in bearing faithful witness to the justice and compassion of God in these situations'. They know what they ought to be doing but they lack the power and the will to do it. What then is the basis of the Christian life and the basis or foundation of Christian service?

Our life, our service for God must be grounded on Jesus Christ and union with Christ. Christian life and service has a theological foundation, and Gary Deddo quotes with approval Ray Anderson when he says, 'Burn out in the Christian life and ministry is essentially a theological problem.' He says that:

this truth was hidden from me until well into my 20 years of university campus ministry. It turns out that theology, when properly grasped at its centre, is the most practical thing in the Christian life. It must undergird and direct all other Christian practice: whether prayer or the practice of spiritual disciplines, social justice, racial reconciliation, worship, evangelism, compassion for the poor, church renewal, or the *missio Dei*.

Being a Christian means being united with Christ in his life and ministry. 'The Christian life is living out and manifesting the reality of our union with Christ.'

Being united with Christ does not mean that we lose our particular, personal identity. Being united with him means that we come through the Holy Spirit to realize our full humanity and become the men and women that God has created us to be. In identifying himself with us, Christ at the same time remains himself, the incarnate saviour, both God and man. In our identification with Christ through the Holy Spirit we remain, or rather become, the new persons, disciples, servants and apostles that God intended and we were created to be.

We are called to obey Christ and to share in his continuing ministry. Being united or identified with Christ does not mean that we cease to be called to obey Christ. We do not escape from our responsibilities living in a sinful and needy world. The whole of the Christian life is a summons to be obedient in Christ and to share in and with him in his continuing ministry to the world.

As each contributor to this volume argues, Jesus lived for all of us, from first to last and indeed for all eternity, a vicarious human life. Jesus our high priest and representative was resurrected in the body. He ascended in the body. As our high priest he entered the holy of holies, and sat down in the presence of the Father. From there he exercises his heavenly ministry. He is still and for all eternity our incarnate saviour, both God and man. Through the Holy Spirit given by the Father and the Son together, Jesus although reigning in heaven is at one and the same time *continuing* his ministry here on earth, seeking among men and women everywhere to reap the fruits of the salvation he has accomplished for us. We are called to discover what Christ is seeking to do in his world today and to seek through the Holy Spirit, in union with Christ, to share with Christ in his ministry. Gary Deddo mentions that among the youth of America a brief revival for faithful Christian living has been taking place. It is 'embodied in the motto: What Would Jesus Do? WWJD, printed on thousands of armbands worn by teenagers and admired by adults'. However commendable and much to be encouraged theologically, should the motto not better read: WIJD? What *is* Jesus Doing?

The joy of the Lord. We sing the well-known hymn, 'Man of Sorrows'. Yet, as we look closer we see that throughout his ministry Jesus, living in continuous communion with the Father, experienced real joy and the spirit of thanksgiving, even in the midst of fierce hostility and suffering. 'Jesus rejoiced in the Holy Spirit and said, "I thank you, Father, Lord of heaven and earth, that you have hidden these things from the wise and understanding, and revealed them to little children"' (Lk. 10:21). Elsewhere, Jesus said, 'Abide in my love . . . These things I have spoken to you, that my joy may be in you and that your joy may be full' (Jn 15:9, 11). In his prayer to the Father, Jesus said, 'But now I am coming to you, and these things I speak in the world, that they may have my joy fulfilled in themselves' (Jn 17:13). Jesus, 'for the joy that was set before him endured the cross' (Heb. 12:2). As W. M. Clow has said, 'In no other religion and in no literature other than the Bible is joy so conspicuous.'[14] In the New Testament, the word 'joy' occurs 63 times, 'rejoice' 43 times, 'sorrow' 15 times and 'sadness' never. Lack of joy comes in Christian service when our focus is not on Christ but on ourselves.

How often have *we* decided what to do in the Church and in mission and have *we* asked God to bless us and to go with us and strengthen us in what *we* are seeking to do for God? That is to say, *we* are the ones who decide what to do, *we* do the work and *we* are asking God to help us and bless what *we* are doing! The emphasis is on us, on our doing, our serving! The focus is not on Christ but on ourselves. The result leads to frustration, failure and a lack of the real joy of the Lord.

Christian assurance. Because of this focus on ourselves there is frequently in the Christian life a lack of assurance of salvation so that we are not really set free to serve! Many years ago following a very fruitful Billy Graham crusade in Scotland, I spoke to a good and sincere elder of the Church of Scotland. He told me that he had gone forward at a crusade meeting and been counselled. He told me that he tried to do all that was asked. He tried to repent, to believe and receive Christ's salvation. He prayed but somehow he was unable to succeed. In his own words, he 'never seemed to get there'. After listening to him, I startled him by saying, 'What you have to learn is to do nothing at all!' I went on and said to him Christ has accomplished your salvation. When Christ said on the cross 'It is finished', he was saying 'I have done everything for your salvation. There is nothing left for you to do. Your salvation is complete and assured. The only thing left for you to do is simply to say Thank You! And then go on saying Thank You!' As the man listened, a spirit of relief came over him. His face relaxed. The struggle was over. I think he laughed.

---

14 *The Bible Reader's Encylopaedia and Concordance*, ed. W. M. Clow (London and New York: Collins Cleartype Press, 1962), 222.

The worry and stress was over in the joyful recognition that Christ had done everything. He knew that his salvation was assured. He was now for the first time set free to serve God. Many in our churches are like that elder. They believe in Christ. They try hard but peace, the assurance of salvation, the joy in Christian service eludes them. The focus is not altogether on Christ and on what he has done, is doing and will do.

Christian service and Christ's wondrous exchange. Some years ago a colleague of mine spoke to me about a Christian friend who was a keen football player. His friend told him that he looked on the Christian life as a game of football. He said for years it was as if he was playing football and Jesus was standing on the touchline watching him. Whenever the opportunity came he always missed the goal. He felt frustrated and defeated. Then suddenly something wonderful happened. Through the Holy Spirit, Jesus exchanged places with him. Now Jesus was playing and he was standing on the touchline watching. Every time that opportunity arose Jesus scored a goal and all he could do was stand and cheer. By the grace of God my colleague's friend had discovered the true theological basis of the Christian life and the way that we are called to live and serve. He discovered with Paul what it means to be able to say, 'It is not I who live and serve. It is Christ who lives in and serves through me.'

C. Baxter Kruger: 'The Hermeneutical Nightmare and the Reconciling Work of Jesus Christ'

In this final chapter, Baxter Kruger gathers up in a fresh and powerful way much of what has already been said, using his own inimitable language and finding vivid new ways to express the gospel and introduce people to theology. He explains how Jesus wants to make his Father known and wants to reveal him to his rebellious, prodigal children. He wants them to know what the Father is really like, for he wants them to know the love, the compassion, the forgiveness of the Father and the Father's longing that his prodigal children will return. He wants them to know how in his love the Father will give them a royal welcome and rejoice over their return.

No one other than Jesus can reveal the Father, for Jesus alone knows the Father and comes from him to make him known. To know Jesus, then, is to know the Father and to know him is to have eternal life. This is the passionate desire of the Son and the Father, that a lost humanity should be restored to the knowledge of God and so be renewed in mind and heart and be saved.

The obstacle is our sin and the blindness created by it. When humankind sinned, fellowship with God was immediately broken and God became hidden. Humankind was plunged into spiritual darkness.

Everything in the mind and imagination of human beings became corrupt and skewed. Unable any longer to see, hear or understand God, men and women created false images of God out of their own sinful imagination. These false gods bore no semblance to reality. They were not gods in any real sense of the word. They were not living, yet people feared them and became enslaved to them. They blocked any possibility of hearing or understanding God. Moreover, not only was their relationship with God broken, their relationships with one another were hopelessly broken. If it had not been for the arresting and restraining grace of God, the world in blindness would have hurtled to destruction.

Only the action of God could save us, and to do that he had to reach us in the midst of our blindness. He did that by becoming man in Jesus and sharing in our darkness, so that he could himself feel our lostness and look through our blind eyes. Into the very heart of our darkness, he brought his own knowledge of the Father, and by sharing our blindness but finding the Father in the very midst of it he overcame our blindness and revealed the true nature of God.

With Tom and James, Kruger expounds the relationship between knowing God and the undoing of sin, the inseparable connection between revelation and reconciliation, between knowing God as he really is in Christ and forgiveness and restoration to fellowship with God.

The New Testament uses two different words for God's making himself known, *phaneroo* and *apokalupto*. The Authorized Version preserves the distinction these words convey, translating *phaneroo* as 'manifest' and *apokalupto* as 'reveal'. The distinction is frequently not so clear in more modern versions. *Apokalupto* means literally to uncover or unveil. When God manifests (*phaneroo*) himself to sinful men and women, they 'by their unrighteousness suppress the truth' (Rom. 1:18) and so God is not known or understood. They remain in darkness under divine condemnation. In revelation (*apokalupto*) there is a twofold unveiling. The heart of God is unveiled and so are the hearts of natural, sinful men and women. In that twofold unveiling, darkness is banished, men and women are in Christ transformed, recreated in the image of God and restored to fellowship with the Father. Kruger's essay strikingly unfolds how in his human life, clothed with our humanity, Jesus achieves that twofold unveiling, from the side of God and from the side of man. Through him we are brought to share in his own knowledge of the Father and so to share with Christ in the love and fellowship of the Triune God.

Each of the contributors in this book has explored in considerable depth and understanding aspects of what the Bible teaches about the incarnate saviour. Each has written with insight from their own knowledge and experience, and readers will find their own Christian thinking being challenged and developed. There is a fascinating range of material here which will help Christians to deepen and enrich their understanding of the Bible and their appreciation of the inseparability both of Christ's person and work, and of Christ from the Father and the Spirit. A study of these essays will serve to enrich the Church and inspire a fresh vision of the love of God and the universal implications of the gospel.

Chapter 1

WHO *IS* THE INCARNATE SAVIOUR OF THE WORLD?

Andrew Purves

There is a noticeable groundswell of interest in the Torrance tradition in theology, both in the United States and also, it seems, in Asia and Australia. Published work on the theology of the brothers Torrance and reprints of the books of Thomas F. Torrance are now quite readily available. The Torrance project is carried forward not only within the family, but by the work of a subsequent generation of theologians. Not infrequently I hear from a pastor, wanting a Torrance bibliography or the chance to sit and talk about this theology and the practice of ministry. At least two of our PCUSA seminaries – Pittsburgh and Dubuque – offer regular courses on the Torrance theological tradition. The T. F. Torrance Theological Fellowship of the American Academy of Religion is also an encouraging sign that the work moves forward.

I recall with fondness and gratitude the 'Dogmatics 2' class in New College, in the early 1970s, where James B. Torrance, with characteristic enthusiasm and clarity, on a near daily basis, used to insist on the priority of the '*Who?*' question over the '*How?*' question for our reflections on Christology. Everything in theology depends on knowing who Jesus Christ is, on what it means that he is confessed as Lord and saviour. For if we go astray right there at the beginning, by asking the wrong question, we will never grasp the radical heart and significance of the gospel. Christianity's central doctrine – Jesus is Lord! – is given as the answer to the question: Who *is* the incarnate saviour of the world?

This question, then, is our subject: 'Who *is* the incarnate saviour of the world?' Of course, it would take a book rather than a lecture to answer the question in an adequate manner. Nevertheless, setting out the priority of the 'Who?' question places us on the trajectory of thought that characterizes the theology of the brothers Torrance. James Torrance, of course, was instructed on this point by Dietrich Bonhoeffer, and the latter's *Christology* was assigned reading. In the early part of that book – its publication title in the US is *Christ the Center* – Bonhoeffer opens up for us in a remarkably insightful way the core methodological issues we deal with in Christology. As Tom Torrance has always insisted, the method of enquiry in theology must be appropriate to its subject.

Asking the Right Question

Bonhoeffer's starting point is the required beginning for what today we would call a non-foundationalist Christology. That is to say, the Enlightenment philosophers do not set the boundaries for our Christian reflections on the identity of Jesus Christ. They do not allocate for us which parts of our thinking are allowable or not. Bonhoeffer puts it very clearly: when the word that is other than the human word, the counter-word, as he calls it, 'appears in history, no longer as an idea, but as "Word" become flesh, there is no longer any possibility of assimilating him into the existing order of the human logos. The only real question which now remains is: "Who are you? Speak for yourself!"'[1] It is this question, 'Who are you?' that Christology is concerned to answer, and that sets our enquiry on its own proper ground. Thus to ask, 'How are you possible?' is a question posed on some human ground, a ground other than Jesus Christ. It is just not adequate, for a question about immanence, says Bonhoeffer, cannot address a reality concerning transcendence. To ask, 'How are you possible?' is, as Tom Torrance used to say, an unscientific question, a remark that often bewildered us until we understood the point, for such a question does not arise out of our knowledge of the subject of study. It is a question that we impose upon it. Thus, we do not begin Christology with a question about the capacity of history to receive transcendence; rather, we begin with the fact that it did, and go on from there. When we ask 'Who are you?' of the incarnate saviour of the world, the answer cannot be given in terms of reflection on human experience, but only on the ground which the Lord Jesus gives himself. As always in theology, actuality is prior to and constrains that which subsequently becomes possible.

Let me explain that a bit further. It is only after the fact that Jesus Christ has revealed himself and confronted us, and by his Spirit drawn us into a relationship with himself, that we ask aright, 'Who are you?' The enquiry is conducted on *his* terms, on the terms by which *he* has established us, not on our terms. There is no ground for knowing Jesus outside of Jesus himself, and what it means that by his Spirit he has brought us into union with himself, thereby to share in his life. There can be no independent reason for Jesus Christ which might have authority to ratify him as the truth of God.[2] He is self-attesting. Thus a basic principle

---

1 Dietrich Bonhoeffer, *Christ the Center*, tr. Edwin H. Robinson (New York: Harper & Row, 1978), 30.
2 Ibid., 32.

in theology is set forth: it is only through God and on God's terms that God can be known. With Jesus Christ, autonomous human reason has reached its limits. Apart from who he is in his own identity and being, and as he gives himself to be known, Christology has no possibility.

So it is that the 'Who?' question which we put to Christ is an ontological rather than a phenomenological question, a question that is concerned to discover more fully the person, identity and meaning of a risen Lord who has already addressed us and claimed us as his own. Thus, theology pursues its questions a posteriori rather than a priori. That is to say, we pursue our Christological enquiries after the fact of Christ, and not according to a previously determined metaphysical or epistemological necessity established independently of Jesus Christ, and to which standard of knowing he must be accommodated.

What happens when we are confronted by the risen Word? Says Bonhoeffer, 'There are only two ways possible of encountering Jesus: man must die or he must put Jesus to death.'[3] For Bonhoeffer, the answer to the 'Who?' question means that it is not we who have dealt with Jesus, but Jesus who has dealt with us. 'So long as the Christological question is the question of the human logos, it remains imprisoned in the ambiguity of the question, "How?" But when it is given voice in the act of faith, there is real possibility of posing the question, "Who?"'[4] And, we might add, the question has as its subject both Jesus and ourselves. Thus, the anthropological question, 'Who am I?' is understood as a derivative question, for in asking 'Who?' of Jesus I accept that I have already been encountered from beyond myself by the One who is the Truth and must now either understand myself in terms of that encounter and surrender to it in faith, or try to force it to be what it is not, which is to live in untruth. In losing Christ I also lose myself.

One final brief point from Bonhoeffer is important to notice, namely, that Christology is not soteriology.[5] We do not know Christ from his works. The reason is that he did what he did in the incognito of the incarnation. Argue, on the one hand, that Jesus was a man, and the argument back from his works to his person is ambiguous. Argue, on the other hand, that Jesus was God, and the argument back from history to God is impossible.[6] Thus is set the priority of the Christological question over soteriology, of 'Who?' over 'What?'. When we know who Christ is, as God and a man, we will know what it is that he does and what that means. The person and work of Christ are not separated, of course, but they are

---

3 Ibid., 35.
4 Ibid., 36.
5 Ibid., 37.
6 Ibid., 39.

established in theological method in this way in the unity of his divine and human personhood.

Who is the incarnate saviour of the world? This, then, is not a quizzical question, one speculative in origin. His personhood is not a neutral datum of experience that we can manipulate at will. Rather, in this question we are trying more faithfully to understand who God is who has revealed himself to us, encountered us and brought us into relationship with himself precisely in, through and as this man, Jesus of Nazareth. It is a question put by faith, not by unfaith. It is a question put *en Christo*, 'in Christ,' and not apart from Christ. It is a heuristic question that arises out of the person of Jesus in his being as the incarnate saviour of the world, already whom we know as Lord because he has encountered us as such. Or to put it differently, in asking, 'Who is the incarnate saviour of the world?' we affirm that in some measure we already know the answer to what we ask. In the question we seek now to enter more deeply into the reality to which we have already testified in asking the question in the first place. We test our knowledge in the light of our continuing and deepening enquiry into God in his action towards us in, through and as Jesus Christ. It is in as much as Jesus Christ has revealed himself to us as the incarnate saviour, and therefore as the answer to our questions before we even know what our questions are, that we pose our questions in order to enter more deeply into knowledge of the one whom we know to be our saviour. Thomas F. Torrance has expressed what we are about here in this way: 'In scientific theology we begin with actual knowledge of God, and seek to test and clarify this knowledge by inquiring carefully into the relation between our knowing God and God Himself in His being and nature.'[7]

Clearly, to ask, 'Who is the incarnate saviour of the world?' is immediately to enter into the great mystery that is central to Christian faith, namely, the incarnation itself. The Church and Christian faith stand or fall on the reality and truth of the incarnation. It is the event in which faith associates the eternal God with a contingent fact of history, and attributes a saving significance to it.

THE WORD BECAME

Tom Torrance, in his earliest systematic work, *The Doctrine of Jesus Christ*, given as lectures at Auburn Theological Seminary, New York, in 1939, and only recently published in book form, suggests that the significant words in the doctrine of the incarnation are 'became' and 'flesh'.[8] *Ho logos sarx egeneto* – 'the Word became flesh' (Jn 1:14). God as the man

---

7   Thomas F. Torrance, *Theological Science* (London: Oxford University Press, 1969), 9.
8   Thomas F. Torrance, *The Doctrine of Jesus Christ* (Eugene, OR: Wipf and Stock, 2002), 73.

Jesus, the movement of the Eternal One into time as this particular man, are expressed in the notion of God's becoming. Fifty years or so later Torrance would write that 'the incarnation is to be understood, then, as a real becoming on the part of God, in which God comes *as man* and acts *as man*, all for our sake – from beginning to end God the Son acts among us in a human way'.[9] With the incarnation we have to think together both God and human nature in the one movement of thought. This is the challenge set for Christology by Jesus Christ.

God and nature: becoming is a counter-intuitive concept to use with respect to God, whom we think of conventionally in terms of immutability, impassibility, incomprehensibility, almightiness and eternity. Basically, God is unchangeable. This is the opposite of how we think about what we identify as nature, which is a social construct and is characterized precisely as a fluid entity. But God was not always incarnate, just as God was not always creator. God becoming a man means a revolution both for our concept of God, and for our understanding of the significance of nature in time/space. It means, as Torrance shows in his early work, that movement is part of God's eternity, and the becoming of Eternity is henceforth part of our understanding of time/space. 'Eternity', he writes, 'is God-in-action . . . Eternity is not static.'[10] Thus we have to hold in our minds these seeming antinomies: God is eternal – God relates; God is unchanging – God becomes; God is ever free to be himself – without ceasing to be God, the Word became flesh and dwelt among us; God is God and creation is contingent – the Word entered creation, but God did not cease to be God, nor did creation cease to be creation.

These antinomies mean at least this: our thinking concerning God and creation must be adapted to the significance of the incarnation. The doctrine of God is accountable to the incarnation, the incarnation is not accountable to a previously conceived doctrine of God. Thus, we must think of the incarnation, God becoming flesh, as falling within the being and life of God.[11] Neither can we allow any room in our thinking for a deistic disjunction between God and creation, for the incarnation also falls within the life of creation – notice, by the way, that I have moved from speaking of nature to speaking about creation, which is nature now perceived in terms of God who both created it and interacts with it. Tom Torrance, in his *Space, Time and Incarnation* observes that:

> the Incarnation (is) to be understood as the chosen path of God's rationality in which He interacts with the world and establishes such

---

9 Thomas F. Torrance, *The Trinitarian Faith* (Edinburgh: T&T Clark, 1988), 150.
10 Torrance, *The Doctrine of Jesus Christ*, 74.
11 Torrance, *The Trinitarian Faith*, 155.

a relation between creaturely being and Himself that He will not allow it to slip away from Him into futility or nothingness . . . Thus while the Incarnation does not mean that God is limited by space and time, it asserts the reality of space and time for God in the actuality of His relations with us, and at the same time binds us to space and time in all our relations with Him.[12]

As the Father of the incarnate saviour, God is not an immutable and impassible deity – unchangeable and devoid of the suffering of love. In love God freely wills to be God with us rather than apart from us. And who God is towards us and for us in Christ, God chooses to be as the One who loves in freedom, as Karl Barth used to put it. In and as the man Jesus, God both loves us as God and receives our love in return as a man, all in the unity of the one personhood of Jesus. If we were to insist otherwise, the incarnation would have to be seen as an event in which God did not really come among us, an event that was only apparent rather than real, and the love of God would have to be regarded as an occasional attribute, rather than as God's act in freedom which is who God is as love, the lover and loving. As Tom Torrance has noted, God is not love insofar as God loves us; God is love in the fullness and perfection of his being, out of which plenitude God reaches out to us in love.[13]

STARTING WITH THE SAVIOUR

One very helpful theme developed by both James and Tom Torrance is the need to free our understanding of God from the vice-like grip of predetermined metaphysical categories of thought. A well-developed example of the critique is Tom Torrance's pointed discussion of the Westminster tradition in his book *Scottish Theology*. It is in part an unrelenting critical review of Federal Calvinism across the loci of doctrine. The sum of the criticism is given in Torrance's analysis of Westminster's tendency to trace the ground of belief back to eternal divine decrees behind the back of the incarnation of the Word. It meant, among other things, the loss of the love of God precisely because the *Confession* does not have a Trinitarian, Christological or soteriological structure. As he states: 'the doctrine of God, thus presented within the framework of the Confession, is strictly not a fully *Christian* doctrine of God, that is, of God the Father made known to us definitively through Christ and his Spirit in the

---

[12] Thomas F. Torrance, *Space, Time and Incarnation* (Oxford: Oxford University Press, 1969), 67.
[13] Thomas F. Torrance, *The Christian Doctrine of God: One Being Three Persons* (Edinburgh: T&T Clark, 1996), 5.

Gospel'.[14] In a similar vein, Alan J. Torrance illustrates the insight of his father, James, when he noted that:

> It is interesting that Calvin himself saw and stated explicitly that, as a result of sin, no human being will now see God as Creator who has not first seen Christ as Redeemer. This means that theologically we should start with God the Redeemer in order to know God the Creator.[15]

As an aside, allow me a brief comment on the call that a number of people in the Presbyterian Church (USA) have made recently for a list of essential tenets of Reformed faith. Recently I was asked to write an article on Jesus Christ for such a statement. The point of interest is that Jesus was sixth on the list of so-called essential tenets! The person and work of Jesus were to be developed in terms of the prior doctrines of Scripture, God, election, creation and human nature. I responded critically, arguing that Jesus Christ was not an item on a list, and certainly not in sixth place, but that he was in a sense the whole list, for everything had to be worked out in terms of who he is as the incarnate saviour of the world. Evangelicals, I sometimes fear, are not radical enough in thinking through the meaning and significance of Jesus Christ, too ready at times to replace him in priority with foundationalist, that is, previously determined and independently derived, theistic and metaphysical assumptions that are then clamped down upon the gospel. This too is the view that Tom Torrance set out clearly in the introduction to his *Reality and Evangelical Theology*. Torrance's revered teacher, H. R. Mackintosh, once summed up the matter thus: 'faith in God means faith in Jesus . . . We cannot state the Christian thought of God except as we include Christ in our statement. He is an integral constituent of what, for us, God means.'[16] That is to say, Jesus is Lord over our doctrine of God, election, Scripture and so on.

THE WORD BECAME *FLESH*

Now let us turn to consider the becoming *flesh*. The human agency of the incarnate Son, his undiminished historical human life, is critically important. The salvation we have in Christ depends precisely on the unity of his being and agency in the flesh of his humanity. Thus, Tom Torrance writes that:

---

14 Thomas F. Torrance, *Scottish Theology: From John Knox to John McLeod Campbell* (Edinburgh: T&T Clark, 1996), 133.
15 Alan J. Torrance, *Persons in Communion: Trinitarian Description and Human Participation* (Edinburgh: T&T Clark, 1996), 62.
16 H. R. Mackintosh, *The Doctrine of the Person of Jesus Christ* (Edinburgh: T&T Clark, 1912), 288 and 292.

while everything pivots upon the downright act of God himself in Christ, that act of God takes the concrete form of the actual historical man Jesus . . . *Only God can save, but he saves precisely as man* – Jesus Christ is God's act, God acting personally and immediately as man in and through him, and thus at once in a divine and human manner.[17]

God saves as this man – this is the staggering claim of Christian faith, and we must not back away from its particularity and universality one bit.

This man, Jesus, in his flesh is God the Son who is saviour. Had the Word not become incarnate, Jesus would not have existed. But the One who is the incarnate saviour of the world is truly a human being. (Here we have the patristic doctrines of the *anhypostasis* and the *enhypostasis*.[18]) Biblically, the humanity of Jesus is expressed in words James Torrance often used to cite to us when we were his students, conflating the words of Paul, 'bone of our bone, flesh of our flesh, born of a woman, born under the law'. The incarnate Word is this man, Jesus, son of Mary. The consequence of this *egeneto sarx* is God *as* Jesus, and the rejection thereby of the idea that the humanity of Christ was instrumental, that is, a functional necessity but not obtaining to the work of salvation itself. God saves not just in and through, but supremely as the man Jesus.

This insight, which comes from Athanasius's mature work *Four Discourses Against the Arians*, came into Scottish theology through John Knox and those who followed after him. Thus, for example, Robert Bruce (1554–1631), Knox's successor at St Giles, referred often to 'the whole Christ', thereby stressing the significance of the incarnate life of Jesus Christ for the atonement and our salvation.[19] Christ is in himself our salvation. For this reason, the incarnation must be understood in both a personal and vicarious way.[20] Let us now turn specifically but briefly to what this means.

ATONEMENT

It is not incarnation by itself that affects our redemption. We have to keep in mind that as the incarnate Word, Jesus Christ acts personally on our behalf. He is saviour as what he is as well as in what he does. Too often, I

---

17 Torrance, *The Trinitarian Faith*, 148–9.
18 See, for example, Thomas F. Torrance, *Theology in Reconstruction* (London: SCM Press, 1965), 131.
19 This point is made by Robert R. Redman, Jr, *Reformulating Reformed Theology: Jesus Christ in the Theology of Hugh Ross Mackintosh* (Lanham, NY: University Press of America, Inc., 1997), 70.
20 Torrance, *The Trinitarian Faith*, 151.

think, theologies of the atonement fail to see this. The atonement takes place within his incarnate life,[21] within the unity of his person, falling thereby within both the life of God and our human lives. The relation between the Father and the Son is not merely an external, moral or juridical relation, as we find often in penal theories of the atonement, but a profoundly personal and ontological relation so that it is God who saves as the man Jesus, and which salvation penetrates to the depths of the human condition. The atonement then is not a work of God upon us as an external transaction, but an act of God from within our humanity and on our behalf.[22] Nowhere is this more magisterially worked out than in the great book of the Scottish theologian John McLeod Campbell, *The Nature of the Atonement*. Published in 1856, this book deeply influenced the Torrance brothers and is one I wish more ministers would struggle with. That is to say, the atonement is worked out within or as the person of the incarnate saviour so that within the unity of his personhood as God and a man the inner ontological relations between Christ and the Father and between Christ and us are held together as a healing restoration to communion.

The Torrance tradition in theology is notable, I think, for underscoring the range of the vicarious life of the incarnate saviour. There is nothing here of an incarnation and atonement only for some, but not for all. Tom Torrance writes that 'it is precisely in Jesus . . . that we are to think of the whole human race, and indeed the whole of creation, as in a profound sense already redeemed, resurrected, and consecrated for the glory and worship of God'.[23] That, frankly, is a remarkable statement both for its boldness as for its grasp of the radical implications of the incarnation upon the whole created order. Thus the ontological relations between all humankind and God are to be understood from within the frame of the vicarious person and work of Christ. When we attempt an answer to the question, 'Who is the incarnate saviour of the world?', we must without reserve maintain commitment to the staggering magnitude of both God's unilateral grace and the enormity of the company of the saved.

It was Tom Torrance's teacher, H. R. Macintosh, I think, who once said that we should press as far towards universalism as we can without actually ending up there. If we are thinking about the incarnate saviour of the *world*, and not about the incarnate saviour of some of the world, then we are thinking in global, indeed, cosmic, and universal terms. I am thinking here of our need to appropriate the doctrine of Christ as *pantokrator* which is found in Orthodox theology, in which he is depicted as the almighty ruler of all things. This lordship is symbolized in the dome

---

21 Torrance, *The Trinitarian Faith*, 161.
22 Torrance, *The Trinitarian Faith*, 158.
23 Torrance, *The Trinitarian Faith*, 183.

painting found in many Orthodox churches, of Christ sitting on the throne of glory with his arms outstretched to include all people and all things in his gathering embrace. The gospel perspective is graciously inclusive – for all. Here we bring to mind that the gospel is about grace upon grace, an overflowing grace.

And yet right here too the Church insists on a degree of soteriological reserve, in some measure always aware of the ugly messiness of our sin and of the consequences for both God and us, not the least of which is Calvary's cross. We are confronted with a great mystery that is certainly not reducible to our theological formulas, or indeed ever adequately solvable, and which we can only talk about under our breath with quiet respect for the staggering sweep of the grace, the holiness and the majesty of the Lord God, who, while he loves us in freedom, will not be mocked. The problem may be stated thus: Jesus lived, died, rose again, and ascended for all; union with Christ and faith in Jesus our Lord is by the gift of the Holy Spirit; the faithless, those who resist life in Christ and refuse to confess him, will be judged unto damnation by God. Given that God actualizes his relation with us and our relation with himself through union with Christ,[24] which is the principal work of the Holy Spirit, why does God not enable everyone to hear and receive the gospel? Here, it seems, there is a terrible limit to our theology, for we have to say that, on the one hand, Jesus Christ is all in all, the beginning and the end, *pantokrator*, and on the other, that there is a human freedom to confess or reject Jesus as Lord. The limitation of our minds means we live within the antinomy of an irresistible universal grace and a human freedom that can be terrible in its consequences, and we cannot collapse the antinomy into either Arminianism or limited atonement.

The Torrance tradition has unfailingly and rightly, I believe, placed the entire soteriological emphasis upon the incarnate saviour of the world, Jesus Christ our Lord. When asked once in class what the human percentage was in the saving equation, Tom Torrance answered, 'one hundred percent God, no percent man'.[25] Our task then, while it is day, is to proclaim the gospel that Jesus Christ is the incarnate saviour of the world, and to pray for the grace of the Holy Spirit upon those who hear us preach, for the night will come when no one can work, and when, perhaps, it will be too late for response. The mystery of the final judgement is not for us to unravel. But of this there is no doubt: 'There is no other name under heaven . . . by which we must be saved' (Acts 4:12), for Jesus Christ, son of Mary, is the incarnate saviour of the world.

---

24 Torrance, *The Christian Doctrine of God*, 152.
25 Torrance, *The Doctrine of Jesus Christ*, 199.

Chapter 2

THE INCARNATE SAVIOUR:
T. F. TORRANCE ON THE ATONEMENT

Elmer M. Colyer

We needed an incarnate God, a God put to death, that we might live. We were put to death together with him, that we might be cleansed; we rose again with him, because we were put to death with him; we were glorified with him, because we rose again with him.[1]

Gregory of Nazianzen

INTRODUCTION

Over many years of teaching T. F. Torrance's theology, and not the least his understanding of the incarnational atoning reconciliation, I have repeatedly witnessed seminary students', pastors' and lay persons' Christian lives transformed as a result of encountering Torrance's vision of the incarnate saviour. The reason for this is Torrance's astonishing grasp of the theological deep-structures that make the gospel, our Lord's incarnational atoning reconciliation, what it is: the power of the Triune God for the salvation of the world. Clarifying the deep-structures embedded in the very reality of the gospel has been Torrance's intent throughout his career. He develops a participatory scientific theology in which our actual knowledge of God, that comes to us in and with God's atoning self-communication through Jesus Christ and in his Spirit, calls into question all alien presuppositions and prior conceptual frameworks embodying what we think we know about God, for everything in theology has to be related to God's Trinitarian self-revelation and self-communication to us in the gospel.[2]

This kind of participatory approach involves probing the essential connections embodied in the very essence and reality of Christ's atoning incarnational redemption itself[3] and presenting what we discover in a

---

1 See Thomas F. Torrance, *The Trinitarian Faith* (Edinburgh: T&T Clark, 1988), 142.
2 Thomas F. Torrance, 'My Interaction with Karl Barth', in *How Karl Barth Changed My Mind*, ed. Donald K. McKim (Grand Rapids: Eerdmans, 1986), 53.
3 Ibid.

core set of central theological relations and concepts that enable us to grasp something of the essence and reality of that redemption with unparalleled theological depth and clarity.[4] What Torrance means by scientific theology is a theology appropriate to and determined from beginning to end by the activity of the Triune God in and through the incarnate saviour.

Of course, this places significant, indeed at times transformative, demands on us, for Torrance's kind of theology can only be rightly undertaken when we enter into an intensely personal and saving relationship with God through Jesus Christ and his incarnational atonement in the Spirit. Revelation, or knowing God, and reconciliation, or being restored to a right relationship with God, are inseparable in Torrance's theology. We cannot know God in an impersonal manner or apart from Christ's atoning reconciliation actually taking hold of and transforming our lives, including our minds.

Our theology, including our thinking about the atonement, can never be more than a refinement and extension of our knowledge of the gospel that arises at the evangelical and doxological level of a living and personal relationship with God through Jesus Christ's atoning reconciliation in the Holy Spirit within the worshipping life of the Church.[5]

Thus for us to enquire into the character of the incarnate saviour in Torrance's theology, especially the atonement, is for us to take an intensely personal journey into the most profound and astonishing of all subjects, the reality and character of the love of the Triune God manifest in the cross. For it is especially on the cross that we come to know that the Triune God loves us with the very love that God is, indeed, loves us even more than God loves himself, as Torrance often asserts.

Furthermore, we cannot but approach this subject in holy reverence and awe, always remembering the famous principle of the early church, to which Torrance regularly appeals, *Deus Semper Maior*, the love of God in the cross is always greater than all we can ever think and everything we can say about it. We can apprehend, though we cannot fully *comprehend* it, for to know the love of God in Christ's death on the cross of Christ is

---

4   Thomas F. Torrance, *Reality and Scientific Theology* (Edinburgh: Scottish Academic Press, 1985), 156.
5   Thus Christian Dogmatics from beginning to end is an empirical and personal engagement of the tangible reality of Jesus Christ. Torrance is quoting H. R. Mackintosh with approval. See Thomas F. Torrance, 'Hugh Ross Mackintosh: Theologian of the Cross', *The Scottish Bulletin of Evangelical Theology* 5, no. 2 (Autumn 1987), 161. For Torrance, in genuine theology the coherent body of informal truth embedded in the foundation of the Church in Christ and his gospel 'comes to formal expression as it presses upon the mind of the Church in its worship of God and in the fulfilment of its mission to mankind'. See Thomas F. Torrance, 'The Deposit of Faith', *Scottish Journal of Theology* 36, no. 1 (1983), 12.

to know that this love surpasses knowledge and leads to thanksgiving, faith, obedience and worship that must permeate all that we think and say about it. So when we talk about Christ's incarnation and atoning reconciliation what we say is linked to a depth of Truth that is far greater than we can ever bring to formal articulation.

This means that when we approach this subject we must do so, as it were, on our knees in prayer and adoration before this absolutely astonishing mystery of divine love. Such a love has chosen to reconcile us sinful earthly creatures of dust. We come to know something of the mystery of the love of God in the cross of Christ and even enter into fellowship with the Trinitarian God and the Triune Life of this wondrous God who has loved us with the very love that God is. Torrance says it this way: 'The saving act of God in the blood of Christ is an unfathomable mystery before which the angels veil their faces . . . before which our minds must bow in wonder, worship and praise.'[6]

THE UNITY OF THE ATONEMENT AND INCARNATION IN CHRIST'S PERSON AND WORK

As we focus on how Torrance can deepen our understanding of the atonement or Christ's atoning reconciliation we must begin with his emphasis on the unity of Christ's person and work. For Torrance, the incarnation and the atonement are intimately, indeed inextricably, interconnected throughout the earthly life, death, resurrection and ascension of Jesus Christ.[7]

Jesus Christ is fully God and wholly human in one person. The two natures are so deeply united in the incarnation that all of Christ's divine and human activity flow from his one person. This includes the atonement or atoning reconciliation which Christ accomplishes for us *within* his own being and life as the incarnate saviour throughout his life culminating in the apex of the atoning reconciliation in the cross and resurrection. None of what the incarnate saviour accomplishes for us in atoning reconciliation, including the cross, takes place *outside* of Christ as something external to who he *is*, external to the incarnate reality of Christ's person as mediator or saviour of the world.[8] Let us examine what Torrance means by this.

---

6   Thomas F. Torrance, *Karl Barth: Biblical and Evangelical Theologian* (Edinburgh: T&T Clark, 1990), 239.
7   See Torrance, *Trinitarian Faith*, 155–90, Thomas F. Torrance, *The Mediation of Christ*, 2nd edn (Colorado Springs: Helmers & Howard, 1992), 62–72, and Torrance, *Karl Barth*, 177–9, 201–5 and 229–36.
8   Torrance, *Trinitarian Faith*, 155.

In the hypostatic, or personal, union between the divine and human natures in the incarnation, the Son of God assumes our actual diseased, sinful and corrupt humanity in conflict with God. This does not mean that Jesus Christ the incarnate Son sinned himself or became contaminated by our fallen and corrupt condition. Rather it signifies that the hypostatic or personal union between the divine nature and our actual sinful human nature in the incarnation is a *reconciling union*. In it, the incarnate Son condemns sin in our sinful humanity and overcomes the estrangement, sin, guilt and death entrenched in our humanity through an atoning and transforming relation between the divine and the human natures. This takes place within the incarnate person of the saviour throughout his life, death and resurrection.[9] So, the incarnation is inherently atoning and the atonement is intrinsically incarnational. Atoning reconciliation takes place from Jesus's birth throughout his life and ministry and comes to its apex in the atoning reconciliation in the cross and resurrection and ascension.

Think of what this means! Our blessed Lord and Saviour took upon himself in the incarnation the fearful tensions, the destructive contradictions, the fears, the doubts, the unbelief entrenched in our sinful and rebellious humanity that lead each of us and all of us to be the broken, guilty and sinful people we are apart from Christ. He did so in such a way that atoning reconciliation takes dynamic form and is worked out within the actual historical relations and structures of our actual human existence all through our Lord's life from birth to death, resurrection and ascension.[10]

The incarnate saviour shared all our human experience. He endured fearful temptations and the onslaught of the forces of darkness. He wept beside the grave of a loved one, had a prostitute kiss his feet and wet them with her tears. He pleaded with his heavenly Father in the Garden to let the cup of suffering pass from him. Yet our Lord overcame it all in a life of purity and faithfulness. He withstood the strain of human sin and God's judgement upon it, especially on the cross. Thus, he sanctified every phase of human life within the hypostatic, or personal, union of his divine nature and our sinful human nature in the oneness of his person as our incarnate saviour.[11] Is it any wonder that Heb. 5:7 says that during

---

9 Torrance, *Mediation*, 65. By making our sin and guilt, our condemnation and death, his own, the Son of God through the hypostatic union brought God's perfect holiness and power to bear upon our fallen nature, reconciling and redeeming it and converting our disobedient humanity back to communion with God. See Torrance, *Karl Barth*, 178–9, 202–4 and 230–1.
10 Torrance, *Mediation*, 65.
11 See Torrance, *Trinitarian Faith*, 166–7. 'Thus there took place in Christ as Mediator', Torrance argues, 'an agonizing union between God the Judge and man under judgement

the days of his earthly life, Jesus offered up prayers and petitions with loud cries and tears? Is it any wonder that Scripture portrays our Lord as a man of sorrow, acquainted with grief; one who took up our infirmities and carried our sorrows; one who was pierced for our transgressions and bruised for our iniquities so that by his stripes we are healed, as the Servant Song of Isa. 53 asserts so graphically?

Think of Heb. 2 and 4, in which we read that Christ shared in our humanity:

> to deliver those who . . . were subject to slavery . . . therefore he had to be made like his brothers in every respect so that he might become a merciful and faithful high priest in service to God, to make propitiation for the sins of the people. For because he himself has suffered when he was tempted, he is able to help those who are being tempted. (Heb. 2: 14–18)

> For we do not have a high priest who is unable to sympathize with our weakness, but one who in every respect has been tempted as we are, yet without sin. (Heb. 4:15)

All of our temptations and sufferings are implied in this text!

In fact, our blessed Lord was tempted even more than we are, because we so often give in before the temptation reaches its full and horrible extreme, as it did with our Lord in the desert, in the Garden and on the cross. '*Eloi, Eloi, Lama sabachthani?* My God, my God, why have you forsaken me?' (Mt. 27:45) is the fearful cry of our Lord in our place, in our stead, out of our very humanity with its bottomless pit of sin, guilt, fear, doubt, despair and profound sense of God-forsakenness.

So for T. F. Torrance, this atoning reconciliation between God and humanity that takes place from Christ's birth to its consummation in his death and resurrection must be understood in terms of 'a continuous vicarious sacrifice in which his incarnate life and his redeeming activity . . . [are] completely interwoven in such a way that his Person, his Word, and his Act are one and undivided'.[12] The incarnation and the

---

in a continuous movement of atoning reconciliation running throughout his obedient and sinless life and passion into the resurrection and ascension when he presented himself to the Father on our behalf and presented us in him as those he had redeemed and consecrated to be his brethren.' Thomas F. Torrance, 'Karl Barth and the Latin Heresy', in the *Scottish Journal of Theology* 39 (1986), 475.

12 Thomas F. Torrance, 'The Atonement, the Singularity of Christ and the Finality of the Cross: The Atonement and the Moral Order', in *Universalism and the Doctrine of Hell*, ed. Nigel M. de S. Cameron (Grand Rapids, MI: Baker Books, 1993), 232 and 236. Torrance sees God's saving act in Jesus Christ as continuous and indivisible. Torrance, *Karl Barth*, 200.

atonement, the personal union of the Son's divine nature and our sinful human nature and the atoning reconciliation, interpenetrate and imply one another within his life, ministry, death, resurrection and ascension of our incarnate saviour.[13]

Given the absolutely perilous condition of our corrupt and sinful humanity, guilty and standing under the utterly real judgement of God, the hypostatic union of Christ's divine nature and our human nature in the incarnation could not be actualized without its overcoming human sin and guilt. This occurred through Christ's atonement for sin and through the sanctification our sinful human nature he assumed in union with his divine nature.[14] Such atoning reconciliation could not take place within the depths of our corrupt and sinful humanity unless Christ penetrated into those depths in the personal union of Christ's divine nature with our diseased, alienated and sinful human nature.[15]

Thus, the hypostatic union of the divine and human natures within the one person of the incarnate Son is always and everywhere the source for all of Christ's atoning activity on our behalf.[16] Jesus Christ as mediator is the ultimate ground of all aspects of our salvation, including our justification, sanctification, glorification and all the rest, which have to be understood as taking place in Christ and mediated to us by the Holy Spirit who unites us to Christ, and through Christ with the Father. For Torrance, Christ's person and work are one and have to be viewed together.

To help us grasp what is at stake in all of this, it is helpful to examine what it is that Torrance is guarding against: a gospel, a conceptualization of atoning reconciliation, understood in merely external, moral or juridical terms characteristic of much Christian faith in North American, indeed in much of the Latin or Western tradition of Christian faith, Protestant and Catholic.

---

13 Torrance can say that the hypostatic union between the divine and human natures in Jesus Christ is the ontological aspect of atoning reconciliation and the atoning reconciliation is the dynamic aspect of hypostatic union. (Torrance is describing Barth's position, though it is clear that Torrance is sympathetic with Barth on this point.) Thomas F. Torrance, 'Karl Barth and Patristic Theology' in *Theology Beyond Christendom: Essays on the Centenary of the Birth of Karl Barth May 10, 1886*, ed. John Thompson (Allison Park, Penn.: Pickwick Publications, 1986), 229.
14 Torrance, *Mediation*, 66.
15 Ibid., 66.
16 Ibid., 64–5.

What Torrance is Against: A Gospel of External Relations

Torrance sees a growing tendency in Western theology from the fifth century on to reject the idea that Christ assumed our sinful, alienated and fallen humanity, and to embrace the notion that Christ assumed a neutral or perfect human nature from the Virgin Mary.[17] This understanding of the incarnation, however, conflicts with that basic principle of salvation found in so many of the Church Fathers, especially the theologians associated with the Nicene Creed, the most revered ecumenical expression of the faith in history. The Fathers asserted that the unassumed is the unhealed: any part of our actual humanity that the Son of God has not taken upon himself in the incarnation is left untouched by the atoning reconciliation effected throughout Christ's life, ministry, death, resurrection and ascension.

So if the Son of God has not assumed our *actual* fallen humanity, but a perfect and sinless humanity different from our own, this cannot but shift how we understand salvation from beginning to end.[18] If the incarnate saviour did not assume our fallen and sinful human nature, Torrance points out that Christ's atoning sacrifice inevitably can only be understood in terms of *external* relations between Christ and humanity's sins.[19] Then the incarnation and atonement, Christ's person and work, begin to drift apart.

The incarnation thus becomes merely *instrumental* in relation to the atonement. It is simply the means of providing a sinless human being capable of living in perfect obedience to God's law, and of taking our place on the cross and enduring the judgement and wrath of God which we deserve because of our sin. In such an understanding, Christ's cries and tears seem somehow less than real, certainly not of the same sort that we *sinful* human beings encounter due to the depths of our broken and sinful human nature. In turn, Christ's suffering and death become merely an external judicial or juridical transaction in which the penalty for sin and the judgement and wrath of God against sin are somehow transferred from sinners like us to the sinless incarnate saviour with his neutral humanity different than our own who dies fulfilling the just and inexorable penalty against those who transgress God's laws.[20]

---

17 See ibid., 40, and Torrance, *Karl Barth*, 203 and 231–2. Torrance sees Leo's *Tome* as one of the chief sources.
18 According to Torrance this also forced the Roman Catholic tradition into the notion of the immaculate conception of Mary to ensure the sinless humanity of Christ. Torrance, *Mediation*, 40.
19 Torrance, *Mediation*, 40, and Torrance, *Karl Barth*, 178.
20 Torrance, *Mediation*, 40.

Now, to be sure there are juridical elements found in Scripture that have to be incorporated into our understanding of the atonement. We will see how Torrance does so in a moment. Yet, if this juridical account is all there is to atoning reconciliation, then this way of understanding of salvation in external relations creates a series of insuperable problems that have infected our understanding of Christian faith in the Western tradition right up until today.

THE JURIDICAL THEORY AT WORK IN WESTERN THEOLOGY

First, this juridical theory of the atonement frees us from the *penalty* for sin, but the actual *root* of our alienation and sin in the ontological depths of our corrupt and fallen humanity is left untouched by Christ's atoning sacrifice. Christ's death on the cross deals only with our *actual* sins, but not our sinful nature.[21] This can lead to a reductionist understanding of salvation as forgiveness now and heaven in the hereafter, or pie in the sky when we die, as some have humorously stated it. Torrance finds a similar tendency in Roman Catholic theology which has also often understood the atonement in external juridical categories. Original sin is cured through the healing medicine of a transferable grace. This spiritual substance dispensed by the Church through the sacraments aids us in overcoming the sin entrenched in our fallen nature untouched by an incarnate saviour who assumed a sinless humanity different from our own, whose death on the cross takes away the guilt of actual sin, but leaves the power of sin unaddressed.[22]

Protestantism has its own ways of dealing with the problem of original sin entrenched in our fallen humanity within the framework of this forensic or juridical model of the atonement. It often attempts to overcome the problem of our sinful nature by an appeal to an additional, subsequent and disconnected source for regeneration in the person and work of the Holy Spirit.

Even John Wesley, the founder of Methodism, occasionally succumbed to this kind of characterization of the order of salvation, saying that justification implies what God *does for* us through his Son, whereas sanctification signifies what God *works in* by his Spirit. Here, Christ's atonement deals with our standing before God, providing pardon for actual sins. The overcoming of sin in our fallen nature is the prerogative of the third person of the Trinity, thus driving a wedge between the activities of the Trinitarian persons so that these activities are entirely disconnected and serial. First Christ provides justification, then the Spirit follows with

---

21 Torrance, *Karl Barth*, 203.
22 Ibid., 232

sanctification. Wesley's theology, of course, is far better than this, but the transition from the atonement of Christ interpreted in external juridical terms to the work of Spirit understood as the inner transformation of the sinful human nature has had a significant impact on Protestantism.

What becomes of the resurrection in this juridical model of the atonement? It is difficult to integrate the resurrection into this understanding of salvation other than as the verdict of the Father that the cross has been successful. Since it is a *neutral* humanity that Christ carries through death to resurrection, different from our own, this theory has difficulty providing any plausible explanation of how Christ's bodily resurrection is related to our own bodily resurrection and final transformation when Christ returns at the end of time. Indeed, it becomes difficult to make much sense at all of the significance of the *bodily ascension* of our Lord. Does it contribute anything at all to our salvation? If so, what? In what way is it related to justification and the rest of our salvation? Usually it is of no practical significance at all.

The Juridical Theory at Work in Liberalism

Modern liberal Protestantism, Torrance contends, has also been infected with a gospel conceived in terms of external relations and corollary theories of the atonement. Here Jesus is viewed as a great moral/religious leader/teacher whose principles and/or example of love/justice/consciousness of God/solidarity with the poor exert a powerful and transforming influence upon the disciples, the apostolic community and us today through the New Testament witness. This Liberalism requires its scholars, like those in the infamous Jesus seminar, to cut out all the theological overlays encrusted upon the authentic original witness by later Christians influenced by Graeco-Roman philosophical categories and other misconceptions.[23]

So in liberal Protestantism, Christ's death on the cross becomes a *model* of suffering love or solidarity in the struggle for justice. Yet note that the cross is still interpreted in extrinsic categories, in terms of the external social-moral, personal or spiritual influence Jesus's example can have on others. It is an external influence that provides the motivation that we ourselves must internalize and then re-embody in our own lives. Once again the Spirit, often merely God's universal presence already in all persons and identical with the deepest self within us (of which Christ is the supreme example), is brought in to provide the subsequent additional help we need to live this reconceived version of Christian faith and

---

23 See Torrance, *Mediation*, 61–2.

life, set free from all mythological-poetic talk about bodily resurrection, miracles and the incarnation of the second person of the Trinity.[24]

THE JURIDICAL THEORY AT WORK IN CATHOLICISM

Yet the most tragic way this juridical model adversely affects Roman Catholicism (and in its own way conservative Protestantism) is in the area of spirituality. In order to guard and explain the sinless humanity that the Son of God assumed in the incarnation, the Roman Catholic Church felt compelled to assert the immaculate conception of the blessed Virgin Mary. Yet, in so doing, Jesus Christ seemed to become more and more divine and at the same time less and less human. Can a sinless saviour born of an immaculately conceived mother really ever be tempted like we are, we who are so heavily laden by the sin entrenched in the fallen nature in which we are all conceived? Do we have a high priest in Christ who can really sympathize with us in our weaknesses?

If you want to understand one of the deep spiritual and theological roots of the doctrine of the saints and prayers to the saints in popular Roman Catholic spirituality, it lies right here. In the depth of their awareness of their broken and sinful humanity, pious Roman Catholic laity know that a sinless saviour born of an immaculately conceived mother cannot really understand the depth of their struggles. Even the Blessed Virgin's humanity is different from their own. So in the sheer depth of their profound spiritual need for a high priest who has been tempted like they are, pious Roman Catholic laity turn to the saints for help in time of need.

We see this every week in Dubuque where I teach. The community is heavily Roman Catholic and every week in a local advertising paper there is a column of printed prayers of thanksgiving paid for and placed in the paper by Roman Catholic lay persons in gratitude for the help they have found in the midst of their dire need for a high priest who can empathize with their weakness.

THE JURIDICAL THEORY AT WORK AMONG CONSERVATIVES

Among conservative Protestants, who do not believe in this kind of doctrine of the saints, the same spiritual and theological problem can play out even more destructively. They are acutely aware of their sin and need. They perceive that Christ is far more divine and far less human than they are because Christ assumed a neutral and perfect humanity different from their own. With this understanding of Christ embedded in

---

24 Ibid.

the juridical model of the atonement they inherited from conservative Protestant sub-culture, they are left bereft of any high priest who can sympathize with them. So they internalize their sin, guilt and fear. This turns into a destructive and deep terror in the presence of the high and holy God before whom the angels veil their faces, as well as into self-loathing and a whole host of other self-destructive tendencies. I have dealt with countless lay persons trapped in this kind of fear and spiritual bondage because they do not have a high priest tempted in every way just as we are.

If we learn nothing else from T. F. Torrance's understanding of the incarnate saviour and Christ's atoning reconciliation, it is this: the Triune God has loved us to the uttermost, has taken up our cause, and in Jesus Christ has assumed our actual diseased, sinful, alienated, fallen human nature, faced every single temptation we face and ever will face day after day. Our blessed Lord suffered more than we will ever know under the load of it all, and yet at every point Christ overcame the sin, death, alienation and temptation in our humanity. He took our sin and guilt to the cross, cried our cry of dereliction in our place, conquered death, resurrected our humanity to newness of life, and even carried that humanity into union and communion with the blessed Trinitarian life of God in his ascension back to the Father.

Through it all the incarnate saviour by his atoning reconciliation healed, cleansed, sanctified and consecrated our humanity, setting it free from actual sin, free from our fallen sinful nature, and free *for* fellowship, union and communion through the Son in the Spirit with the Father and with one another in him. We have a high priest who is able to sympathize with our weakness, tempted in every way just as we are. Therefore let us always approach the throne of grace with confidence that we will receive mercy and find help in our time of need from our blessed incarnate saviour and his great act of atoning reconciliation.

In each of these theories, and their many variations, Torrance sees a gospel of external relations in which the sacrifice of Christ on the cross is interpreted merely in terms of moral influence or a juridical transaction between Jesus Christ and the rest of humanity. Collectively, Torrance refers to all these various forms of this gospel of external relations as the *Latin heresy*.[25]

---

[25] See Thomas F. Torrance, 'Karl Barth and the Latin Heresy', *Scottish Journal of Theology* 39 (1986), 461–82.

Personal and Ontological Redemption

In contrast to these reduced views of the atonement, Torrance argues for an atoning reconciliation that takes place *within* the one person of Jesus Christ, the incarnate saviour.[26] In the incarnation the Son of God has penetrated the dark depths of human sin and alienation from God, taking our fallen and diseased humanity upon himself in order to get at the very ontological roots of the sin and guilt entrenched in the recesses of our fallen human existence. Throughout his vicarious life, ministry, death, resurrection and ascension, atoning reconciliation was accomplished by Jesus Christ within the hypostatic or personal union of his divine and human natures lived out dynamically from cradle to cross and empty tomb.[27]

This entails a profound and intense personalization of salvation. For the Son of God himself acts personally on our behalf, not at a distance, but from within the very depths of our actual diseased, sinful, alienated and fallen humanity, which the incarnate saviour assumed and gathered to himself from birth to cross and resurrection. So for Torrance, the incarnate saviour effected atoning reconciliation for us by actually working out our salvation in himself, in our very humanity that he assumed from us. Atoning reconciliation takes place within the personal life and being of Jesus Christ. So while there are forensic and exemplar elements within Torrance's incarnational atoning reconciliation, Jesus Christ embodies the reality of our salvation in his divine-human person.[28] Christ does not mediate an atoning reconciliation other than what he is. He is in his own incarnate person the reality and content of the atoning redemption that he mediates to us. This is why Torrance is so adamant that all of the salvation Christ accomplished for us, including forgiveness of sin and our justification, comes to us through union with Christ, through participation in Christ in the Holy Spirit.

This means that being crucified with Christ and Christ living his life through us, as Paul describes the Christian life in Gal. 2:20, is talking about the exact same reality as our being filled by the Spirit in Eph. 5:18: one is looking at our salvation in terms of the activity of the second person of the Trinity, the other is looking at the very same salvation from the perspective of the activity of the third person of the Trinity.

---

26 See Torrance, *Trinitarian Faith*, 154–5.
27 Torrance asserts that the hypostatic union is the immediate ground of all Christ's mediatorial and reconciling activity in our human existence (Torrance, *Mediation*, 64–5).
28 Torrance, *Trinitarian Faith*, 156.

THE PRECISE NATURE OF VICARIOUS ATONING RECONCILIATION

By now it should be clear that for Torrance Christ's atoning reconciliation on the cross is to be conceived in closest relation to his personal incarnational assumption of our fallen humanity. Without a unifying centre in the Son of God assuming our actual fallen humanity, the various aspects of the atonement in the biblical witness break up into various theories of the atonement, each stressing one element or another found within Scripture, as has been the case repeatedly in the history of Christian faith.[29]

Torrance finds a far more realist and holistic understanding of the atonement in the New Testament especially through the 'Christological reinterpretation' of God's redemptive acts in the Passover and Exodus delivering Israel out of bondage in Egypt that we find at various points in the NT, as in Hebrews. This holistic understanding unifies the various aspects of the atonement found in the New Testament.[30]

It was Jesus's own interpretation of his Passion, revealed in his words to his disciples about his mission, and in the institution of the Holy Supper on the night he was betrayed, that provided the Church with its point of reference for interpreting the atonement according to Torrance.[31] Jesus told his disciples that the Son of Man came to serve and give his life a ransom for lost humanity, and the cup Jesus offered them represented the new covenant in his blood poured out for the forgiveness of sins.[32] In this way Christ interpreted his life and his Passion in light of the suffering servant and cultic atonement in the Hebrew Scriptures.[33] It is important to note that for T. F. Torrance, if we are to know Jesus Christ and understand his incarnational atoning reconciliation, we must view him within the dynamic inter-relations of God's interaction with Israel, for this is the matrix within which Jesus Christ actually lived, died and rose again.[34] This is the matrix within which the significance of the atonement comes into view. Apart from the Old Testament and Israel the cross would have been a bewildering enigma.[35]

So Torrance sees the New Testament understanding of redemption developed in light of Jesus's own self-interpretation through an appropriation of the three Hebrew terms (*pdh*, *kpr* and *g'l*) and their cognates

---

29 See ibid., 159–60, and also Torrance, 'The Atonement', 239.
30 Torrance, *Trinitarian Faith*, 171, and Torrance, 'The Atonement', 239.
31 Torrance, *Trinitarian Faith*, 168–70.
32 See Mk 10:45 and Mt. 20:28; and Mk 14:24, Mt. 26:28 and Lk. 22:20.
33 Torrance, *Trinitarian Faith*, 169.
34 Torrance, *Mediation*, 2–3, 5 and 60.
35 Ibid., 18.

associated with redemption in the Old Testament.[36] They relate to three crucial aspects of Torrance's understanding of the atonement, which he calls the dramatic, the priestly and the ontological. These concepts and images had already been used by the great prophets and applied to God's anointed Servant who would mediate a new covenant, bearing the sins of God's people and providing God's ultimate redemption.[37]

Under the impact of the life, death and resurrection of Jesus Christ, these three basic themes are transformed and utilized by Christ and the Church 'in expressing something of the indescribable mystery of Christ's Passion and the ineffable truth of atonement in its various but profoundly interrelated aspects'.[38] Torrance develops his realist and holistic doctrine of the atonement by drawing together these three aspects (the dramatic or dynamic, the priestly or cultic, and the ontological), with the ontological (incarnational) providing the overall pattern.[39] But we must always remember that in the end Torrance understands the reality of the atonement as so replete with depth and breadth of content that we can never render the reality of Christ's atoning reconciliation entirely explicit within the confines of our human thought and speech. We can apprehend it, but we cannot fully comprehend it, as Torrance repeatedly asserts.

The Dramatic Aspect of Redemption

The dramatic aspect or theme (*pdh*) refers to redemption as a mighty act of God delivering God's people from bondage or oppression and God's judgement upon it, as in the case of God's delivering Israel out of Egypt. In its fulfilment in the incarnate saviour, this dramatic aspect of the atonement points to the reality of Christ delivering us from the threat of the law, the power of death, the forces of evil, and even the judgement of God.[40] This is no ransom paid to the devil. Rather, the dramatic dimension refers to the mighty and victorious act of God in Christ's obedience unto death and triumphing over the powers of darkness, sin and death through the cross and the resurrection, disarming the powers and principalities, making a public spectacle of them in his victory over them (Col. 2:15).

---

36   See Torrance, 'The Atonement', 239–40, and Torrance, *Trinitarian Faith*, 170–2, for discussion of these three Hebrew terms.
37   Torrance, 'The Atonement', 240, and Torrance, *Trinitarian Faith*, 171.
38   Torrance, 'The Atonement', 239. Also see Torrance, *Trinitarian Faith*, 158.
39   Torrance, *Trinitarian Faith*, 173, and Torrance, 'The Atonement', 240. Torrance develops these three themes in the Old Testament and in the early church up through the Nicene theologians in significant detail in Torrance, *Trinitarian Faith*, 170–9.
40   Torrance, *Trinitarian Faith*, 175.

In his yet unpublished Edinburgh lectures, Torrance can speak in utterly astonishing realism about this, saying that, in Christ Jesus his incarnate Son, God himself enters into the destructive power of evil and so hazards, as it were, his very existence and being as God for the sake of overcoming the sin and evil entrenched in our world and in our fallen humanity.[41] Our predicament is far more perilous than we are often willing to concede. Nothing short of the presence and Passion of the Triune God there on the cross can overcome our dire situation.

So often when we face the inexplicable suffering and evil of this world, the untimely death of a loved one, cancer, sexual abuse of children, or the atrocities of war, we cry out for a theodicy, an explanation of how God can be all powerful, all good, and yet permit evil. We forget that evil, pain and suffering are far more real and deadly than we think and they cannot be explained or overcome simply by some theory or theodicy. Nothing short of God's becoming incarnate, suffering and dying can wrench the evil and suffering of this fallen world out of God's good creation and set it free for newness of life. If there was any hazard or risk on God's part, as T. F. Torrance suggests on occasion in his various publications, then truly horrendous and perilous is our situation and that of this fallen world in the thrall of evil and sin.

THE PRIESTLY ASPECT OF REDEMPTION

Closely related to the dramatic dimension is the priestly (*kpr*) aspect of redemption. In Torrance's own words, through atoning sacrifice for the expiation of sin and guilt, 'God incarnate in Christ draws near to us and draws us near to himself, cleansing us through his blood, sanctifying and healing us . . . ransoming us from servitude to the world, delivering us from slavery into liberty . . . thereby constituting us as a . . . special people belonging to himself.'[42] This aspect of Christ's atonement, of course, draws upon the ritual acts of sacrifice in the Old Testament and reveals again how profoundly important the Old Testament and the people of Israel are for any proper understanding of Christ's atoning reconciliation.

When we say that Jesus Christ is the Lamb of God that takes away the sin of the world, we are not saying that Jesus is like the little white lambs eating grass beside a babbling stream that we know about through our general human experience. Jesus as the Lamb of God draws its meaning from God's dealing with Israel in history as inscribed in the Old Testament. In the Exodus account, at God's command, the people of Israel

---

41   Thomas F. Torrance, 'Edinburgh Lectures in Dogmatics' (unpublished), ch. 7, 7.
42   Torrance, 'The Atonement', 240–1.

slaughtered spotless lambs, spreading the blood over the doorposts of their homes so the angel of death would pass over them. Jesus as the Lamb of God draws also from the countless lambs slaughtered throughout the history of Israel in obedience to the LORD's command, as part of the liturgical, priestly, covenanted way of response that God provided Israel. Through such sacrifices, Israel could come before God and receive forgiveness and restoration to covenant partnership with God even when Israel repeatedly broke the covenant. Of course the whole Old Testament sacrificial system points forward in time to the final and true Lamb of God, Christ himself, and his ultimate sacrifice on the cross. So the New Testament interprets Christ's atoning reconciliation in the midst of Israel in light of the Israel and the Old Testament. In this priestly aspect of atoning reconciliation culminating in the cross Torrance incorporates forensic elements within his understanding of the atonement.[43] Torrance can even speak of this aspect as an expiatory sacrifice offered in atonement for sin and in propitiatory reconciliation with God.[44] While Torrance is adamant that God is always the subject of this act of reconciliation and atonement and never the object of it, he even makes a place for the wrath of God against human sin and guilt on the cross.[45]

Here is how Torrance states it in his unpublished Edinburgh lectures:

> The menaced and threatened existence of humanity into which God the Son enters and within which he lives as son of man is an existence under the threat of destruction not only from the inherent negation of evil but the negation of it through the divine judgement . . . It is into our very existence under divine judgement and into its corruption and destruction under divine negation that God enters himself in order to save humanity. That is why the hazard, so to speak, to which God submits as he stakes his own being in our salvation, comes not from the attack of evil by itself but from the divine judgement and negation of evil. It is that fact that makes the cross and the *Eli, Eli, lama sabachthani* of the Lord Jesus so indescribably terrible, makes it the sheer anguish of God bowed under his own judgement on sin, judgement not mitigated but utterly fulfilled. . . . God resists sin in the full Godness of God. That is the meaning of the *wrath* of God . . . But let us be quite clear about what the wrath of God means. It is . . . the wrath of redeeming love. As such the very wrath of God is a sign of hope, not of utter destruction . . .[46]

---

43   See Torrance, *Trinitarian Faith*, 161, 170 and 173, and Torrance, 'The Atonement', 239–42.
44   Torrance, 'The Atonement', 239.
45   Torrance, *Trinitarian Faith*, 170.
46   Torrance, 'Edinburgh Lectures', chs 7, 8–9 and 13.

What Torrance is saying here is that Jesus's cry of dereliction is no mere cry ushering forth solely from his human nature, as if only his humanity suffered in our place. There on the cross, it is the cry of God the Son as the very righteous and holy judgement and wrath of God against human sin fell upon our blessed incarnate saviour. That cry, 'My God, my God, why have you forsaken me?' is an inter-Trinitarian event in which God, our incarnate saviour, bows under God's own unmitigated judgement and wrath against our sin which the Son of God assumed from us when he took upon our sinful alienated nature. How can we do anything else but clasp our hands over our mouths, bow our heads in wonder and astonishment at the sheer depth and breadth of the love of God in Christ that would go to such an extreme because the blessed Triune God has willed not to be God without us.

THE ONTOLOGICAL ASPECT OF REDEMPTION

Finally the ontological (*g'l*) aspect of the atonement in Torrance's theology refers to redemption out of bondage, destitution, or forfeited rights through the advocacy of someone with a kinship, affinity or bond to the person in need. The emphasis is on the person and nature of this redeemer (called the *go'el* in the Old Testament) who claims the cause of the person in need and stands in for that person. This Old Testament concept of redeemer is even applied to God who takes up the cause of God's people, as in Deutero-Isaiah where we find the promise of a new Exodus when the Divine Redeemer will rescue Israel through an anointed Suffering Servant who bears the iniquities of God's people.[47]

While the Old Testament never identifies this Suffering Servant with the divine redeemer, this identification is precisely what Torrance sees taking place in Jesus Christ, the incarnate saviour in the New Testament. The incarnate Son of God is simultaneously Suffering Servant and Divine Redeemer. He is *homoousios* (of one being) with God, but has also established an ontological covenant bond with us in our lost condition and is therefore *homoousios*, of one being, with us through assuming our diseased and sinful humanity to himself in the incarnation. The incarnate Son identifies with us in our diseased, destitute, damned and dying condition, and makes our cause his own by taking our fallen and sinful humanity upon himself.[48]

This incarnational aspect provides the overall framework for Torrance's doctrine of the atonement, for the incarnate saviour in his very person in his oneness with us, 'sums up and is intensively in himself

---

47 Torrance, *Trinitarian Faith*, 171.
48 Torrance, 'The Atonement', 241.

all that he undertakes in atoning activity on our behalf'.[49] By virtue of this ontological identification with us in the incarnation, Christ claims us for the redemption he has accomplished in his overcoming of sin, judgement and death, and the offering of himself in propitiatory sacrifice to God on our behalf and in our place.[50]

All the elements of Christ's atoning work interpenetrate one another in a dynamic whole within Christ's one Person as both Suffering Servant and Divine Redeemer.[51] This is why Torrance repeatedly emphasizes that Christ is always priest and sacrifice, offerer and offering, who not only suffers and dies in our place on the cross but carries our sinful humanity through judgement and death to resurrection and new life, indeed ascends back to the Father as the incarnate saviour who continues to unite in his one person our forgiven, reconciled and redeemed human nature with his divine nature. So in the ascension Christ unites our very humanity in his one person in union and communion with the Triune God. Jesus Christ is our Great High Priest even now still incarnate in the very the presence of the Father on our behalf.[52]

Here we see how Torrance's understanding of incarnational atoning reconciliation unites not only the incarnation and the atonement, but also unites the cross and resurrection and ascension in a seamless holistic understanding of how the Triune God brings about our salvation from birth through life, ministry and death to resurrection and ascension. This brings us to a final point in Torrance's understanding of atoning reconciliation: what he calls the blessed or atoning exchange.

THE BLESSED OR ATONING EXCHANGE

This exchange involves the redemptive translation of humanity '*from* one state *into* another brought about by Christ who in his self-abnegating love took our place that we might have his place, becoming what we are that we might become what he is'.[53] Atoning exchange is at the centre of Torrance's understanding of incarnational atoning redemption for Christ's union with us in our actual broken and sinful nature. It entails

---

49 Ibid.
50 See ibid., and Torrance, *Trinitarian Faith*, 176.
51 Torrance, 'The Atonement', 241–2, and Torrance, *Trinitarian Faith*, 175.
52 Torrance, *Trinitarian Faith*, 154, 170, 173 and 177.
53 Ibid., 179. Torrance finds support for this in the early church through the Nicene Fathers and in Calvin and Karl Barth, as well as in the New Testament (2 Cor. 8:9 for example). See ibid., 179–81 and Torrance, *Karl Barth*, 204 and 223. Torrance, however, is critical of Reformed theology on this point since he thinks that, on the whole, Reformed theology tends to formulate the blessed exchange within a rather Latin conception of the incarnation. Ibid., 231.

the humiliation and self-sacrifice of the incarnate Son in life and death, but also the transformation and the exaltation of our humanity which is lifted up in and through Christ in his resurrection and ascension to share in the communion which God is in God's own Trinitarian life. Thus the descent and ascent, the humiliation and exaltation, the death and resurrection of the Son of God are inseparable and involve from beginning to end this blessed exchange between Christ and ourselves.

This point brings out the decisive significance of Jesus Christ's resurrection and ascension in Torrance's theology, for they are more than simply the verdict of the Father's complete approval of the self-offering of Son on the cross. Torrance argues that redemption takes place through Jesus Christ's resurrection and ascension and not just Christ's death on the cross. Incarnational atoning reconciliation involves not only forgiveness and freedom from bondage, but also new life in union with God.[54] The end and ultimate goal of the atonement is more than the restoration of relations between God and humanity; for it includes union with God in and through Jesus Christ in whom our human nature is not only saved, healed and renewed but lifted up to participate in the very light, life and love of the Holy Trinity.[55]

It is also important to note that for Torrance this is *bodily* resurrection and ascension in which Jesus Christ in his risen *humanity* is exalted into the immediate presence of God the Father where Christ 'presented himself to the Father on our behalf and presented us in himself as those he had redeemed and consecrated to be his brethren'.[56] This is another way of expressing what is conveyed in the concept *theosis* or *theopoiesis*, by which we mean not the divinization of humanity, but the recreation of our lost humanity in the dynamic, atoning interaction between the divine and human natures within the one person of Jesus Christ. Through him we enter into the very communion which God is in God's Trinitarian Life.[57] So we are brought into union and communion with the divine Life and Love of God, yet preserved in our humanity, not transmuted into divinity.

For Torrance, this blessed exchange involves the entire relationship between Jesus Christ and ourselves: 'between his obedience and our disobedience, his holiness and our sin, his life and our death, his strength and our weakness . . . his wisdom and our ignorance, his joy and our misery . . .'[58] The atoning exchange *is* incarnational redemption and

---

54 Torrance, *Trinitarian Faith*, 180.
55 Torrance, *Mediation*, 66.
56 Torrance, 'Latin Heresy', 477.
57 Torrance, *Trinitarian Faith*, 189.
58 Ibid., 181.

incarnational redemption *is* atoning exchange, all worked out in the one person of the incarnate Son of God within the twisted depths of our fallen humanity.

While this blessed exchange reaches its apex in the humiliation and death of Christ on the cross and his exaltation in the resurrection and ascension, it is ongoing throughout his earthly life. Let me point to just one example of what Torrance has in mind and how it illumines the New Testament: Jesus's baptism by John in the Jordan river.

Why did Jesus submit to John's baptism, which both Mt. 3 and Mk 1 indicate was a baptism of *repentance*? Jesus never sinned. He had nothing to repent of. So why undergo this pointless baptism of repentance by John the Baptist? For Torrance it was not *his* sins but *our* sins that Jesus repented of and confessed there before the Father at the hands of John as he went under the water. Humanity does not even repent aright. Our blessed incarnate saviour even does that for us in self-humiliation on our behalf, in our place and in our stead there in the Jordan as part of this blessed exchange.

According to Mark's Gospel, when Jesus came up out of the water, heaven was torn open, the Spirit descended upon Jesus like a dove, and the voice of the Father spoke from heaven, 'You are my beloved Son; with you I am well pleased' (Mk 1:10–11). This means that the Father accepts the incarnate Son's self-humiliation, repentance and confession of sin on our behalf and pours out the Spirit upon him. Though the incarnate Son of God was never without the Spirit, he receives the Holy Spirit into our humanity, the humanity he took from us in the incarnation. And the Father's words of pleasure in the Son extend to us as well though our union with the incarnate Son by that same Holy Spirit who is sent by the Father through the Son to us at Pentecost and ever after.

Elsewhere, following Irenaeus, Torrance argues that this blessed exchange includes especially the gift of the Holy Spirit. In the union of divine and human natures in the Son the eternal Spirit of the living God has composed himself, as it were, to dwell with human nature, and human nature has been adapted and become accustomed to receive and bear that same Holy Spirit.[59] The Holy Spirit in his new coming at Pentecost does not simply proceed eternally from the Father, but is mediated through the blessed exchange that takes place in the earthly life and atoning reconciliation of the incarnate saviour on our behalf. As the Spirit of Jesus, Torrance sees the Holy Spirit not as an isolated and naked Spirit, 'but rather as the Spirit charged with all the experience of Jesus as he shared to the full our mortal nature and weakness, and endured its temptation and grief and suffering and death'.[60]

---

59 Torrance, *Reconstruction*, 246.
60 Ibid., 247.

Thus, every baptism that the Church does in the Trinitarian name is finally at its greatest depth a union with and participation in Christ's own baptism in the Jordan and Christ's own baptism in the cross and resurrection. Torrance views all of the earthly life and ministry of the incarnate saviour in terms of this blessed exchange. He thinks out the doctrine of ministry and the gifts of the Spirit also in terms of this blessed exchange and our union with and participation in it via the Holy Spirit. At its core the blessed exchange involved in Christ's atoning reconciliation tells us that the Triune God has loved us to the uttermost and has entered the dark depths of our sinful humanity within this fallen creation in order to make our misery, shame, sin, guilt, alienation and godlessness his own, substituting himself for us, thwarting evil, forgiving, reconciling, redeeming and restoring us to union and communion with the Triune God who loves us more than he loves himself.

THE RANGE OF CHRIST'S ATONING REDEMPTION

The range and significance of the atoning exchange that took place in Jesus Christ, according to Torrance, is as comprehensive and boundless as the eternal nature, being and love of the Triune God incarnate in Jesus Christ.[61] If God did not spare his own Son but gives us with him all things (Rom. 8:32), then the benefits of God's gift of Christ to humanity are inexhaustible.[62] Torrance sees the redemptive exchange as opening the door to all of God's creative and sanctifying purposes for humanity.

Following Athanasius, Torrance also emphasizes the universal range of Christ's redemptive activity, for Christ's life, death and resurrection on our behalf and in our stead, 'Christ as Man represents all mankind ... all who belong to human nature are involved and represented – all human beings without exception'.[63] Torrance rejects any and every idea of limited atonement, for if in the incarnation the Son of God assumed the actual fallen nature of humanity, then all human beings without exception are involved and represented.[64] Only if Christ's humanity (and atoning reconciliation) has no inner ontological connection with those for whom he died, but is regarded as an external instrument used by God as he wills, in effecting salvation for all those whom God chooses can the atonement be limited to only some people.[65]

---

61 Torrance, *Trinitarian Faith*, 181–2, and Torrance, 'The Atonement', 244–7.
62 Torrance, *Trinitarian Faith*, 181.
63 Torrance, 'The Atonement', 245.
64 Ibid.
65 Torrance, 'Latin Heresy', 481. Torrance has a detailed and sophisticated analysis of limited atonement and universal salvation which he sees as both bound up with the 'Latin Heresy'. See ibid., 481–2.

The universal range of Christ's effective incarnational redemption, Torrance contends, includes not only all people, but the entire universe: the universal range of the redemptive work of Christ takes in not only all humanity, but the whole created universe of space and time, including all things (*ta panta*) visible and invisible, earthly and heavenly alike.[66] This includes the fulfilment of salvation for all time until the final consummation when Christ returns, for Christ's incarnation, death and resurrection are not a momentary episode, but rather a perfected event within the divine-human reality and person of Jesus Christ who is even now in the presence of God the Father and remains unceasingly present and active as God incarnate.[67]

In light of statements like these some might think that Torrance embraces universal salvation. This, however, would be a grave misunderstanding of his position. Torrance sees universalism and limited atonement as twin heresies which rest on a deeper heresy, the recourse to a logico-causal explanation of why the atoning death of the Lord Jesus Christ avails or does not avail for all people.[68] Torrance rejects universalism because we cannot explain why some people believe and others do not, any more than we can explain why evil came into the world.[69] The gospel, Torrance argues, does not even tell us precisely how evil is vanquished by Christ and the cross. It is a mystery before which the angels veil their faces. But the gospel tells us that God has loved us to the uttermost and has entered the dark depths of our sinful humanity within this fallen creation in order to make our misery, shame, sin, guilt, alienation and godlessness his own, substituting himself for us, thwarting evil, redeeming and restoring us to union and communion with the Triune God who loves us more than he loves himself.

---

66 Torrance, 'The Atonement', 249.
67 Ibid., 232.
68 Ibid., 248.
69 Torrance, *Karl Barth*, 239.

Chapter 3

FAR AS THE CURSE IS FOUND: THE SIGNIFICANCE OF CHRIST'S ASSUMING A *FALLEN* HUMAN NATURE IN THE TORRANCE THEOLOGY

Gerrit Scott Dawson

1. PERSONAL INTRODUCTION

'Last of all, as to one untimely born, he appeared also to me' (1 Cor. 15:8). So Paul wrote concerning the resurrection appearances of our Lord. He was not there among the original apostles when Jesus ate breakfast with them on the beach, nor when Christ breathed the blessing of the Spirit on them in the upper room. Paul felt like something of an interloper after he had a revelation of the risen Christ along the Damascus Road. He was the last one to see the resurrected Jesus.

'Last of all, as to one untimely born.' Of the hundreds and hundreds of students Thomas and James Torrance had, I was one of the last. While Tom gave the Warfield Lectures at Princeton Seminary that would become his masterwork, *The Trinitarian Faith*, I was on campus. But too stupid to go and sit at his feet. I would need more than a dozen years to be ready for what these brothers offer the Church. Then I became their student. Though never officially or formally, I was a disciple nonetheless, taken within a circle of friendship and mentoring by which I consider these men my fathers in the faith.

In 1996, my wife Rhonda and I returned to Edinburgh with our friends Parker and Patty Williamson. Though we had met Tom and James two years earlier, it was on this second visit that the eyes of my mind and heart began to open. First, I read James' book, *Worship, Community and the Triune God of Grace* on the train from London. A spark began to ignite. Then, that night, we enjoyed an extraordinary three-hour dinner with Tom and Margaret, James and Mary at the Prestonfield House. I can still feel the touch of James' hand on my sleeve and the worship in his voice as he spoke of the 'Triune God of Grace'. Tom had brought along copies of his two latest books. To me he handed *Scottish Theology*. Through its pages, a love for theology would be fanned into flame. And the subject of this essay would be raised.

2. Redeeming Us from the Moment of Conception

Several months after that dinner, deep into the text, my eyes fell on a particular paragraph in the section on Thomas Erskine. It seemed that suddenly the depths opened up before me. Here was something I had never thought of before, but something that rang true:

> Of considerable theological importance for Erskine was the teaching of St. Paul 'about God sending his own Son in the likeness of sinful flesh' . . . This is not to say that Christ was a sinner, far from it, for the very contrary was the case: he condemned sin in the flesh he assumed from us, our flesh, the flesh of sinners, that he might redeem it from sin, and lift it up to God. 'It was a fallen nature, a nature which had fallen by sin, and he thus condemned sin in the flesh. He came into it as a new head, that he might take it out of the fall, and redeem it from sin, and lift it up to God.' That is to say Erskine held strongly to the truth that in assuming flesh from fallen and sinful humanity, far from being contaminated by it, Christ redeemed and sanctified it at the same time – the very assumption of Adamic humanity was essentially redemptive from the moment of its conception in the Virgin Mary.[1]

In assuming flesh from fallen humanity, Christ was not contaminated by our sin. Far from it. Even as he assumed our human nature, Jesus began redeeming us. From the moment of conception the incarnate Son of God was forging our salvation. Thus, the accomplishment of our eternally purposed redemption did not begin on the cross. It began in the incarnation, in the miraculous conception within the womb of Mary by which humanity and God were joined as one person in two natures. He took from Mary a *real* humanity. Yet the stain of human sin which passed through every generation did not stain Christ Jesus. No, in taking our humanity, by the work of the Holy Spirit, he immediately began cleansing it. He continued to do so throughout what Calvin called 'the whole course of his obedience':[2] through his baptism, his ministry, his crucifixion, his resurrection and glorious ascension.

It had never occurred to me how our salvation was being worked out *within* Christ's life from the moment of his conception. For I had not grasped the significance of the incarnation for the atonement. I would

---

1 Thomas F. Torrance, *Scottish Theology* (Edinburgh: T&T Clark, 1996), 279.
2 John Calvin, *Institutes of the Christian Religion*, ed. John T. McNeill, trans. Ford Lewis Battles (Philadelphia: Westminster Press, 1960), 2.16.5.

later realize that what so captivated my imagination was an essential, distinctive element of the Torrance theology.

Central to the teaching of Thomas, James and David Torrance is the recovery of the incarnation in all its fullness. The ancient church, especially in the East, understood that our redemption is in the cross, certainly, but not only in the cross. Moreover, the cross only makes sense in light of the incarnation. The enfleshment of the eternal Son of God in Jesus Christ gives to the cross the depth and the height of its meaning. In other words, through the eyes of the Torrance brothers, I began to see that my Jesus had been too small. My theology was too shallow. Richer theological jewels than I had imagined possible were being revealed.

In short, the story goes like this. The Son of God came to us as the man Jesus to restart the human race. He took to himself our very bone and skin, heart and mind. Jesus was the root out of which a new humanity could arise. This is possible because in Jesus God truly joined himself to our ruined, wrecked, sin-sick, fallen humanity, then transformed it. In our flesh he won the victory of perfect obedience even through the agony of Gethsemane and death upon the cross. Then, passing through death into resurrection, Jesus in our flesh was transformed. He was outfitted for heaven, the realm of God, clothed with a body fit for life in the intimate and immediate presence of his Father. Even now, he remains in our skin, glorified yet still essentially *us*. For, in his ascension, he has taken what we are, in our embodied, besouled existence, into the eternal Triune life of God.

On this basis of all he is and has done in our humanity, Christ joins us to himself. He unites us to his new humanity by sending the Holy Spirit into our hearts. The blessed Spirit quickens us to new life, creates faith in us, and enables us to be born from above into the body of Christ our head. Our hope is that in Christ, we, too, are a new creation right now (2 Cor. 5:17). Then, on the last day, even our lowly bodies will be transformed to be like Christ's glorious body (Phil. 3:21). We, too, will be outfitted for perfect communion in the Triune God.

The Torrance tradition, in distinction from many others, emphasizes that in the incarnation, *Jesus took up a fallen human nature*. Of course, by the agency of the Spirit, he bore this fallen nature sinlessly. But nevertheless it was the actual humanity which you and I indwell to which Jesus united himself. This, as we shall see below, was a crucial aspect of how Jesus could redeem us.

But is this insistence on the fallen humanity which Jesus took compatible with historic orthodoxy? Before we attempt to explore the Torrance position and its relationship to the apostolic faith, we must first back up to consider a crucial, yet broader, theological question. What difference does it make that Jesus took up the humanity that we really are?

3. The Curse

To grasp the significance of *that* question, we have to plumb for a while the depth of our need. Only in view of our desperate situation can we understand why God had to go to such lengths to rescue us. The third stanza of Isaac Watts' beloved Christmas carol 'Joy to the World!' declares:

> No more let sins and sorrow grow.
> Nor thorns infest the ground.
> He comes to make his blessings flow,
> Far as the curse is found . . .

How far is that? The ancient curse for Adam's disobedience included thorns in the ground and bones in the grave. The toil of work, the pain of childbirth, the dysfunction in family relationships and ever present mortality followed upon our disobedience. This theme of our curse is played out through the pages of Scripture.

We read in Gen. 2:17, 'Cursed is the ground because of you; in pain shall you eat of it all the days of your life; thorns and thistles it shall bring forth from you . . . in the sweat of your face you shall eat bread, till you return to the ground, for out of it you were taken. For you are dust and to dust shall you return.' So we recall every Ash Wednesday. As we enter Lent, we contemplate both our sin and the mortal frailty which flows from it. 'You are dust and to dust you shall return.'

The preacher in Ecclesiastes laments, 'Man's fate is like that of the animals; the same fate awaits them both: As one dies, so dies the other. All have the same breath; man has no advantage over the animal. Everything is meaningless. All go to the same place; all come from dust, and to dust all return' (Eccl. 3:19–21).

From the curse came our frailty and finitude, our isolation and lostness. But the problem is more than these symptoms of our mortality. It is the root of our disease, the thorn that infests the ground of our very lives: our sinfulness. We read in the prophets:

> All of us have become like one who is unclean,
> and all our righteous acts are like filthy rags;
> we all shrivel up like a leaf,
> and like the wind our sins sweep us away. (Isa. 64:6)

And:

> The heart is deceitful above all things,
> and desperately sick;
> who can understand it? (Jer. 17:9)

This problem is located in the very centre of our being. Jesus confirmed, 'But the things that come out of the mouth come from the heart, and these make a man "unclean". For out of the heart come evil thoughts, murder, adultery, sexual immorality, theft, false testimony, slander' (Mt. 15:18–19).

Even more, though, our heart condition has implications for all creation. Paul wrote:

> The creation waits in eager expectation for the sons of God to be revealed. For the creation was subjected to futility not by its own choice, but by the will of the one who subjected it, in hope that the creation itself will be liberated from its bondage to decay and brought into the glorious freedom of the children of God. (Rom. 8:19–21)

Paul recognized the subjection to futility which was felt from Adam through Ecclesiastes into the present moment. It is not limited to humanity. All creation is in bondage to decay. The earth groans under the curse which followed our disobedience. The thorn is deep indeed.

But Paul has mentioned this groaning in the context of hope. As through humanity the curse came on creation, so in the liberation of humanity will come the restoration of all creation as well. Through our redemption will come the fulfilment of the created order.

4. THE CURE

This raises the next question. How, then, has God worked out the removal of such a deeply embedded thorn of death and futility? We return to the prophet:

> I looked, but there was no one to help;
> I was appalled, but there was no one to uphold;
> so my own arm brought me salvation,
> and my wrath upheld me. (Isa. 63:5)

We were not, and are not, capable of saving ourselves. The disease at the core of our humanity is beyond our skill to heal. God, however, did not leave us alone to wallow in the devices and desires of our own hearts. The LORD our God determined that he would bring salvation to a helpless race. He would do so by coming himself to his people.

In what way would he appear? As triumphant, conquering king? No, first he would visit us as the Suffering Servant, the one who bears the weight and grief of this world all on his shoulders:

> Surely he has borne our griefs
> and carried our sorrows;
> yet we esteemed him stricken by God,
> smitten by God, and afflicted.
> But he was wounded for our transgressions;
> he was crushed for our iniquities;
> upon him was the chastisement that brought us peace,
> and with his stripes we are healed.
> All we like sheep have gone astray;
> we have turned every one of us to his own way;
> and the LORD has laid on him
> the iniquity of us all. (Isa. 53:4–6)

The Suffering Servant took upon himself the worst that we are. Moreover, he received into himself the consequences of having our wicked hearts' desires fully worked out to their natural result which is death and hell.

Paul connected this prophecy to Jesus in 2 Cor. 5:21: 'For our sake he made him to be sin who knew no sin, so that in him we might become the righteousness of God.' His arrival in our midst was our salvation. The LORD himself came to save us. He came to us *as a man* in Jesus Christ, who took upon himself the sin and separation of humanity, made it his own in the terrible moment of dereliction on the cross, and then healed the breach. The patristic shorthand for this reads, 'He became what we are that we might become what he is.'[3] Without himself sinning, he became on the cross the sin at the root of our ancient curse that we might have, from the inside out, the righteousness he lived from the centre of his being.

---

3   This thought is deeply rooted in the Church Fathers; see, for example Irenaeus (*Against Heresies* 5. Pref.) in *The Ante-Nicene Fathers* (*ANF*), ed. Alexander Roberts and James Donaldson, American edn, A. Cleveland Coxe (Edinburgh: T&T Clark and Grand Rapids: William B. Eerdmans, 1993) and Athanasius (*Against the Arians*, 4.7) and Gregory of Nazianzen (*Oration* 1.5) in *A Select Library of Nicene and Post Nicene Fathers of the Christian Church* (*NPNF*), ed. Phillip Schaff and Henry Wace (Edinburgh: T&T Clark and Grand Rapids: William B. Eerdmans, 1993), second series.

Thus, in his union with us, Jesus healed us. By becoming what we are, the eternal Son of God could act from within our humanity for the sake of all humanity. The one who stands as creator in relationship to all human beings did a creative work within the humanity he took from us. In turn, joined to him by the Spirit, united to his new humanity, we may thus receive the benefits of all he accomplished in our flesh.[4]

So we think through this redemption in terms of the saving union of Christ with us and our union with Christ. As we do so, we hold together the Triune purpose for our salvation conceived before the foundation of the world with the continuing incarnation of Christ. We stretch our minds to keep the particular moment of incarnation at Christ's conception in Mary's womb together with the finished work of the cross. We consider as one grand act the 33 years of Jesus's perfect intimacy with his Father as it was enacted from within our humanity. We go on to realize how even in this moment he appears before the Father in our name and on our behalf – in our skin – as our faithful High Priest. Thus, we do not separate Jesus's ministry from his sacrifice. We do not divide his active obedience in prayer, love, teaching and healing from his passive obedience in going willingly to the cross where the sins of the world were laid upon him. We keep the necessity of his circumcision, baptism, temptations, transfiguration, institution of the Supper and fidelity both in Gethsemane and before Pilate to the meaning of his crucifixion. All these events are interlocked. Of course, without the ultimate obedience enacted in the crucifixion, the previous years would have been nullified. There is no salvation without the cross. But the cross is not an isolated transaction. It is part of the whole incarnate person of Christ who saves us by means of his work on our behalf.[5]

---

4   See Thomas F. Torrance, *The Trinitarian Faith* (Edinburgh: T&T Clark, 1988), 155:

> As the Head of creation, in whom all things consist, he is the only one who really can act on behalf of all and save them. When he took our human nature upon himself, and in complete somatic solidarity with us offered himself up to death in atoning sacrifice for man, he acted instead of all and on behalf of all. Thus the redemptive work of Christ was fully representative and truly universal in its rage. [range]

5   Thomas F. Torrance, *The Trinitarian Faith* (Edinburgh: T&T Clark, 1988), 180:

> It is, then, upon this concept of atoning exchange as its inner hinge that the whole doctrine of incarnational redemption through the descent and ascent, the death and resurrection, the humiliation and exaltation, of the Son of God rests. It lies at the heart of the Nicene theological orientation in which the death and resurrection of Christ were never treated in isolation from each other, and in which therefore redemption was thought of as taking place through the resurrection and ascension as well as the death of Christ, not just from death, bondage and judgment, but into new life, freedom and blessedness in God.

John Calvin helps us here:

> Now someone asks, How has Christ abolished sin, banished the separation between us and God, and acquired righteousness to render God favorable and kindly toward us? To this we can in general reply that he has achieved this for us by the *whole course of his obedience* . . . In short, from the time when he took on the form of a servant, he began to pay the price of liberation in order to redeem us.[6]

Leaning on what the Church Fathers had established, Calvin went on to describe how Christ's union with us and our union with him is part of a miraculous commerce between God and humanity:

> This is the *wonderful exchange* which, out of his measureless benevolence, he has made with us; that, becoming Son of man with us, he has made us sons of God with him; that, by his descent to earth, he has prepared an ascent to heaven for us; that, by taking on our mortality, he has conferred his immortality upon us; that, accepting our weakness, he has strengthened us by his power; that, receiving our poverty unto himself, he has transferred his wealth to us; that, taking the weight of our iniquity upon himself (which oppressed us), he has clothed us with his righteousness.[7]

This *wonderful exchange* occurred within the life of the incarnate Son of God among us. Jesus the Suffering Servant absorbed the poison of our sin unto death, but the life-giving health of his eternal life and perfect obedience overcame that death. He took our killing blows full on and returned them as forgiving love. He absorbed the rage of our guilty lostness and transformed it into the peace that passes understanding.

Thomas Torrance has explained so ardently, 'Jesus Christ [is] God himself incarnate, who refused to be alone or without us, but insisted on penetrating into the heart of our sin and violence and unappeasable agony in order to take it all upon himself and to save us.'[8] The entire incarnate life was, and remains, necessary to our salvation: from conception through obedient, Spirit-empowered ministry to atoning death on the cross; through victorious resurrection in the body to triumphant ascension to pouring out the life-giving Spirit to present intercession as

---

6 Calvin, *Institutes*, 2.16.5.
7 Calvin, *Institutes*, 4.17.2. See also Thomas F. Torrance, *The Trinitarian Faith*, 179.
8 Thomas F. Torrance, 'The Christ Who Loves Us', in Thomas Torrance, James Torrance and David Torrance, *A Passion for Christ: The Vision that Ignites Ministry*, ed. Gerrit Dawson and Jock Stein (Edinburgh: Handsel Press, and Lenoir, NC: PLC Publications, 1999), 13.

our great High Priest. From the beginning to the present, and even into the future, Jesus makes this full, yet sinless, identification with who we are in the midst of our lostness. He does this in order to dig beneath the thorn of our sinfulness, draw it out, and then recreate us in himself. He takes from us the horrible thorn and returns to us the healing fullness of the Triune God of grace.

5. What Kind of Man?

So, we have seen that the depth of our need required a salvation that would issue from within the depth of our being. That made reply to the question of why it was necessary that Christ took up a *real* humanity. Though today there is much general amnesia about the breadth of this grand salvation, there is yet agreement in historic orthodoxy about what Jesus has accomplished. He took our sins upon himself and returned to us forgiveness and new life. We agree that he did this as one who was, and is, both fully human and fully divine, fully the Son of Man and the Son of God. Further, there is no disagreement on the question of whether or not Jesus was sinless. The Church and her theologians have through the centuries affirmed with Scripture: Jesus was without sin (Heb. 4:15). He did not sin in thought or deed, so that he might offer himself as a perfect, pure sacrifice in our place.

But there has not been agreement over how to answer our original question about what *kind* of man the Son of God became. Was he an ordinary man, a person like us? Or did his divine nature make him a kind of superman? We read in Heb. 4:15: 'For we have not an high priest which cannot be touched with the feeling of our infirmities; but was in all points tempted like *as we are, yet* without sin' (AV). These texts seem to answer both our questions with a Yes. Jesus is, on the one hand, 'as we are'. Yet, on the other hand, is 'without sin', and in that sense definitely *not* as we are.

For the Torrances, the emphasis lands on the 'as we are', including the assertion that God took up sinful flesh which he wore sinlessly in Jesus. This Torrance position may well be controversial. For the idea that Jesus took up a *fallen* humanity has seemed at first glance to compromise the sinlessness of Jesus. Still more questions are raised. If Jesus had a predisposition to sin, even though he beat it back, would that not in itself be the sin called concupiscence, an expression of the sinful heart? Moreover, how could the Son of God take a sin-stained humanity into union within himself? For how could a holy God coexist with sinful humanity?

Such questions aim to protect the holiness of the Son of God in our humanity. Yet they drive us once again to ask prior questions. We have to consider the way forward between two poles: (a) if Jesus was not sinful, and he was fully God in the flesh, then wasn't it actually *impossible* for him to sin? Yet, (b) if it is necessary to our redemption that the redeemer be fully human, didn't Jesus have to be of the same 'lump of Adam' as we are? Didn't his temptations have to be real if his humanity was real?

6. WAS IT *IMPOSSIBLE* FOR HIM TO SIN?

Some theologians take the possibility of Jesus's sinning out of play. For example, the theological notes in the *Reformation Study Bible* declare:

> Jesus could not sin, but He was able to be tempted . . . Since His human nature was conformed to his divine nature, it was impossible that He should fall in the course of His resistance. It was inevitable that He would endure temptation to the end, feeling their entire force, and emerge victorious for His people.[9]

Jesus has two natures united in one person. He is fully God and fully human. For the theologians of the *Study Bible*, the divine nature so controlled the human nature that the human nature of Jesus could do nothing contrary to the will of Jesus's divine nature. He could not compromise his Godhood by the acts of his manhood. The presence of divinity made it inevitable that Jesus's humanity would not fail.

Loraine Boettner, a fine theologian, in *Studies in Theology*, explains further:

> As a matter of fact, it was impossible for Christ to commit sin. For in His essential nature, He was God, and God cannot sin . . . In order for us to understand how Christ could have been tempted while at the same time there was no possibility that He would fall, it is necessary that we keep in mind the real nature of temptation.[10]

Boettner goes on to describe temptation as a testing to prove genuineness. Real gold may be tested, but because it is genuine, it always stands the test, there is no possibility of its being other than what it is.

The logic in this position is consistent. It relies on classic a priori definitions of God as perfect and holy. It interprets Rom. 8:3, 'the likeness of sinful flesh' (*homoiomati sarkos hamartias*) as maintaining a necessary

---

[9] R. C. Sproul (ed.), *The Reformation Study Bible* (Orlando: Ligonier Ministries, 2002), p. 1836.
[10] Loraine Boettner, *Studies in Theology* (Phillipsburg, NJ: Presbyterian and Reformed Publishers, 1946), 211.

distance between the incarnate Son and our corrupt nature. But is such theology deep enough to express the reality of the incarnation adequately? Does a Jesus who simply *cannot* sin truly have a genuine humanity? Such a Jesus would be a man in a category higher even than our first parents before their fall. Is that a person who comes as far as the curse is found?

At this point in our discussion, it might be helpful to bring in Augustine's famous formula about the stages of humanity in relation to sin. Augustine described human nature as passing through several phases in regard to our capacity for sin and obedience:

1. Before the fall, we were *able to sin or not to sin*. Adam and Eve had genuine choice in the Garden. They had complete freedom. They had the capacity to choose obedience.
2. After the fall, however, the thorn that infested the ground of our being was so great that everything we thought, felt or did has been laced with sin. We are *not able not* to sin. We can't help but sin. Even our best deeds are tainted with self-interest.
3. With the coming of God in Christ, humanity has been remade. Jesus is the new Adam, the head of a new human race. Jesus's perfect obedience has rewired our humanity so that in union with Christ, our capacity for obedience is restored. Through the indwelling Holy Spirit, *we are able, by his grace, not to sin*. We are also able, by the presence of the old nature still within us, to sin and do so frequently.
4. After Christ's return and the resurrection of the dead, we will enter our life in heaven. In this state of blessedness, when our salvation is fully realized, we will be free from temptation. We will *no longer be able to sin*. Our free choice will always and ever be the will of God.[11]

By this formula, it seems that according to the Sproul/Boettner view, Jesus in his humanity was already at stage 4, unable to sin. This would mean that he skipped entering our condition altogether. Now if pressed, perhaps advocates of this position would assert that Jesus was actually at stage 1, the stage of humanity's innocence, with all possibilities before him. Thus, in this classic Reformed understanding, Jesus assumed a kind of 'neutral' human nature, of the kind possessed by Adam and Eve before the fall. But in the divine/human union in Christ, in his life lived empowered by and in constant reliance on the Holy Spirit, it was inconceivable that Jesus should ever disobey.

---

11 Augustine, *The City of God*, 22.30, *NPNF*, 1st series, vol. 2; *Treatise On Rebuke and Grace to Valentinus*, 33–5, *NPNF*, 1st series, vol. 5.

This position creates visceral objections. If I am to relate to Jesus as my faithful High Priest because he was indeed tempted as I am, how could he not have had the possibility to disobey? Worse, why go through the 40 days in the wilderness if his confrontation with the devil was merely an exhibition and not the real game? Sweating blood in Gethsemane if the universe did not truly hang in the balance seems a hideous charade. The trial and scourging become just a stop on the way to the cross, itself reduced merely to a means of atonement transaction.

The Gospel accounts, however, imply real choice for Jesus. For example, during his arrest, Jesus commanded Peter to put away his sword with these words, 'Do you think that I cannot appeal to my Father, and he will at once send me more than twelve legions of angels?' (Mt. 26:53). Doing so would have interrupted his sacrifice and sent our salvation into ruins. But Jesus certainly communicated the potency in the choice to quit that was ever before him. Indeed, he could have sinned. We could have been lost.

7. Was Jesus Truly From 'The Lump of Adam'?

The Torrances assert that Jesus took up our *real* humanity. As Basil wrote in the fourth century, the flesh of the Son of God was 'assumed of the lump of Adam'.[12] In being conceived by the Holy Spirit within the womb of the Virgin Mary, the Son took from her a humanity like hers, and so just like ours. The Torrance tradition discerns in Jesus then, not a superman unable to sin, but a real man, God come to us in the midst of our fallen humanity. Support for this view may be found in both Scripture and the Greek Fathers.

a. Scripture

Thomas Torrance has cited the genealogy of Jesus in Mt. 1 which shows a long line of sinners in his bloodline, such as: Tamar, made pregnant by Judah her father-in-law, Rahab the harlot, Ruth who had been raised a pagan Moabite, David who fathered Solomon by taking Bathsheba the wife of Uriah for his own. Of this lump of sinful humanity there came Mary the mother of Jesus through whom his humanity came.[13]

He also notes Lk. 2:52 which says, 'And Jesus grew in wisdom and stature, and in favour with God and men.' T. F. leans on the etymology of

---

12 Basil, *Letters, NPNF*, 2nd series, vol. 8, 261. See also Torrance, *The Trinitarian Faith*, 153.
13 See Thomas F. Torrance, *The Mediation of Christ* (Edinburgh: T&T Clark, 1983), 40.

the word for 'grow' in that passage, as the old image of beating out metal with blows. Effort is required to shape something the right way which has a tendency to stay in the wrong shape:

> As the Son of Adam he was born into our alienation, our God-forsakenness and darkness, and grew up within our bondage and ignorance, so that he had to beat his way forward by blows, as St Luke puts it, growing in wisdom and growing in grace, before God as well as before man.[14]

Heb. 5:7–9 is also important:

> During the days of Jesus' life on earth, he offered up prayers and petitions with loud cries and tears to the one who could save him from death, and he was heard because of his reverent submission. Although he was a son, he learned obedience from what he suffered and, once made perfect, he became the source of eternal salvation for all who obey him.

Jesus's sinlessness was not a static, untouchable state. He did not coast through his days on earth. Rather, his perfection grew through his moment-by-moment choices of obedience, often made in the face of intense spiritual opposition. The strain of temptation, the tension of being obedient in the midst of sinful people, the weariness of beings surrounded by so much perversion and distortion, the pressure to collapse his resistance to sin, all sent Jesus into loud, tearful prayer, even to the point of sweating great drops of blood in Gethsemane.[15]

---

14 Thomas F. Torrance, *Theology in Reconstruction* (London: SCM Press, 1965), 132.
15 Ibid.:

> He learned obedience by the things which he suffered, for that obedience from within our alienated humanity was a struggle with our sin and temptation; it had to be fought out with strong crying and tears and achieved in desperate anguish and weakness under the crushing load of the world's sin and the divine judgment. Throughout the whole course of his life he bent the will of man in perfect submission to the will of God, bowing under the divine judgment against our unrighteousness, and offered a perfect obedience to the Father, that we might be redeemed and reconciled to him.

b. The Church Fathers

The Torrances also find support from the fourth-century Cappadocian Church Fathers.[16] A sampling of those passages can deepen our explorations:

Gregory of Nazianzus in the fourth century combated those who asserted that Christ had a divine, not human mind. He wrote:

> If anyone has put his trust in Him as a Man without a human mind, he is really bereft of mind, and quite unworthy of salvation. *For that which He has not assumed He has not healed*; but that which is united to His Godhead is also saved. If only half Adam fell, then that which Christ assumes and saves may be half also; but if the whole of his nature fell, it must be united to the whole nature of Him that was begotten, and so be saved as a whole. Let them not, then, begrudge us our complete salvation . . .[17]

Gregory employed a theological formula used by the Torrances, 'The unassumed is the unhealed'.[18] In order to be wholly saved, our complete humanity had to be taken up. If any essential part of us was left outside of Christ's incarnation, then it did not fall under his redemptive work. We would be only partly saved if all we are was not truly taken up in the humanity of Christ.

In one of his theological orations, Gregory dramatically considered how Christ took our place in judgement:

---

16 Torrance, *The Mediation of Christ*, 40:

> That was the doctrine taken up by the Greek Fathers especially, but before long in the fourth century there began a revolt against the idea that Christ took our fallen humanity including our depraved mind upon himself in order to redeem it from within. Thus there developed especially in Latin theology from the fifth century a steadily growing rejection of the fact that it was our alienated, fallen, and sinful humanity that the Holy Son of God assumed, and there was taught instead the idea that it was humanity in its perfect original state that Jesus took over from the Virgin Mary, which of course forced Roman Catholic theology into the strange notion of immaculate conception which divided the Latin from the Greek Church.

17 Gregory of Nazianzus, *To Cleodonius the Priest Against Apollinarius*, NPNF, 2nd series, vol. 8 (Edinburgh: T&T Clark and Grand Rapids: William B. Eerdmans, 1989), esp. 101.

18 See *The Trinitarian Faith*, 167 and *The Mediation of Christ*, 39. See also James B. Torrance, 'Christ in our Place', in *A Passion for Christ*, 47: '[Christ] becomes the patient! He assumes that very humanity which is in need of redemption, and by being anointed by the Holy Spirit in our humanity, by a life of perfect obedience, by dying and rising again for us, our humanity is healed in him.'

But look at it in this manner: that as for my sake He was called a curse, Who destroyed my curse; and sin, who taketh away the sin of the world; and became a new Adam to take the place of the old, just so He makes my disobedience His own as Head of the whole body. As long then as I am disobedient and rebellious, both by denial of God and by my passions, so long Christ also is called disobedient on my account . . . And thus He Who subjects presents to God that which he has subjected, making our condition His own. Of the same kind, it appears to me, is the expression, 'My God, My God, why hast Thou forsaken Me?' It was not He who was forsaken either by the Father, or by His own Godhead, as some have thought, as if It were afraid of the Passion, and therefore withdrew Itself from Him in His Sufferings . . . But as I said, He was in His own Person representing us. For we were the forsaken and despised before, but now by the Sufferings of Him Who could not suffer, we were taken up and saved. Similarly, He makes His own our folly and our transgressions . . .[19]

Christ is 'called disobedient on my account' and 'makes His own our folly'. He takes as his own our fallen nature and receives in himself the consequence of such rebellion as he enters the state of God-forsakenness. He does so not for his own sins but in substitution for us. For our sakes, he is called a curse.

About the same time, Basil wrote:

For if what was reigned over by death was not that which was assumed by the Lord death would not have ceased working his own ends, nor would the sufferings of the God-bearing flesh have been our gain; He would not have killed sin in the flesh: we who had died in Adam should not have been made alive in Christ; the fallen to pieces would not have been framed again; the shattered would not have been set up again; that which by the serpent's trick had been estranged from God would never have been made once more His own. All these boons are undone by those that assert that it was with a heavenly body that the Lord came among us. And if the God-bearing flesh was not ordained to be assumed of the lump of Adam, what need was there of the Holy Virgin?[20]

---

19 Gregory of Nazianzus, *Orations*, *NPNF*, 30.5 (*Theological Oration* 4.5). See also, Torrance, *The Trinitarian Faith*, 162–3, 'No one used stronger language than Gregory Nazianzen in reinforcing St. Paul's teaching about Christ being made a curse and sin on our behalf.'
20 Basil, *Letters*, *NPNF*, 261.2.

Our salvation required the assumption of our full humanity. As the Torrances read the ancient Fathers, this meant the very humanity we are in our sin-prone nature. Christ took up a fallen human nature but did not sin it. To the West, but still in the fourth century, Hilary of Poitiers commented, 'For He took upon Him the flesh in which we have sinned that by wearing our flesh He might forgive sins; a flesh which He shares with us by wearing it, not by sinning in it.'[21] For the Torrances, the question 'What kind of man was and is Jesus Christ?' has to be answered, 'A real man, a man who took up fallen human nature and, from the moment of his conception through his ascension, wore that flesh sinlessly. He has now redeemed us so thoroughly that he has taken our humanity into Augustine's category of being unable to sin. Christ holds in heaven this gloriously perfected humanity as a pledge for what we shall one day be.[22]

8. Cleansing Us from the Root: Why It Matters

One more aspect must be explored concerning why the nature of Christ's humanity matters to our salvation. This involves considering whether the atonement Christ made for sin was an event *external* to the life and being of the Triune God and our humanity, or something that happened *within* the Son of God's very being as fully human and fully God. Was atonement primarily a transaction by which our sinful acts were paid for and God's justice was satisfied? Or did it involve forgiving, reconciling and changing us in the very depths of our being so that God and we could once more enter intimate communion? If the latter, how important is the kind of humanity Christ assumed to such an ontologically grounded salvation?

Even in his earlier writings, T. F. was probing these depths:

---

21 Hilary of Poitiers, *On the Trinity*, *NPNF*, 1.13.
22 See Thomas F. Torrance, *The School of Faith* (London: James Clarke and Co. Limited, 1958), lxxxiv:

> In the very heart of Christ's atoning work we are concerned with the union He wrought out in His birth, life, death and resurrection between the human nature He assumed from us and His holy divine nature. That concerns the reconciling and sanctifying work carried on throughout the whole course of His human and historical life, but it also concerns the union wrought in the assumption of our fallen and estranged humanity which He sanctified in His very act of assuming it. Thus the incarnation, even in the narrower sense of that term, is redeeming event from the very birth of Jesus. In His holy assumption of our unholy humanity His purity wipes away our impurity, His Holiness covers our uncleanness, His divine life heals our corruption.

Now in this active and passive obedience we are to think of Christ as dealing with our *actual sins* through the atoning exchange of His life and death and resurrection, but we cannot do that without also thinking of His incarnational union of our human nature with His divine nature as dealing with our *original sin,* or as sanctifying our fallen human nature through bringing it into healing and sanctifying union with His holy divine nature. This is also supremely important, for it is only through this union of our human nature with His divine nature that Jesus Christ gives us not only the negative righteousness of the remission of sins but to share in the positive righteousness of His obedient and loving life lived in perfect filial relation on earth to the heavenly Father. If we neglect this essential element in the obedience of the Son, then not only do the active and passive obedience of Christ fall apart in our theology, but we are unable to understand justification in Christ as anything more than merely forensic non-imputation of sin. (*School of Faith,* lxxxvi)

Torrance wants us to understand that Jesus won more than just payment for sins. He effected a uniting of humanity with God. This occurred because he entered the depths of our fallen existence and from *within* our humanity lived in perfect filial love and obedience before his Father. Justification indeed involves the forensic, or legal, forgiveness of sins. But it goes further than legal status to penetrate the heart and soul. Jesus dealt with our original sin because he sinlessly took up a humanity tainted with original sin and bent that humanity in its depths back to obedience to his Father. That is why Torrance can say that through Christ's union with our humanity we receive more than the 'negative righteousness of the remission of sins'. We are given to share, as the Spirit unites us to the one who has already united himself to us, in 'the positive righteousness of His obedient and loving life'.

Three decades later, writing at the height of his theological powers in *The Trinitarian Faith,* T. F. clarified how Jesus sanctified our *fallen human nature* through bringing it into healing and sanctifying union with his holy divine nature. We need to hear it in his own words:

Moreover, since Jesus Christ is himself God and man in one Person, and all his divine and human acts issue from his one Person, the atoning mediation and redemption which he wrought for us, fall *within* his own being and life as the one Mediator between God and man . . .

Through his incarnation the Son of God has made himself one with us as we are, and indeed made himself what we are, thereby not only making our nature his own but taking on himself our lost condition subject to condemnation and death, all in order that he might substitute himself in our place, discharge our debt, and offer himself in atoning sacrifice to God on our behalf.

> ... atoning reconciliation must be understood as having taken place within the personal being of Jesus Christ as the one Mediator between God and man, and thus within the ontological roots and actual condition of the human and creaturely existence which he assumed in order to save. In this event, atonement is not an act of God done *ab extra* upon man, but an act of God become man, done *ab intra*, in his stead and on his behalf; it is an act of God as man, translated into human actuality and made to issue out of the depths of man's being and life toward God.[23]

If the saving act of God in Christ were something external to Christ, something merely between Christ and us or between Christ and the world, then when completed it would be over and done with. But if the soteriological exchange takes place within the constitution of the incarnate person of the Mediator, then it is as eternal as Jesus Christ himself, the eternal Son.

Our salvation has occurred within the life of God. It is as secure as his own eternal being! As long as Jesus the eternal Son of God is united to our humanity, so long is he our new and living way to the Father. In as much as we are in Christ by the work of the Holy Spirit, we have been united to the one in whom salvation was wrought once for all, yes, but also in whom the reconciliation of humanity to God continues in the dynamic intercession of our High Priest. He has laid hold of our humanity in the awful depths, sanctified it and carried it to the throne of his Father. He appears not only in our name but in our skin. So we, in Christ, enter the same communion which Jesus enjoys with the Father in the Spirit. Atonement as an act within the life of God means our inclusion now in the joyful Triune life.

9. The Awful Moment of Judgement and Fidelity

Finally, we make one more foray into T. F. Torrance's writing to attempt to grasp the fearsome price Jesus paid to lay hold of our fallen nature and redeem it.

We consider two quotations from the Psalms which Jesus uttered from the cross:

---

23   Torrance, *The Trinitarian Faith*, 155–9.

1. 'My God, my God, why hast thou forsaken me?' (Ps. 22:1, Mt. 27:46) and
2. 'Father, into your hands, I commit my spirit!' (Ps. 31:5; Lk. 23:46).

No paraphrase of mine could recapture the theological poetry from *Theology in Reconstruction*, so we follow a lengthy but powerful quotation:

> It is just at this point that we come up against the essence of the Gospel. What man cannot do of himself, God has done for him, in the Man on the Cross. 'My God, my God, why hast thou forsaken me?'
>
> Theological inquiry cannot hurry past that terrible cry of God-forsakenness of the Man on the Cross; for it is there that we are carried to the extreme edges of our existence, to the very brink of the abysmal chasm that separates us from God. It is there that we see the end of all *our* theologizing, in sheer God-forsakenness, in the desolate waste where God is hidden from us by our sin and self-will and self-inflicted blindness and where, as it were, God has 'died out on us', and is nowhere to be found by man.
>
> In Jesus Christ the Son of God entered into our rebellious humanity, laid hold of the human nature which we had alienated from the Father in disobedience and sin, and by living out from within it the life of the perfectly obedient Son, he bent our human nature in himself back to the obedience to the Father. Standing in our place, in life and in death, not only to be questioned but to give a faithful and true answer, he answered for us to God; even in his terrible descent into our God-forsakenness in which he plumbed the deepest depths of our estrangement and antagonism, he reconstructed and altered the existence of man, by yielding himself in perfect love and trust to the Father. 'Father into thy hands I commend my spirit.' 'Father' – that had been the answer of his whole life on earth, the answer of the obedient Son, for through the whole course of his obedience from birth to death he bent our human nature back into a perfectly filial relation of faith and truth toward the Father. 'Not my will, but thine be done.'
>
> And the Father answered the cry of his Son from the depths, answered not in word only but in deed, answered by resurrecting Jesus from the dead as his own Son with whom he kept faith and truth even in the midst of judgment and death. 'Thou art my beloved Son.' But that is the answer that God directs to us all in the Gospel for Jesus' sake, that through Jesus the Son of God become our Brother, we may be restored to faith and trust in the heavenly

Father. Through sharing brotherhood with the incarnate Son of God, we share with him also one and the same Father Almighty.[24]

At the moment of God-forsakenness, Jesus yet made faithful answer. In the horrifying hell of finding no trace of his Father's presence, Jesus yet said, 'Father'. And so 'he reconstructed and altered the existence' of humanity. Jesus yielded his will in fidelity from the very state that is the consequence of stubbornly asserting our human will against God. He saved us from the eternal inside out.

The Son of God took up a real, fallen human nature in assuming flesh from Mary. He became what we are. Yet, because he is the Son of God, he was cleansing that humanity from the moment of conception. Our uncleanness did not stain him. Rather his holiness sanctified our human nature from the beginning. He wore our sinful flesh so sinlessly that it was not sinful any more, but remade. This cleansing, re-creating work was not static but dynamic, continuing through all stages of human life. Jesus strode through the wreckage of the world remaking humanity. Through the eyes of the Torrance brothers, I have come to glimpse something of how great is this salvation.

He came as far as the curse is found. He dug beneath the thorn in order to lift it out and remove it. He wore the thorns as his crown, taking as he took them, the sting out of death and the shame out of humanity. Thanks be to God.

---

24 Torrance, *Theology in Reconstruction*, 124–6.

Chapter 4

THE REALIST EPISTEMOLOGY OF THOMAS F. TORRANCE

Douglas F. Kelly

It is appropriate to begin this lecture with a prayer that Professor Torrance so often prayed at the beginning of our classes in Edinburgh University in the 1960s and 1970s: 'Our heavenly Father, we pray Thee to send the Holy Spirit, so that in thy light, we may see light, through Jesus Christ our Lord. Amen.'

As a former student of T. F. Torrance, a friend and decades-long reader of his theology, I believe that his Christian realist epistemology, that is to say, his *biblical and scientific realism*, is his greatest contribution to the theological life and mission of the Church for ages to come. In my view, he was providentially raised up at this juncture in history to enable the Church to speak the saving gospel into today's heavily scientific culture. To neglect his theological contribution would be to miss one of the major gifts God has given his people in our time to spread the evangel to the ends of the earth.

SCIENCE AND CHRISTIAN REALISM

Now by 'epistemology', I mean the relationship between knowing and being: that is, how do we know reality, or can we? Are truth-claims merely power assertions of competing groups, with the assumption that we cannot really know what is outside our own heads? A large part of the significance of Professor Torrance is that he asserts traditional Christian realism (i.e. we can know things outside ourselves, including ultimate truths, and him who is 'the way, the truth and the life), but he expresses it in dialogue with the best insights of science, especially modern physics. This is important because we live in a culture where people come close to worshipping certain views of science. For the Church to ignore science would be self-defeating, as far as getting people in our culture to take our message seriously, and it is also incorrect and unnecessary to view all science as an atheistic enemy of the faith.

Yet many otherwise literate people do indeed see science as

implacably opposed to Christianity, and oddly enough, some of the very ones who say that no man can know truth, then turn around and assert that the truths of science exclude traditional Christian beliefs! But Torrance, never one 'to suffer fools gladly', will not easily let them by with this. His long research into both scriptural teaching on how we relate to reality, along with his research into the basic scientific method, penetrates to the heart and roots of our scientific culture in light of the Word of God incarnate and written. His Christian epistemology, which is part and parcel of his realist theology, provides us with one of the sharpest tools for the harvest of souls since Calvin and Luther, or perhaps even Athanasius. Far from being a philosophical nicety or an arcane theological technicality, his teaching on how knowing is related to being has the most direct implications for the Church's work of preaching, sacraments, evangelism, missions and cultural renewal. That is why I have chosen this particular topic.

Our good professor always taught us that 'knowing follows being' (or as the medieval scholastics said it: *operari sequitur esse*). Epistemology follows ontology.[1] True rationality never seeks to impose a preconceived pattern on to the material it wishes to know. Instead, it humbly enquires of a given field of reality; it puts questions to it, and then – as Torrance so often says – it lets its questions be questioned. As Torrance writes in *Transformation & Convergence*:

> . . . while knowledge of God is grounded in his own intelligible revelation to us, it requires for its actualisation an appropriate rational structure in our cognising of it, but that rational structure does not arise within us unless we allow our minds to fall under the compulsion of God's being who he really is in the act of his self-revelation and grace, and as such cannot be derived from an analysis of our autonomous subjectivity.[2]

What T. F. Torrance says in the preface to his book, *Theological Science* (which put him 'on the map' with many leading physicists throughout the world, and led to his winning a coveted prize a year after its publication in 1969), is extremely significant for how and why he approaches the question of knowing in both theology and science. Moreover, these words that I am about to quote greatly upset the then soon-to-be Bishop of Durham, the very liberal Dr Jenkins, who reviewed the book soon after it came out! The offending words of Professor Torrance were:

---

1 This is discussed by Karl Barth in *Church Dogmatics* I/2, 5ff.
2 Thomas F. Torrance, *Transformation & Convergence in the Frame of Knowledge* (Grand Rapids: William B. Eerdmans, 1984), p. 294.

> Science and meta-science are required not because God is a problem but because *we* are. It is because *our* relations with God have become problematic that we must have a scientific theology. If I may be allowed to speak personally for a moment, I find the presence and being of God bearing upon my experience and thought so powerfully that I cannot but be convinced of His overwhelming reality and rationality. To doubt the existence of God would be an act of sheer irrationality, for it would mean that my reason had become unhinged from its bond with real being. Yet in knowing God I am deeply aware that my relation to Him has been damaged, that disorder has resulted in my mind, and that it is I who obstruct knowledge of God by getting in between Him and myself, as it were. But I am also aware that His presence presses unrelentingly upon me through the disorder of my mind, for He will not let Himself be thwarted by it, challenging and repairing it, and requiring of me on my part to yield my thoughts to His healing and controlling revelation.[3]

In his moderatorial address to the General Assembly of the Church of Scotland in May of 1977, Torrance stated:

> I do not believe that the Christian Church has anything to fear from the advance of science. Indeed the more truly scientific inquiry discloses the structures of the created world, the more at home we Christians ought to be in it, for this is the creation which came into being through the Word of God and in which that Word has been made flesh in Jesus Christ our Lord. The more I engage in dialogue with scientists and understand the implications of their startling discoveries, the more I find that, far from contradicting the fundamental beliefs, they open up the whole field for a deeper grasp of the Christian doctrines of creation, incarnation, reconciliation, resurrection and not least the doctrine of the Holy Spirit.[4]

Now *how* could Torrance say that 'the advance of science . . . far from contradicting the fundamental beliefs . . . opens up the whole field'? Is this not the precise opposite of how many believers, especially since the Fundamentalist/Modernist controversy of the 1920s, have assessed the situation? Do not people from the high register of the intellectual culture in prestigious universities, media and think tanks down to the ordinary

---

3 Thomas F. Torrance, *Theological Science* (London: Oxford University Press, 1969), p. ix.
4 Elmer Colyer (ed.), *The Promise of Trinitarian Theology: Theologians in Dialogue with T.F. Torrance* (Lanham, MD: Rowan and Littlefield Publishers, Inc., 2002), 25.

blue-collar worker, downing his beer as he watches professional sports at the weekend, generally agree that 'science has long since disproved Christianity' (e.g. evolution disproves Genesis creation accounts; science teaches us that the Virgin Birth and bodily resurrection could not happen, since miracles violate natural law, etc.)?

How then can a highly educated scholar like T. F. Torrance (who is competent in both physics and theology) seriously claim that science, which so many assume to be antithetical to every fundamental doctrine of the Word of God, instead of 'contradicting fundamental beliefs' actually opens up the way for them?

To answer this not insignificant question, let us look first at what Torrance means by the knowing involved in theology; secondly at what he means by the knowing involved in science; and thirdly why, properly understood, these two work together, rather than contradict each other. Attempting to answer these questions will get us, I hope, into the heart of Torrance's theological contribution to the future Church: his epistemological realism.

1. How we Know from Theology

The Hypostatic Union

Since knowing follows being, we must first examine his teaching about the ultimate meaning of *being*. This must be addressed before discussing epistemology or knowing. The heart of his theological teaching is that Jesus Christ is Lord and Saviour; fully God, fully man; two natures in one person. Three of his class handouts will be known already to some of you: 'The Patristic Doctrine of Christ', 'The Reformed Doctrine of Christ' and 'The Hypostatic Union'. I am glad to report that Dr Robert Walker of Edinburgh, nephew of T. F. Torrance and a classmate of mine, is preparing these for imminent publication. After well over 20 years of teaching theology, I still think that 'The Hypostatic Union' is by far the best single writing on who Jesus Christ is and what difference it makes for us sinners, and I have required many hundreds of students to read it over these years. It is best to start there to grasp Torrance's understanding of being.

By way of illustrating his central theology of being, I will take a few moments to go through this remarkable Christological essay. Here, as throughout this essay, I'd like as much as possible to allow Torrance to speak in his own words. With simple profundity, he discusses first *the Humanity* of Christ. He shows how the manhood of Christ is absolutely essential to our salvation:

> If Jesus Christ were not Man as well as God, that would mean that God had not actually come all the way to man . . . within the time-series in which we are, and that God would still be far away from us . . . Any docetic view of the Humanity of Christ snaps the life-line between God and man, and destroys the relevance of the divine acts in Jesus for men of flesh and blood.[5]

He then shows that the humanity of Christ is essential to two matters inherent in our salvation: (1) Revelation and (2) Reconciliation.

(1) The true humanity of Christ is essential to *Revelation*, for:

> In Jesus Christ, God's Truth has become actual . . . The astounding thing is that the Eternal Word by whom all things were created became a creature, became man, certainly without ceasing to be that Eternal Word, and therefore its very creatureliness constitutes the act of Revelation, and is the guarantee that Revelation is here within creation and accessible to human creatures . . . Because the eternal has become temporal, man can know the eternal Truth in creaturely form, the Eternal Truth in time.[6]

(2) Torrance goes on to demonstrate that the humanity of Christ is also essential to God's *Reconciliation*, for:

> the actuality of atonement is grounded upon the fact that in actual human nature, it is God acting on our behalf. Thus any docetic view of the humanity of Christ would mean that God only appears to act within our human existence . . . If the manhood of Christ is imperfect, atonement is imperfect, and we would still be in our sins . . . apart from His human sacrifice, we have nothing at all to offer to God, nothing with which we can stand before God, but our sin and guilt.[7]

Then, in his lecture on 'The Hypostatic Union', Torrance goes on to show the necessity of the full *Deity* of Christ for sinners to be saved:

> If the Humanity of Christ is the guarantee of the action of God among men, revealing Himself and reconciling sinners to Himself, the Deity of Christ is the guarantee that that work of revelation and

---

5 Thomas F. Torrance, 'The Hypostatic Union' (Edinburgh: Unpublished University Lecture, 1968), 3.
6 Ibid., 4.
7 Ibid., 4–5.

reconciliation is not hollow and empty on its objective side; it is the guarantee that in Jesus Christ we have to do with the reality of God Himself. What Jesus does in forgiveness is not just the work of man, but the work of God, and is therefore of final and ultimate validity . . . The significance of His Deity lies in the fact that it is God Himself who acts in Jesus Christ, in His teaching and reconciliation. 'He that hath seen me hath seen the Father.' We worship and adore Christ as very God of very God, for He is God . . . The Deity of Christ is thus the guarantee that the actions of Christ are not in time only, only just temporary or temporal actions, but the eternal action of God, eternally real in the Godhead.[8]

As he had done with Christ's full humanity, Torrance next shows how Christ's full deity is essential, first to Revelation and then to Reconciliation.
(1) Revelation:

To reveal God, the revealer must take the place of God, and only God can take His own place. This identity of Christ's Revelation with God's self-revelation is the ground of our assurance and certainty that what we know in and through Jesus Christ, is none other than God, and that there is nothing in God essential to our knowledge of Him which is hid from us, and that God as He is in Himself, is not a reality other than the God revealed to us in and through Jesus Christ. Thus the weakening in the affirmation of the Deity of Christ, results in indecision and uncertainty. It is indeed because of this weakness that men are engulfed in relativity, and are not sure about what they believe. How do you know that you are right, and you are not wrong? How do you know that they are not right, and you are not wrong? Such is the uncertainty that is born of clouded vision of the Deity of Christ. When the Deity of Christ is denied, the bottom falls out of Christianity. When the Deity of Christ is denied, His humanity is denied as well, because Jesus is made out to be a liar, and if Jesus is adrift from the Truth, then we are all hopelessly at sea . . .[9]

---

[8] Ibid., 5.
[9] Ibid., 6.

(2) Reconciliation:

It is important to see that if the Deity of Christ is denied, then the Cross becomes a terrible monstrosity. If Jesus Christ is man only and not also God, then we lose faith in God and man . . . for that means that man is such that when he sees the very best, the very highest and noblest the world has ever known, he crucifies it in spite, and will have nothing to do with it except to hate it. Put God in heaven and Jesus a man only on the Cross, and you destroy all hope and trust, and preach a doctrine of the blackest and most abysmal despair . . . But put God on the Cross, and the Cross becomes the world's salvation . . .[10]

The third part of Torrance's lecture discusses how both Christ's Humanity and His Deity must be *held together* (i.e. in the hypostatic union) for lost sinners to be eternally saved. This is '. . . the doctrine of the hypostatic union, in which we assert of the mystery of Christ that divine and human natures and acts are truly and completely united in one Person or Hypostasis. That hypostatic union is also known as 'personal union', but personal union means union in the *One Person*'.[11] As in the sections of Christ's true humanity and his true deity being essential for both revelation and reconciliation, Torrance shows that *the humanity and deity together in personal union* are essential for these to become real for us.

(1) The hypostatic union is essential for revelation:

No, not even in Jesus can we get across from man to God, unless in Jesus Christ there is hypostatic union between Him and God, unless the human forms and speech and acts of Jesus are predicates of the one Divine Person (as Hilary says). It is only because Christ is Himself personally God that his human speech and human actions, and his human forms of thought, are also divine Revelation. The language of Jesus was creaturely language, and creaturely language is only capable of speaking of creaturely things. If here God's language has become human and creaturely language, we would not hear God in Jesus' creaturely speech, unless there was hypostatic union between His creaturely language and God's own godly language. It is only in that union in which God's language

---

10 Ibid., 7.
11 Ibid., 8.

condescends to take on creaturely form, and human language is joined to God's language, that there is real Revelation.[12]

(2) The hypostatic union is essential to Reconciliation:

> In Jesus Christ, God has come in the humble form of a servant, veiling His divine majesty, for we could not look on the face of God and live. If God came openly in his glory and majesty, we would be smitten to the ground in sin and death; the last judgment would be upon us, with no time to repent, no opportunity for personal decision in faith. The very humanity of Christ is the veiling of God. The flesh of sin, the humiliation and the form of a servant, and the death of Christ all veil God – and so God draws near under that veil in order to reveal himself and save us. It is sometimes asked if God cannot reveal Himself to us apart from or without Christ, without the humble form of a servant. But if Revelation were to take place apart from the veiling of Christ, or in a form totally unknown to us, it would disrupt the conditions of our world and of our humanity, and instead of saving us, it would mean our disintegration . . .
>
> The humanity of Christ is the actuality of God's presence among men, but this humanity holds man at arm's length away from God, in order to give man breathing space, time, and possibility for surrender to God's challenge in grace, time for decision and faith in Him.[13]

Torrance then summarizes the absolute necessity for our salvation of the personal union of the two natures of Christ:

> If we could divide between the two natures of Christ, His divine and his human nature, into a nature of a divine person and a nature of a human person, then the human acts would not be acts of the divine person, and the divine acts would not be in the human person. In the event, the accomplishment of reconciliation would be illusory, for its ultimate achievement would not have been carried through. It is the doctrine of the union of two natures in One Person which is thus the mainstay of a doctrine of atoning reconciliation . . . It is the hypostatic union, therefore, which lies embedded in the very heart of atonement; and all that is done in the judgment of sin, expiation of guilt, in the oblation of obedience

---

12 Ibid., 9–10.
13 Ibid., 10–11.

to the Father is in order to bring back to union with God, and to anchor that union within the eternal union of the Son and the Father, and the Father and the Son through the communion of the Holy Spirit.[14]

The Doctrine of the Trinity

If we want to penetrate the heart of Torrance's evangelical faith and his doctrine of being, we will start, as we have done, with his teaching on the hypostatic union of Christ, and that will lead us immediately to the doctrine of the Trinity, which he refers to as '. . . the ultimate ground of intelligible relations in God himself . . . the ultimate unitary basis on which a clarification and simplification of all theology may be carried. Thus it is finally in our understanding of the Trinitarian relations in God himself that we have the ground and grammar of a realist theology.'[15]

In two of his very greatest books, *The Trinitarian Faith* (1988) and *The Christian Doctrine of God: One Being, Three Persons* (1996), Torrance shows that the Christian Church had to work out the doctrine of the Trinity because it had to think through the Father/Son relationship, especially in light of the Nicene Creed's timely summation of the true gospel in the phrase that the Son is *homoousios* (of the same reality, substance or essence) with God the Father Almighty.

Following in the track of his favourite theologian, Athanasius, he states: 'Through the *homoousion* the incarnational and saving self-revelation of God as Father, Son and Holy Spirit was traced back to what God is enhypostatically and coinherently in himself, in his own eternal being as Father, Son and Holy Spirit.'[16] In contrast with other religions, Torrance shows that the Trinity is *the* Christian conception of God:

> The doctrine of the Trinity enshrines the essentially Christian conception of God: it constitutes the ultimate evangelical expression of *the grace of the Lord Jesus Christ* who though he was rich for our sakes became poor that we through his poverty might become rich, of *the love of God* who did not spare his own Son but delivered him up for us all, for it is in that personal sacrifice of the Father to which everything in the Gospel goes back, and of *the communion of the Holy Spirit* through whom and in whom we are made to participate in the one

---

14 Ibid., 12.
15 Thomas F. Torrance, *The Ground and Grammar of Theology* (Charlottesville, VA: The University of Virginia Press and Belfast: Christian Journals, 1980), xi.
16 Thomas F. Torrance, *The Trinitarian Faith: The Evangelical Theology of the Ancient Catholic Church* (Edinburgh: T&T Clark, 1988), 199.

eternal Communion of the Father and the Son and are united with one another in the redeemed life of the people of God. Through Christ and in the Spirit God has communicated himself to us in such a wonderful way that we may really know him and have communion with him in his inner life as Father, Son and Holy Spirit . . .

In sharp contrast with every other religion, Christianity stands for the fact that in Jesus Christ God has communicated to us his *Word* and has imparted to us his *Spirit,* so that we may really know him as he is in himself although not apart from his saving activity in history, for what he is toward us and for us in history he is in himself, and what he is in himself he is toward us and for us in history. The Word of God and the Spirit of God are not just ephemeral modes of God's presence to us in history; nor are they transient media external to himself through which God has revealed to us something about himself; they belong to what God ever is in his communion with us . . . That is why we believe that what God is toward us in Jesus Christ, the Word made flesh, he is in himself, antecedently and eternally in himself; and that what he imparts to us through the Spirit who sheds the love of God into our hearts, he is in himself, antecedently and eternally in himself.[17]

Torrance's profound Trinitarian teaching shows us that the homoousial or perichoretic relationship of the three divine persons with one another was not a mere 'linking or intercommunication of the distinctive properties of the three divine Persons but a completely mutual indwelling in which each Person, while remaining what he is by himself as Father, Son or Holy Spirit, is wholly in the others as the others are wholly in him'.[18]

Of greatest significance in Torrance's theological contribution to the whole Church is the way he affirms the total and absolute ontological equality of the three divine persons, and avoids all lingering subordinationism, by following closely the teaching on the subject of Athanasius, Gregory of Nazianzus and Epiphanius, who taught that within the Godhead there is no before or after, and no causation of one person by another; that the whole Trinity is the source of the persons; no one person is 'caused' by another person. To reach this important point, Torrance had to avoid some of the concepts of Basil and Gregory of Nyssa. In place of these two Cappadocians, Torrance recommends

---

17 Thomas F. Torrance, *The Christian Doctrine of God: One Being, Three Persons* (Edinburgh: T&T Clark, 1996), 2–4.
18 Torrance, *Trinitarian Faith,* 305.

returning to the earlier Athanasius, to the other Cappadocian, Gregory of Nazianzus, as well as to Cyril of Alexandria and Epiphanius.

In Chapters 6 and 8 of *The Trinitarian Faith*, Torrance, for the first time in theological history (as far as I know), cuts behind the *filioque* controversy and gets at the absolute equality of Father and Son in sending the Spirit (the basic concern of the West) without having to invoke the added-in phrase to the Nicene Creed of 'and the Son' (a standing affront to the East). Remarkably, several leaders of the Eastern Orthodox Churches agreed to his general approach, more or less, no small achievement in potentially settling a millennium-long divisive issue![19]

Further, in line with his realist epistemology, that central to Torrance's concern that the Son of God is *autotheos* (and thus fully equal to the Father), is the fact that for us to know truly the Father is to know truly his Son. If the Son is essentially different from (or less than) the Father, then when we meet Jesus, it is not at all clear that we know who the Father really is in his essence. But, Torrance follows his beloved mentor, H. R. Mackintosh of Edinburgh University, who said that it is in the face of Jesus Christ that we see most clearly revealed the heart of the heavenly Father. That is why Torrance so strongly rejects certain types of Eastern 'apophatic' theology, for this approach (as in Pseudo-Dionysius) holds that God the Father is finally unnamable and thus unknowable by us. If they are right, then it could not be said that in Christ we really do know who God the Father is. But how does that Neoplatonic assumption square with Christ's words to Philip in Jn 14:9: 'Whoever has seen me has seen the Father'? Or with Heb. 1:3, that Christ is 'the exact imprint' (*to xaraktar*) of God's person? Of course, Torrance is at pains to show with Hilary, Calvin and all good theologians that we know God truly, but not exhaustively; that is, we finite persons apprehend him, but do not comprehend the Infinite One. But the problem with the Neoplatonist strand of thought that came into Eastern Orthodoxy through 'Dionysius the Aeropagite' is that it denies that we can even *apprehend* who the Father is. (Of course, much of the best thought of Eastern Orthodoxy does *not* follow Dionysius at this point.)

Vicarious Humanity

Both in his classroom teaching, which I so gratefully remember, and also in his multifarious writings, Torrance takes great pains to discuss the

---

19 See Thomas F. Torrance (ed.), *Theological Dialogue Between Orthodox & Reformed Churches* (Edinburgh: Scottish Academic Press, 1985) and 'Historic Agreement by Reformed and Orthodox on the Doctrine of the Holy Trinity' in Thomas F. Torrance, *Trinitarian Perspectives: Toward Doctrinal Agreement* (Edinburgh, T&T Clark, 1994).

vicarious humanity of Christ as the only way the heavenly Father has appointed for us humans truly to know the Father, whom to know is life eternal (Jn 17:3). That is to say, the eternal Son of God takes on true human flesh as both our substitute and our representative, standing in for Adam's fallen progeny, in the words of Irenaeus (to whom Torrance often refers) 'recapitulating in Himself', our broken, failed humanity, and leading it back through every stage of life (conception, infancy, childhood and maturity) to deepest love of God and fullest heart obedience to all his will.[20]

In *The Mediation of Christ* Torrance explains:

> in Jesus there was provided for mankind a way of response to God which issued out of the depths of its existence and as its very own and in which each human being was free to share through communion with Jesus. Thus in Jesus the final response of man toward God was taken up, purified through his atoning self-consecration on our behalf, and incorporated into the Word of God as his complete self-communication to mankind, but also as the covenanted way of vicarious response to God which avails for all of us and in which we all may share through the Spirit of Jesus Christ which he freely gives us . . .[21]

Union with Christ

This teaching of vicarious humanity opens the way for us to understand the high significance for Torrance's theology (as for that of Calvin before him) of our *union with Christ*. Let me refer to Torrance's brief but potent statement of the matter in his earlier volume, *Theology in Reconstruction*:

> Let us take as a text for our discussion [Calvin's] answer in the *Geneva Catechism* to Question 342. 'Since the whole affiance of our salvation rests in the obedience which he has rendered to God, his Father, in order that it may be imputed to us as if it were ours, we must possess him: for his blessings are not ours unless he gives

---

20 E. M. Colyer has a helpful chapter on Torrance's understanding of 'vicarious humanity' in his *How to Read T. F. Torrance* (Downer's Grove: InterVarsity Press, 2001), and among many other places, Torrance himself devotes much attention to it in his *The Mediation of Christ* (Edinburgh: T&T Clark, 1983), especially in Chapter 4, 'The Mediation of Christ in our Human Response'. J. B. Torrance, also one of my honoured teachers, has done wonderful work on this. See his 'Christ in Our Place' in *A Passion for Christ: The Vision that Ignites Ministry*, ed. Gerrit Dawson and Jock Stein (Edinburgh: Handsel Press, and Lenoir, NC: PLC Publications, 1999).
21 Torrance, *Mediation of Christ*, 88.

himself to us first.' The same essential point is made by Knox in the *Book of Common Order* in which he says that justification, regeneration, sanctification flow out of *adoption* . . . It is only through union with Christ that we partake of the blessings of Christ, that is through union with him in his holy and obedient life. Through being united to him we share in his judgment and his exaltation, in his passive and active obedience, in his death and also in his resurrection and ascension – but first of all it is necessary that we be united to him, that is, have part in the union which he wrought out between us in his Incarnation and in the whole course of his obedience.[22]

Torrance teaches that 'through the gift of the Holy Spirit [we are given] to share in the relation of mutual knowing between the Father and the Son and thus in God's knowledge of Himself'.[23] Elsewhere he writes, 'By drawing near to us in Jesus Christ who took our human nature upon himself and lived out his divine life within it as a human life, God has opened up to us knowledge of his innermost Self as a fullness of personal being and brought us into intimate personal communion with himself as Father, Son and Holy Spirit.'[24] Or, as he writes in *The Ground and Grammar of Theology*:

Here we have to do with the living God who reveals Himself to us in such a way that he creates in us the capacity to receive and apprehend him; and he communicates himself to us in such a way that he lifts us up into the inner communion of the divine Being so that we are given to share in the mutual knowing of the Father and the Son in the Holy Spirit and thus to know God as he is in himself in the immanent relations of Father, Son and Holy Spirit. Further, this God reveals himself to us where we are in our error and wrong and sin, in our misunderstanding and self-centeredness, in such a way as to strike into the very heart of our being and to turn us inside out, in order to redeem us from sin, reconcile us to himself, and assimilate us into the communion of love in his triune Being. That is why the divine revelation penetrates into our inquiries, takes the initiative in questioning us, and so turns our questions upside down and inside out, reshaping them creatively under the impact of his eloquent Being . . . To know this God . . . is to be lifted out of ourselves, as it were, into God, until we know him and love him and enjoy him in his eternal Reality as Father, Son and Holy Spirit in

---

22 Torrance, *Theology in Reconstruction* (London: SCM Press, 1965), 158.
23 Torrance, *Trinitarian Faith*, 33.
24 *Trinitarian Faith*, 65–6.

such a way that the Trinity enters into the fundamental fabric of our thinking of him, and constitutes the basic grammar of our worship and knowledge of God.[25]

The Holy Scriptures

In any evangelical setting, not least the one in which I teach, which still subscribes to the Westminster Standards, to speak of true knowledge of God automatically raises the question of the place of the inspired Holy Scriptures. I am often asked by students whether or not T. F. Torrance believes in the inspiration of the Scriptures, since he is certainly influenced in many places by Karl Barth, whose teaching on the matter is to say the least very complex. For my part, I do not actually think that *functionally* Torrance's use of Scripture, and his submission to their divine authority, is very much different from those who affirm plenary verbal inspiration (an expression which he rejects as problematic). Over the years it has seemed to me that he is careful never to go against what Scripture plainly teaches; he affirms all of the miracles, and indeed (better than some evangelical scholars who affirm inerrancy and yet teach theistic evolution), he believes in creation. He has generally been much less prepared to welcome Higher Criticism than was his mentor, Karl Barth. Torrance has done some remarkable writing showing the poisonous philosophical roots of much Higher Criticism (not least that which is employed by the followers of Bultmann, as well as the Jesus Seminar). As I remember, Torrance tended to use the conservative *Introduction to the New Testament* of the evangelical British scholar, Donald Guthrie.

However, he does wish to make the point that while the Holy Scriptures are truly given by the Holy Spirit and thus are true to their purpose, still their primary purpose is to witness beyond themselves to the ultimate truth, who is God, the Father, Son and Holy Spirit. That is to say, their truth finally lies in the one to whom they truly and accurately direct us. With Calvin, they are a lens (or spectacles) through which we see reality and ultimate truth. Of considerable relevance here is Torrance's awareness, that 'what we cannot represent in language is the relation of language to the external facts – that is, in the language of Wittengenstein, we cannot produce a picture of the relation of a picture to that which is pictured'.[26] In the same volume he says that: 'Theological statements are so closely bound up with the Word to which they refer and

---

25   *Ground and Grammar of Theology*, 154–5.
26   *Theological Science*, 183.

from which they derive (i.e. as 'heard statements') that they do not have their truth in themselves but in their referents.'[27]

And, in accordance with Calvin's teaching on *the internal testimony of the Holy Spirit* (who causes believers to know that God's written Word is true), Torrance affirms the necessity of regeneration for one to be able to understand the Scriptures. In *The Christian Doctrine of God*, he writes:

> In a faithful interpretation of the New Testament we may not treat the words employed in it as if they were no more than transient linguistic symbols detached from any objective content in divine revelation, and as if they were not lively oracles through which the incarnate Word of God speaks to us in Person. Rather must we treat them as words communicating and interpreting himself to us in the course of his reconciling activity. That is to say, in the words of the Bible through which the Word of God's Trinitarian self-revelation reaches us, we have to do not with some divine Word detached from his Being and Activity, but with the very Being of God speaking to us and acting upon us in an intensely personal way. In and through them we encounter the living Word who is identical with God himself, the Word in whom we have to do with the Person and Act of God, the Son made man in Jesus Christ, and are thereby summoned to personal commitment and faith in Christ and through cognitive union with him to have knowledge of God the Father.[28]

2. Torrance on How we Know from Science

We have looked first at Torrance's teaching on theological knowledge; now we must consider what is his approach to *scientific* ways of knowledge. Let me refer you here first to his *Theological Science* (1969), then to some of his later works: *Space, Time and Incarnation* (1969); *Christian Theology and Scientific Culture* (1981); *The Ground and Grammar of Theology* (1980); *Reality and Scientific Theology* (1985); *Transformation and Convergence in the Frame of Knowledge* (1984); and *Preaching Christ Today: The Gospel and Scientific Thinking* (1994). There are two helpful chapters by Elmer Colyer on Torrance's approach to science (ch. 9 in *How to Read T. F. Torrance*, and ch. 9 in *The Promise of Trinitarian Theology*). Also, Alister McGrath addresses 'Theology and the Natural Sciences' in his *T. F. Torrance: An Intellectual Biography*.

---

27 Ibid., 268.
28 *The Christian Doctrine of God*, 42.

How We Approach Reality

Any decent teacher deeply desires to be able to take profound truths and then state them as clearly as possible, and I hope I can do that in these next pages. It seems to me that one of the clearest statements by T. F. Torrance on what he considers *a truly scientific approach* to be is found in one of his earlier works: the long introduction to *The School of Faith* (1959), written some ten years before his epoch-making *Theological Science* (which opened the hearts of many leaders in the scientific realm to what this Scottish theologian had to say). Let us note a few simple, yet profound and crucial points raised by Torrance in his earlier work on *what attitude and approach the human mind should take in order to know the truth about objective reality.* That is the way I am using 'scientific approach' here as concerns the work of Torrance.

Before noting these points, let me add here that in his classes in Edinburgh, when students felt confused and protested about the complexity of his lectures, I remember how from time to time, and usually with considerable patience, he would say something like: 'Well, I see we must go back to the basics to understand how we approach reality in order to know what is given to us outside ourselves.' Then he would often go over some of the very points that he had made in this *School of Faith* introduction. He lays down a key principle:

> The nature of the content must be allowed to condition not only the form but the method of instruction . . . [in Christian catechism for instance] . . . a proper method of instruction will have to reckon with an event of communication which is also an event of reconciliation and with the transcendent operation of the Holy Spirit who enables man to receive truth beyond his natural powers, and so to be lifted up above himself in communion with God.[29]

Then Torrance discusses general principles of any kind of objective knowing. He notes seven important aspects of all proper scientific enquiry:

(1) **Adaptation to the Object:** All knowing involves an *adaptation of our capacities* in accordance with the nature of the object . . . The learner . . . has to make an effort to relate his reason differently to different kinds of objects – that indeed is the very essence of rationality. It would be just as irrational to apply only the specific mode of

---

29 Thomas F. Torrance, trans. and ed., *The School of Faith: The Catechisms of the Reformed Church* (London: James Clarke and New York: Harper and Row, 1958), xxi–xxiii.

rational activity which is required in mathematics to the knowledge of other human minds, as it would be to try to smell with the ear or see with the nose. Thus the communication of Christian truth requires like all other truth serious adaptation toward it on the part of the receiver.

(2) **Attitude:** One adopts a rather different attitude in biology from that required in archaeology. One does not adopt the same attitude toward a living thing as one does toward a piece of ancient pottery. In all scientific knowledge we must adopt a procedure of impartiality, that is, in this sense, of objectivity. In other words, we do not allow our presuppositions to dictate to us *a priori* anything about the 'what' or 'how' of what we are investigating . . . It belongs to the *scientific attitude* therefore to learn humility and wonder, that is, how to be really open toward the disclosure of entirely new facts and meanings, but it also belongs to the scientific attitude to learn the appropriate attitude required by the nature of the field of study . . .

(3) **The Right Questions:** It is an important step in any branch of scientific research to learn to ask the *right questions* . . . it is essential to ask the questions appropriate to the nature of the object. If we ask only biological questions we can only expect biological answers . . . The really scientific questions are questions which the object that we are studying, through its very nature puts to us, so that we in turn put only those questions which will allow the object to declare itself to us or to yield to us its secrets . . .

(4) **Objectivity:** You cannot think unless you have something to think about . . . If modern science has taught us anything about the reason, it has taught us that reason is nothing without its object, and that truly rational activity is inseparable from learning to behave in accordance with the nature of what is objectively given, for that is the only way to learning what we do not and cannot otherwise know . . .

(5) **Image and Idea:** It belongs to the essence of good education *to hold together the realm of the image and the realm of the idea.* That is natural to the child who is at once both a born 'realist' and a born 'idealist,' as it were. It is one of the most tragic features of modern occidental civilisation that the realm of the image is torn apart from the realm of the idea, and once that happens it is next to impossible to bring them together . . . Christianity, through its doctrine of the Incarnation above all, is committed to the healing of the rift between image and idea . . .

(6) **Proper Tools:** You cannot make anything unless you have the *tools* with which to form and construct it. You cannot think unless

you have tools with which to think and shape the thoughts in your mind and form your judgments. The tools that the mind requires are conceptions and categories and formulated ideas. Nor can you make much progress in instruction and learning unless you have appropriate and adequate tools for rational communication . . .

(7) **Integration:** You cannot make much progress thinking on your own in a vacuum. You cannot think unless you have something to think about. Nor can you think unless you have an environment, unless you have others with whom to think together . . . it is only in the essential *integration* of the Truth with being and action that it can be either received or communicated . . .

Torrance summarizes: 'None of the seven principles we have been discussing is peculiar to Christian knowledge or instruction. They all obtain in every branch of science or knowledge in ways appropriate to each . . .'[30]

In *Theological Science*, ten years later, Torrance says much the same, though with a necessarily different emphasis:

> Communication takes place between minds that are directed to the same or similar objects and so is necessarily indirect . . . This presupposes the rationality of the medium and the context in which communication takes place, that is, not only an intelligible language but an intelligible subject-matter . . . This is something that we assume and operate with continually in ordinary experience and in science without attempting to explain it . . . It is because things are amenable to rational treatment that we can apprehend them at all . . . as we let the realities we investigate disclose themselves to us under our questioning and we on our part submit our minds to their intrinsic connections and order . . . as we seek to penetrate into the rationality of something, our inquiry must also cut back into ourselves and into our presuppositions . . . It is always the nature of things that must prescribe for us the specific mode of rationality that we must adopt toward them.[31]

Throughout his discussions of true scientific methodology, Torrance constantly stresses that the truly rational (and thus faithful) approach for human minds to take towards objective reality outside themselves is one of humility and openness, in which one distinguishes what one knows from one's knowing of it, and seeks to know things in accordance with

---

30   Ibid. xxiv–xxxi. Subtitles and emphasis mine.
31   *Theological Science*, x–xii.

their natures. He writes, 'We know things strictly in accordance with their natures or what they are in themselves and at the same time we allow what things actually are to reveal themselves to us and thereby to determine for us the content and the form of our knowledge of them.'[32]

And as far as the science of pure theology is concerned, the most appropriate, or truly rational, adaptation of the human mind to know God is precisely *faith*. Torrance rejects the Enlightenment (especially Lockean) opposition between reason and faith. On the contrary, faith *is* the proper use of the human reason when it comes to responding to God. He writes in *Christian Theology and Scientific Culture*:

> . . . [Michael] Polanyi set out to clarify the fact that fundamental belief is objectively not subjectively grounded, in direct antithesis to Locke's discrediting of belief as no more than an ungrounded persuasion of the mind or a subjective feeling without evidential certainty. Our fundamental beliefs are . . . basic acts of acknowledgement in response to some intelligibility inherent in the nature of things . . . beliefs arise in us because they are forced upon us by the nature of the reality with which we are in experiential contact . . . Polanyi points out that truth is the external pole of belief and belief, far from being a merely subjective or private concern, is to be regarded as the obedience of the mind to the truth . . . In this event it is unreasonable to throw faith and reason into a Lockean 'contradistinction', for faith is the very mode of rationality which the reason takes in its faithful adaptation to what it seeks to understand and explain.[33]

3. What True Theology and True Science Share in Common for our True Knowledge

In his remarkable essay, 'Newton, Einstein and Scientific Theology', Torrance shows what a similar epistemological struggle had to be faced both by early twentieth-century physics and by contemporaneous biblical Christianity. In a word, both had to overcome the secularist Enlightenment's cosmological and epistemological dualisms. He states it a bit more simply in the first few pages of his *Preaching Christ Today: The Gospel and Scientific Thinking*.

---

32 Thomas F. Torrance, *Christian Theology and Scientific Culture* (Belfast: Christian Journals, 1980), 27–8.
33 Ibid., 67–9.

Beyond Dualism

In these pages, he deals with the deistic dualism embedded within the so-called 'historical critical method' or the 'historical scientific method' almost universally used since the Enlightenment triumph to interpret Holy Scripture. It led to Bultmann's:

> sharp line of distinction between two kinds of history called *Historie* and *Geschichte*, the kind of history that is interpreted in terms of strict causal connections, and the kind of history that is interpreted in terms of how things appear to us. That distinction goes back through Hermann and Kant to Lessing's 'ugly big ditch' between necessary truths of reason and accidental truths of history, but ultimately it derives from the radical dualism between 'absolute mathematical time' and 'relative apparent time' posited by Newton in his system of the world . . . That . . . dualism . . . ruled out of rational consideration anything that could not be explained in terms of physical laws . . . That is why, of course, Bultmann held that *Historie* understood in this natural causalist way ruled out any thought of incarnation or miracles or resurrection, or of God's interaction with us in history . . . His acceptance of the idea of an unbroken continuity of cause and effect governed by natural law made him regard the central Christian beliefs embedded in the Gospels and Epistles of the New Testament as a mythological account of reported this-worldly events in other-worldly ways lacking objective truth and reality . . . Hence Bultmann devised 'a program of demythologizing' and reinterpreting the New Testament existentially in which modern people can make sense of the New Testament in terms of their own self-understanding in the scientific world of classical Newtonian mechanics.[34]

But while nineteenth- and twentieth-century biblical scholars were reworking everything to fit into the mechanistic assumptions of post-Newtonian dualism, a number of leading physicists were going in a very different direction; they were moving away from Newton's closed universe to one that is open. Torrance then goes on to show how the radical dualism in the Newtonian concept of absolute mathematical time and space which splits empirical events and theoretical construction in a rigid closed, causal mechanism, shut off from transcendent interaction, had to be abandoned for the reconstruction of the foundations of

---

34   Thomas F. Torrance, *Preaching Christ Today: The Gospel and Scientific Thinking* (Grand Rapids: William B. Eerdmans, 1994), 4–5.

science – in particular, modern physics – especially through the brilliant work of James Clerk Maxwell and then Albert Einstein:

> That is why our twentieth-century science has made such enormous advance, for it no longer imposes abstract necessary patterns of thought upon nature, but seeks to understand nature out of its own inherent rational order, and is therefore concerned with continuous dynamic fields and with real time . . . This involves a way of thinking in which experiment and theory, empirical and theoretical factors interact with one another and must not be divorced from one another, and therefore a way of thinking in which the historical and the conceptual ingredients must be taken together in the understanding of any historical culture or religion. The extraordinary thing is that our biblical scholars seem to show very little knowledge of this revolution and correction in the foundations of rational and scientific knowledge. They still work with a dichotomy between empirical and theoretical factors in knowledge, and with the old discarded notions of split time expressed in their two kinds of history. I don't know any scientist who accepts what biblical scholars say about *Historie* and *Geschichte*.[35]

What Torrance is showing here is of utmost importance for true epistemology in today's culture. Strangely, the very ones who sceptically deny the possibility of God's intervention into our realm in incarnation and other miracles on the basis of 'science', are a good century behind in the developments of true science! They are working with outmoded dualisms long since surpassed in the research of Clerk Maxwell and Einstein! The amazing advancements of modern physics, as Torrance constantly shows us, long ago overturned the closed mechanistic system of Newton, with its necessarily sceptical epistemology about 'things in themselves' or ultimate truths beyond the imperious human mind. Thus, what Torrance is pleading for, is for theologians and biblical scholars to catch up with the realism of modern science; to abandon a closed, deterministic, antisupernatural epistemology for a mind and heart open to reality outside self and above self. That is why he makes so much reference to the theorem of Kurt Gödel (as in *Space, Time, and Incarnation*) which undid logical positivism with this insight: a system cannot be closed and consistent at the same time. If it is consistent, then it must be opened to a higher level of reality in terms of which it can then be seen to make sense. Hence, to make sense of the Jesus of the New Testament, one must be

---

35 Ibid., 6–7.

opened to the direct intervention of God, or else all is meaningless, and one must go on yet another quest for the so-called historical Jesus! This is the essence of the epistemological realism of T. F. Torrance, and that is why he is so appreciative of the best efforts of modern physics, for they overcome the kind of dualism that precludes any realist theory and practice of knowing.

Nominalism and Idealism

I have spoken several times of Torrance's epistemological *realism*. He believes – with all of the writers of Scripture – that words and sentences point beyond themselves to reality: to true states of affairs in the created order, and to the creator and redeemer himself. But because of the dualisms mentioned above there have been alternative views of epistemology, generally known as *Nominalism* and *Idealism*.

First, nominalist thought. Nominalist theology all but destroyed the late medieval church in the fourteenth and fifteenth centuries, and it periodically emerges when the culture operates with a damaged relation between existence and language. Especially is it strong when cultures wish to avoid ultimate reality by taking refuge in linguistic games and theological systems, rather than facing external reality, which might just cause them to have to face the living God. Here is how T. F. Torrance describes it in *Theological Science*:

> The problem posed here is whether truth is primarily concerned with the reference of statements to the reality of things beyond them, or whether it is concerned rather with the logico-syntactical relations of statements to one another and therefore to be discerned in ideological complexes. A double error appears to lurk here: a) the reduction of truth to ideas, which rests on the mistaken notion that we can express in ideas how ideas are related to being; b) the reduction of truth to statements, which rests on the mistaken notion that we can state in statements how statements are related to what is stated. The one implies the 'conversion' of universals into abstract entities, and the other implies that in the last resort science is about propositions. This represents a mutation from intuitive knowledge of the real to abstractive knowledge either of the ideal or the symbolic, and in both introduces a lapse from the truth of being.[36]

---

36 *Theological Science*, 142.

Similarly, in a chapter on 'Theological Realism', he notes that:

> Nominalism so focuses on the form of the words themselves (which are held to represent only individual phenomena, not universal realities or actual classes) that their reference to the reality above them can only be indirect. But with realism, signs or words fulfil their semantic function properly when we attend away from them to the realities they signify or intend . . . [they] serve as transparent media through which those realities show themselves.[37]

We may note that nominalism has appealed to some groups of theological conservatives, whereas idealism has tended to appeal to liberals.

The second epistemological alternative to Christian realism is *idealism*. In brief, it is the epistemological theory that the mind of man constitutes reality, rather than God himself. Thus, we form a world which suits us, and a God who suits us, rather than One who holds us to his own character and to his creational limits. The modern neo-gnosticism of the so-called 'Jesus Seminar' is in this camp, as Hegelianism and Marxism were in a former day.

But on the contrary, certain groups of conservatives (although definitely a minority), especially after the bruising Liberal/Modernist debates of the 1920s in America, took on board so much Deistic/Rationalistic baggage in their determination to outdo the Modernists in the realm of apologetics, that they became functional nominalists. In other words, they put such emphasis on the words and supposed doctrines of Scripture that they avoided seeing the referents of those words in the Triune God himself. Thus, in a very different way from the Modernist idealists, they too spoke as though they themselves were in control of the words and systems which they put into the place of God. In both cases, these people missed meeting the true God. (Perhaps they somehow knew God, but it was in spite of their system: whether idealist or nominalist. And happily, the grace of God is greater than our little systems!) Both thought that they were in control of the theological position. Neither position seriously believed in ontological and cognitional union with Christ. Both positions are a disaster, as far as true knowledge of God in Christ is concerned. That, I think, is why Torrance has so threatened and angered both idealistic liberals and nominalistic conservatives. And that is why, I believe, his epistemological realism is so needed to guide the Church successfully over these deep intellectual sink-holes.

---

37 Thomas F. Torrance, 'Theological Realism' in B. Hebblethwaite and S. Sutherland (eds), *The Philosophical Frontiers of Christian Theology: Essays Presented to D. M. MacKinnon* (Cambridge: Cambridge University Press, 1982), 196.

In sum, we can say that the epistemology of T. F. Torrance is based on the fact that *we know God where he has given himself to be known: that is, in his Word and by his Spirit*. It is not given to theologians and philosophers to predetermine where and how God shall be known, nor how that knowledge shall be validated. Only God can reveal God, as the Church Fathers said, and so, God alone chooses the place to reveal himself, and that is his Word in the covenant community of his appointing. Thus, that Word (that revelation of who God is) is truly known in a divinely constituted community, first in Old Testament Israel, and then in the New Testament Church.

Although the philosophical mind has found it hard to take in, the majestic Triune God stooped down an infinite distance in order that we may know him. In Calvin's words, God *accommodated* himself to our finite capacities; our creatureliness did not prevent his entrance into our realm. God accommodated himself to us in the frailty of our space–time series, while always remaining who he transcendently is, even in his revelation of the truth in the flesh on earth. He does so in the Holy Scriptures and supremely in the incarnation. For this reason, Torrance often says that we cannot know the ultimate truth unhistorically:

> We cannot know this truth unhistorically or statically, therefore, by seeking to pass behind or beyond His action and life *in time*... The truth of God cannot be separated from the whole historical Jesus Christ, for time, decision, action, history belong to the essential nature of this Truth. Therefore we cannot apprehend or consider the Truth in detachment from relations in space and time without downright falsification.[38]

This is precisely the opposite of Lessing's dictum that 'the necessary truths of reason cannot be expressed in the accidental truths of history'. That kind of preconceptual idealism is rendered null and void in light of the events of creation, incarnation, atonement, resurrection and Pentecost, and as we just saw, its deistic dualism was long ago surpassed by modern physics (although most biblical scholars, not least the Jesus Seminar, have not found out yet).

One cannot repeat it too often: we image-bearers of the divine do not dictate to God how he shall reveal himself. Rather, we know him only where he makes himself known: in the order of creation and conscience, in the Christ-event, and in the inspired prophetic and apostolic testimony to it all. We know him in history, and we know him in a covenant

---

38   *Theological Science*, 208–9.

community. We know him in Word and Spirit, and therefore, we know him in truest realism by his grace.

In *Reality and Evangelical Theology*, Torrance states that:

> ... within the hypostatic union of divine and human nature that took place in Jesus Christ, there is included a union between uncreated and created rationality and between uncreated and created word, so that it is in the rational form of creaturely human word that Jesus Christ mediates God's Word to all mankind.[39]

The Scriptures are the appointed and inspired testimony of the Father to who his Son is. On the basis of the Gospel events, the Holy Spirit baptizes us into union with the Christ who is set before us in the Scriptures, and apprehended in the community of faith – the Christian Church. The Messiah of Israel is the saviour of the world, and in and through him we are lifted into the knowledge and love of Father, Son and Spirit for one another and for us. As Jn 17:3 (AV) tells us: 'This is eternal life that they know thee, the only true God, and Jesus Christ whom thou hast sent.' The Triune God is the supreme reality, and the Church is 'the pillar and ground of the truth' (1 Tim. 3:15, AV).

True Knowledge

This God created us so that we could know accurately those realities that are outside ourselves in the created order and above all else, its mighty creator. So let us think for a moment about true knowledge of the creation and then of true knowledge of the creator.

First, the creation. Torrance has frequently discussed how the advancements of modern physics were only made possible by the assumption of the validity of external reality above the mind of the knower, and by the allied assumption of the coherence and knowability of the created order. He comments on an article by Albert Einstein on James Clerk Maxwell in which Einstein splits with the Kantian denial that we can truly know 'things in themselves':

> In his essay on Clerk Maxwell's influence, he insisted, in sharp contrast to the positivist and conventionalist tradition, that 'The belief in an external world independent of the perceiving subject is the basis of all natural science', but along with that belief went

---

39 Thomas F. Torrance, *Reality and Evangelical Theology: The Realism of Christian Revelation* (Downers Grove, IL: InterVarsity Press, 1982 and 1999), 91.

another belief in the ultimate comprehensibility of the universe. These are beliefs that have to be assumed and put to the test, but they are not open to logical derivation or proof for they are prior to logical reasoning and have to be employed as premises in any attempted proof . . . somehow there is 'a pre-established harmony' between human thought and independent empirical reality, in virtue of which the human mind can discern and grasp the relational structures embedded in nature.[40]

By the way, Torrance believes that while each academic discipline necessarily has its own peculiar methodology, scientific thinking is still not essentially different from true knowing in any field of enquiry, theology included: 'This is the way of acting and thinking that is no more and no less than the rigorous extension of our basic rationality, as we seek to act toward things in ways appropriate to their natures, to understand them through letting them shine in their own light, and to reduce our thinking of them into orderly forms on the presumption of their inherent intelligibility.'[41]

Yes, the Triune God created us to know the external creation (to know created reality) with its marvellous comprehensibility, as 'the theatre of his glory' (in Calvin's words). But above all else, he created us to know *himself*, who is the supreme Reality, the creator/redeemer God, whom it is our privileged honour 'to glorify and to enjoy forever'. He who is supreme reality has Being, which as Professor Torrance often says, is 'eloquent'. God is not a dumb being; he whose Son is the eternal Word is a speaking being. For God to be is to be in relationship within himself, and part of that relationship is communication: speaking, sharing, loving. He made us in his image precisely to be brought up into that loving knowledge that constitutes the eternal joy of Father, Son and Holy Spirit.

Validating the Real

A few concluding observations are now called for on the question of validation of one's knowledge, whether in science or theology. We have been speaking of realist epistemology and realist science and realist theology, and a real relationship with God. But how do we know that these things are real? The impossibility of putting into a syllogistic proof the validation of the external world, its creator, and how one knows such

---

40 *Christian Theology and Scientific Culture*, 57–8.
41 *Theological Science*, 107.

things, was a major concern of British Logical Positivism last century. Ultimate validation of being and our knowing of it is surprisingly similar in both theology and science (though of course very different in detail because what or who is known is on an infinitely different level of reality in physical science and in theology). Torrance succinctly summarizes the position concerning validation of scientific truth:

> Michael Polanyi reminds us in his Gifford lectures that we cannot convince others by formal argument, for so long as we argue within their framework, we can never induce them to abandon it. 'Formal operations relying on one framework of interpretation cannot demonstrate a proposition to persons who rely on another framework' . . . The only proper road to take at that point is to persuade those operating from the other frame to look away at the realities we seek to indicate . . .[42]

It is not essentially different in theology. In *Theological Dialogue Between Orthodox and Reformed Churches*, Torrance says:

> There is no way to demonstrate this Truth outside of the Truth; the only way for the ultimate Truth to prove Himself is to be the truth, and the only way for us to prove the ultimate Truth is to let Him be what He is before us in His *autousia* and *autezousia*. That is the majesty and prerogative of the Truth of God as it is in Jesus, Truth who is ultimate in identity with the Being and Act of God, Truth who is and cannot be established by us, Truth who will not be mastered and yet will not remain closed to us, Truth who unveils Himself for us and who is known only through Word and Grace on God's part and faith and thankfulness on our part . . .[43]

Rather than fruitless arguments (from within unbelieving frameworks) about the possibility of there being a real world and a God, and the possible validity of knowledge, Polanyi counsels people to get others to look outside their limited frameworks to reality itself, and Torrance does the same in the different field which sets before us the Absolute Subject. He urges us to look outside our unbelief up to the ultimate Reality. Not least, Torrance paraphrases Michael Polanyi in advising those who wish to know the truth 'to indwell' the relevant passages of Scripture. That advice cannot be far from the divine word in Heb. 12:2:

---

42   *Theology in Reconstruction*, 27–8).
43   *Theological Dialogue*, 108.

'Looking to Jesus, the founder and perfecter of our faith, who for the joy that was set before him endured the cross, despising the shame, and is seated at the right hand of the throne of God.'

Let us conclude with one brief remark by Torrance in *Theological Science*, and then with two of his prayers. First, he writes:

> What the nature of the Truth requires, then, is *justification by Grace*, and *demonstration of the Spirit*, that is, verification and action by the Truth Himself . . . That may be summarized by saying that justification by the Grace of God in Jesus Christ applies not only to our life and action, but to our knowledge, and is essentially relevant to epistemology.[44]

In his moderatorial year in the Church of Scotland, Torrance offered these two short prayers:

> Heavenly Father . . . we thank thee for our incarnate Saviour, his life on earth and his death on the Cross; we bless Thee that he interceded for us in his life and prayed for us in his death, making his soul an offering for sin, and that he ever lives as our Mediator at thy right hand. Continue to pour out upon us, O Lord . . . the Spirit of thy Son, that joined to him in the life he prayed and the death which he offered on our behalf we may learn daily to pray as he prayed and to live as he lived; that all we do . . . may please thee.

> May the heavenly intercession of thy Beloved Son so prevail on behalf of thy Church that constrained by divine love it may proclaim the Gospel to all the world until every nation becomes his inheritance and the utmost parts of the earth are the possession of his Kingdom. Bless with the mighty aid of thy Holy Spirit those who work to the glory of thy Name in distant lands. Give them wisdom and courage in all their difficulties, and the great joy of gathering men and women and children into the one fold of the Saviour of mankind.[45]

---

44 *Theological Science*, 198.
45 *Promise of Trinitarian Theology*, 30.

Chapter 5

THE BIBLE AS TESTIMONY TO OUR BELONGING: THE THEOLOGICAL VISION OF JAMES B. TORRANCE[1]

Alan J. Torrance

The concern of this chapter is to articulate the central theological concerns and emphases in the theology of James B. Torrance ('JBT'). Not only was he my father, who discussed theology continually and, at times, almost obsessively at home, he was one of my teachers and later, albeit briefly and by an extraordinary turn of events, an academic colleague. To succumb to the temptation to become anecdotal in paying homage to a father one loved and admired would be no tribute to a man who was impatient with theologians and ministers who allowed autobiography to eclipse the gospel of the Triune God of Grace – turning theology into 'me-ology', as he once quipped!

COVENANT NOT CONTRACT

So what were the key biblical and theological themes my father was most keen to articulate and draw out? The first one I should like to consider (and for which he was perhaps best known) concerned the theological concept of covenant and what he considered to be the profound importance of differentiating between a covenant and a contract – two concepts which have been confused by much of our Western theological tradition, a confusion which he believed was profoundly detrimental to the life and mission of the Church. Consequently, he sought to argue that

---

1 This article constitutes an attempt to distil and articulate the theological vision of James B. Torrance utilizing lecture notes, published and unpublished material and, indeed, the conversations of a lifetime. The context of this article means that there will be 'unacknowledged' quotation and semi-quotation throughout. Given the unique character of this theological memoir, I did not consider it necessary to provide detailed references or citations and will simply refer the reader to articles in which he deals with the subject under discussion.
    J. B. Torrance's thought is to be found articulated in a particularly lucid and accessible form in his monograph, *Worship, Community and the Triune God of Grace* (Carlisle: Paternoster, 1996 and Downers Grove, IL: InterVarsity Press, 1996).

God's relationship to humanity required to be understood in covenantal terms and emphatically not in contractual terms. The implications and significance of this and of how the relevant theological terms should be understood were argued with analytic lucidity. Nowhere did he perceive it more important for the mission of the Church to have conceptual and semantic hygiene than on this point!

Biblically speaking, a covenant, he argues, is a promise binding two people or two parties to love one another *unconditionally*. It is for this reason that the word was used of marriage in the English service book of 1549 and has been subsequently retained in the traditional forms of marriage service. A couple promise and covenant to love one another 'for better for worse, for richer for poorer, in sickness and in health . . .'. That is, they promise to love each other unconditionally. For JBT, the marriage service enshrines the fact that all true love and all true forgiveness are unconditional. From a Christian perspective, he argued, to love someone unconditionally is to forgive them unconditionally. Consequently, just as there is no such thing as conditional love, there is no such thing as conditional forgiveness.

It is this that makes a *covenant* so different from a *contract*. A contract is a legal relationship in which two people or two parties make a commitment on mutual conditions to bring about some future result. It denotes a business deal or the result of a process of bargaining that is grounded on certain terms or conditions with a future state of affairs in mind. It takes the form, 'If . . . and if . . . , then . . .'. As such, contracts are the essential tool of business. 'If you provide a building or a computer system or mechanical device to the following specifications by such and such a date, I shall pay you x pounds/dollars.'

Although the words 'covenant' and 'contract' are used interchangeably ('marriage contract' or 'deeds of covenant'), biblically speaking there is an absolutely central conceptual distinction to be made. This is not to suggest that the Bible always means the same thing by the Hebrew term *berith* (*covenant*). Indeed, it speaks of different kinds of covenant. There are mutual, *bilateral* (two-sided) covenants freely made between equals as, for example, between David and Jonathan. Although these covenants are bilateral, they are not contracts, that is, conditional deals: they are unconditional, two-sided covenant commitments. The best example of a bilateral covenant is, of course, marriage.

Central to the biblical witness, however, is the concept of a *unilateral* covenant. Not only is it profoundly important to be clear that God's relationship with Israel was to be understood as a covenant and not a contract, it is equally important to be clear that it was a unilateral covenant and not a bilateral one. In this regard, God's relationship with his people is significantly different from a marriage relationship.

Whereas a marriage cannot take place without each party freely giving themselves to the other, God's relationship with Israel is established unilaterally by God: 'I am and will always be your God and you are and will always remain my people!' In short, God was committed to Israel prior to any response on Israel's part and Israel's belonging to God was not contingent in any way upon a decision or commitment made on the part of Israel. As Paul would argue in Rom. 9–11, God's commitment to Israel remains binding – there are no conditions, temporal or otherwise!

In short, as JBT used to remind his students repeatedly, 'The God of the Bible is a covenant God and not a contract God.' Moreover, God's commitment to humanity is a unilateral commitment that is not contingent upon our response. Furthermore, it is for all time. The New Covenant (*kainē diathēkē*) was made not *with* but *for* humanity in Christ. It was made for us nearly 2,000 years before we were born and is not a response to any virtue that we might exhibit.

This inevitably raised an obvious question. Does emphasizing God's unconditional covenant of grace in this way not have the effect of devaluing or minimizing the significance of the human response? Emphatically not for JBT! Here the difference between a unilateral and bilateral response becomes crucially significant. In a bilateral covenant, there can be no covenant without a response. In marriage, for example, a spouse cannot make a covenant for his or her beloved. There must be a response in the form of 'Yes' to a proposal of marriage before a couple can enter mutually into this two-sided covenant. Such a covenant is free, open-minded and contingent upon the mutual response of both parties. This is *not*, however, the nature of the New Covenant in Christ.

The unilateral covenant (*diathēkē*) articulated in the Bible is quite different. God has made, once and for all, a covenant for us in Christ – the New Covenant 'in my blood'. Although this unilateral and completed commitment still demands a response it is not conditional upon our response – indeed, it inspires the free and joyful response God desires precisely *because* his covenant commitment is not conditional upon our response. So the New Covenant made by God for humanity in Christ is perceived as demanding the joyful, loving, 'Amen' of the whole person – which is what worship is. What is noteworthy about this kind of response is the fact that it is free and joyful – and not driven either by fear or by self-centred desire for gain that would underpin a response conceived in contractual terms.

All this is to say that God's covenant is unconditional and is not conditioned by considerations of whether we are worthy. It is *free* – God's grace is the 'given' under which we live our lives.

INDICATIVES AND IMPERATIVES

God's unconditional commitment makes claims upon our lives – *unconditional* claims indeed. In this respect, it may be said to be 'costly'. As JBT would point out, 'Liberals and Lutherans have tended to stress free grace. Conservatives and Calvinists stressed the costly claims of grace. Liberals can sometimes turn free grace into cheap grace. Puritan Calvinism can sometimes turn costly grace into conditional grace.'

It belongs to the essence of the argument here that the *indicatives* of grace are always prior to the *imperatives* of law and human obligation. The Ten Commandments begin, in Exod. 20, with the Lord's indicative affirmation of his prior, faithful commitment to Israel and his deliverance of Israel from slavery in the land of Egypt. The structure of the law possesses, therefore, the following form: 'I love you and I have redeemed you (indicatives) . . . *Therefore*, be faithful to me and to each other, that is, to all those to whom I am also committed and faithful (imperatives)!'

The universal temptation of humanity, however, is to reverse the order of the indicatives and the imperatives – implying that if we enact the imperatives, God will be faithful. To do this is to turn a covenant into a contract. As JBT argued, the universal sin of the human heart in all ages is to want to do precisely that! Why is that the case? Two reasons stand out. First, it reflects the human desire for control – to be able to condition God's response to us and to earn our deserts, that is, to be in a position to claim credit for the way in which God treats us. To think in this way constitutes nothing less than the quintessential form of human alienation. Second, there is the desire within the Church, both Catholic and Protestant, to control and motivate its adherents – often out of apparently worthy intentions. To translate God's covenantal relationship into contractual terms in order to manipulate people into either repentance or conversion clearly amounts to a betrayal of the life of the Body of Christ and the form of our participation in God's Triune life. It is to supplant the free, loving and transforming activity of the Holy Spirit, with the worldly manipulation of people's self-interest – by either the use of fear or the promise of reward.

There was a *tendency* in the Pharisees of late Judaism (though this has often been over-stressed and erroneously applied to Judaism as a whole) to do precisely this. '*If* you keep the law, God will love you. *If* you keep the Sabbath, the kingdom of God will come.' The imperatives were made prior to the indicatives – and God's grace made conditional upon humankind's obedience. It is precisely against this inversion of the order of grace that Paul protested with such lucidity and cogency in Gal. 3:17–22. In short, love always brings its obligations. But the obligations of love are not the conditions of love. If this is true of human love, JBT would comment, how much more true is it of divine love. The God of the Bible is a covenant-God not a contract-God. God loves us and forgives us unconditionally. God's commitment, of course, demands a response but our response is not a condition of his love and forgiveness.

JBT's exposition of this invariably gave rise to a second concern, namely, that such a theology of grace risked weakening or diluting the force of the law thereby opening the door to a liberal if not licentious attitude towards our God-given obligations. The simplest example suggests why this is surely not the case. Two husbands travel regularly to Amsterdam on theological business at the Free University. Let us imagine that their wives begin to become concerned lest their respective husbands become tempted to engage in untheological activities in the nightspots of Amsterdam. Consequently, each decides to speak to their respective husbands. As John leaves on his next trip, his wife Margaret says, 'John, never forget that if I ever find out that you have so much as nodded in the direction of another woman in the course of your travels, I shall sue you for divorce and ensure that you lose the kids, the house and a substantial proportion of your salary, not to mention your reputation in theological circles!' However, as David heads out of his front door, his wife Jane stops him and says, 'David, I would just like you to know that no matter what circumstances you find yourself in and no matter what happens, I shall always be there for you and will always love you. If you make mistakes, never forget that I shall always forgive you!'

Which of the two husbands is more likely to engage in the aforementioned 'untheological activities' during his trip? One suspects that it would be John for the simple reason that, as he left, his wife Margaret made it clear that she did not love him unconditionally. Contrary to the commitment inherent in their wedding vows, their relationship was a contractual one. She was, in effect, informing him that she did not really love him at all. The withdrawal of unconditional love could only serve to weaken the obligations that stem from it. The obligations on David were, by contrast, profoundly strengthened – and in a way that was both affirming of him and surely freeing. It would not only intensify the obligatory response but inspire and facilitate it.

If God's relationship to Israel requires to be seen as a unilateral, covenantal relationship, what were the implications of this for Israel's relationship to the Gentiles? This was a question with which Israel had to wrestle. In the Suffering Servant songs in Isaiah, however, we find the profoundest grasp of the implications of God's elective purposes articulated in a manner radically consistent with the covenantal theology at the heart of the *Torah* (the law). The true Israel, the remnant, was to fulfil God's covenant purposes by being a light to the nations. Her election meant communicating the all-inclusive covenant purposes of God for all nations (for the '*ethnē*', to use the Pauline term), and doing so in a manner so radically true to the gracious character of God's covenant faithfulness, that a delicate bruised reed would not be broken and a barely lit, smouldering wick would not be put out (Isa. 42:3). In other words, the Suffering Servant would be a witness to God's all-inclusive covenant purposes for the world and in such a way that the very form of its witness would be radically true in character to its content. Sadly, this vision was lost for several centuries until it was fulfilled in Jesus Christ, in whom we find the true Suffering Servant in whom God's all-inclusive election of Israel is fulfilled in the One for whom there is neither Jew nor Gentile, bond nor free, black nor white, male nor female (Gal. 3:28).

If Israel struggled to grasp the full ramifications of the covenant for its dealing with others, the Christian Church has continually misconstrued and misrepresented it – as evidenced throughout the whole span of its history. Reflecting JBT's vision of the vocation to which the Church was elected as the body of Christ, was his own lifelong commitment to opposing apartheid, racism, sexism and all that dehumanizes people. This was grounded not on the basis of an abstract ethical agenda or a theory of natural law but in the recognition of God's covenantal commitment to humanity. The all-inclusive nature of God's election of humanity in Christ places unconditional obligations on Christians as individuals and on the Church as a whole, to embody, and thereby witness to, that all-inclusive purpose in every facet of our dealings in this world, not least our political commitments and affiliations. We cannot witness to a gospel through which God desires to give people their humanity while we simultaneously deprive them of their humanity by political, economic, cultural or, indeed, religious means.

Filial not legal[2]

The covenantal character of God's commitment to humanity has profound ontological implications. Every facet of humanity's relationship to God requires to be interpreted in radically filial rather than legal terms. The tragic tendency of the Federal Calvinist tradition was its inclination to undermine such an understanding by suggesting that God is only related to the elect by grace.[3] Whereas he is related to believers as

---

[2] See James B. Torrance, 'The Contribution of John McLeod Campbell to Scottish Theology', *Scottish Journal of Theology* 26 (1973), 295–310. Also James B. Torrance, 'Introduction' in John McLeod Campbell, *The Nature of the Atonement* (Edinburgh: The Handsel Press, 1996), 1–16.

[3] See James B. Torrance, 'The Concept of Federal Theology – Was Calvin a Federal Theologian?' in *Calvinus Sacrae Scripturae Confessor* (ed. Wilhelm Neuser, Grand Rapids, MI: William B. Eerdmans, 1994), 15–40. Also, James B. Torrance, 'Calvin and Puritanism in

Father, he is related to non-believers as creator. To the faithful he is redeemer, but to society at large, he is simply law-giver and judge. This meant that it was only *if* you repented that God could be deemed your Father and that his relationship towards you could be conceived in filial terms. On this account God is related to non-believers simply as creator – a relation interpreted in terms of law not grace, contractually not covenantally. It is for this reason, JBT argued continually, that the Calvinist tradition has misconstrued the socio-political ramifications of the gospel – because it failed to interpret our obligations Christologically. The doctrine of a limited atonement suggests that those who are not elect are not related to God covenantally or by redemption in Christ. Consequently, political duties are interpreted by appeal to a quasi-doctrine of creation (interpreted in isolation from Christology) and then, utilizing legal or contractual notions, there is an appeal to natural law or 'orders of creation' which are interpreted by our *logoi* (words or reasoning) in isolation from the one Logos[4] who is the embodiment of God's purposes both for humanity and, indeed, for creation as a whole.[5] The result led, in South Africa, to the widespread oppression and dehumanization by Christians of the majority of the population; in Northern Ireland, it underpinned sectarianism. Too often also it has served conceptions of the role of women which are driven by references to the natural order and orders of creation and which are uninformed by the incarnate Lord through whom and for whom all things were created and in whom there is neither male nor female. Suffice to say, the contemporary question which Christians most need to address is whether we are able to think through the political ramifications of confessing the Christ in whom there is neither Jew nor Gentile, Christian nor Muslim and in

---

England and Scotland – Some Basic Concepts in the Development of Federal Theology' in *Calvinus Reformator: His Contribution to Theology, Church and Society*, Institute for Reformational Studies (Potchefstrom: Potchefstrom University for Christian Higher Education, 1982), 264–86. Also James B. Torrance, 'Strengths and Weaknesses of the Westminster Theology' in *The Westminster Confession in the Church Today*, ed. A. I. C. Heron (Edinburgh: Saint Andrew Press, 1982), 127–47.

4   Dietrich Bonhoeffer argued that to affirm with John, in the prologue to his Gospel, that Jesus Christ is the 'Logos' (Word), means that we should regard him from the perspective of *our* concepts, notions and ideas (*logoi*) as the *Counter-logos* or *Anti-logos*. That is, he is to be regarded as the One who redefines and transforms our prior ideas, categories and commitments. Consequently, it is imperative that we ensure that we do not condition or adapt God's self-communication as the incarnate Word to fit *our* preconceived concepts, priorities and agendas! Cf. Dietrich Bonhoeffer, *Christology*, trans. John Bowden (London: Collins, 1966), 29–30.

5   See his essay 'Interpreting the Word by the Light of Christ or the Light of Nature? Calvin, Calvinism and Barth' in *Calviniana: Ideas and Influence of Jean Calvin* (Sixteenth-Century Essays and Studies, vol. 10), ed. R. V. Schnucker (St Louis, MO: Sixteenth-Century Journal Publishers, 1988), 255–67.

whom all are recognized as the beloved sons and daughters of the Father, whether they recognize it or not. The Father desires that all might know the extent of his love and forgiveness – even those who, for the present, 'reject the Lord who (nonetheless) bought them!' (2 Pet. 2:1).

As JBT continually insisted to those who would restrict the compass of God's Fatherhood, God is *essentially* – eternally and antecedently – Father. God is not contingently, functionally or temporally 'Father'. It is as Father that God is love. And to say that God *is* love is incompatible with the suggestion that God is universally just but only selectively loving towards a circumscribed few. It is the mistranslation of the biblical categories of God's righteousness (when the Hebrew *tsedaqah* is translated as 'justice' by the Latin *justitia*), *Torah* (conceived as 'law' in terms of the Roman *lex*') and covenant (where the Hebrew *berith* is translated by the Latin *foedus* – contract) that helps to set up the confused polarization of God's love and God's righteousness. It is God's loving righteousness and faithfulness that defines God's holiness.

It will come as no surprise, therefore, that JBT was so profoundly opposed to contemporary, liberal moves to replace the Trinitarian formula with 'Creator, Redeemer and Sanctifier/Giver of Life'. Aside from the fact that this reduces the persons to 'functions', thereby undermining the very notion of the Triune communion, to replace 'Father' with 'Creator' is to use a term for God which does not, in and of itself, imply loving commitment of any kind – 'Creator' is compatible with a deist account of the creation of objects or playthings. To address God as 'Abba, Father' (Rom. 8:15) constitutes an unambiguous affirmation that we are not the objects of some impersonal divine plan but that we are created to be the sons and daughters of the one Father.

The significance of this point for the transformative impact of the gospel cannot be overstated. Indeed, the essential point here is one appreciated in the secular context as evidenced by a recent British government drugs campaign. A powerful TV advertisement was made aimed not at drug users themselves but at their parents. Viewers were presented with a poignant picture of a teenager lying semi-conscious in a filthy gutter in the middle of the night. It was pouring with rain and drainwater was piling up against the young lad's body. The street lights allowed a glimpse of a syringe on the road beside him. You then see his father kneeling in the ditch and tenderly picking up his son and embracing him. The thrust of the campaign was to encourage fathers to ask whether they were 'man enough' to be there for their kids when they were lost and really needed them. What was clear to the anti-drugs campaigners was that it is only this kind of solidarity that can deliver teenagers from the social evils and addictions lying in wait for them.

Jesus's statement 'Whoever has seen me has seen the Father' (Jn 14:9) suggests neither a remote creator nor an arbitrary progenitor who loves some and hates others – who is, in fact, not a true father at all. Rather, it testifies to One who comes, in the person of his Son, in search of the lost and takes their suffering and the costliness of their alienation to himself in a radical act of 'being there' with and for an alienated and hostile humanity. The father in the anti-drugs advertisement, envisaged as the solution to the problem of alienated families and 'lost children', constitutes an icon of the God presented in the gospel as 'Immanuel'.

EVANGELICAL VERSUS LEGAL REPENTANCE

Do we not run the risk here of presenting a sentimental gospel whose transformative edge is blunted by a failure to take sin and the need for repentance sufficiently seriously? If we eliminate the conditionality of God's forgiveness is this not the thin end of an antinomian wedge?[6] It is here that a further emphasis central to JBT's thought comes to the fore, namely, his distinction between evangelical and legal repentance. This was a distinction to which John Calvin referred[7] – although, frustratingly, it is not one he developed as rigorously or extensively as he might have. Its significance was appreciated more fully by Thomas Boston and the 'marrow men'[8] and taken up again, in the nineteenth century, by F. D. Maurice.

Legal repentance suggests that *metanoia*[9] results from our being confronted with the law which leads us to repent by virtue of the fact that it exposes, judges and condemns. Although such a view does not necessarily involve contractual categories, it is normally associated with a contractual interpretation: '*If* you are to be forgiven and God is to be merciful towards you, *then* you must repent, obey the law!' Such an approach is considerably less effective in upholding righteousness and engendering our repentance/conversion (*metanoia*) than is widely assumed. First, the implication is that God does not love or value persons as they are. Rather, it suggests, God *may* love and forgive sinners if and to

---

6 That is, is this not to oppose or undermine the rule of law by implying that God will love and forgive us whatever we do or fail to do?
7 John Calvin, *Institutes of the Christian Religion*, 3.3.4.
8 The 'marrow men' were a group of theologians who were united around Thomas Boston and his enthusiasm for a work entitled *The Marrow of Modern Divinity*. This was published in the early seventeenth century and proved anathema to the legalistic orientation of the 1720 General Assembly of the Church of Scotland, which consequently condemned the book as heretical and antinomian.
9 The Greek word *metanoia* means literally 'change of mind' though it is usually translated as 'repentance'.

the extent that they manage to deliver the faith and repentance that is required. What is important to appreciate here is that such an approach does not and cannot generate love for God – any more than a contractual imperative encourages children to admire, let alone love, their earthly parents.

Secondly, it is equally ineffective in encouraging or sustaining love and respect for other persons or their human dignity. Given that the driving force in our orientation to the world becomes a form of fear of God – rather than love of God – our orientation towards others is seen as a means to an end. As Luther pointed out, we are not actually doing the will of God until we *desire* to do the will of God. God desires that we love him and love concerns our desires! Neither fear nor self-interest (hope of heaven) can generate the required desire. The love that stems from discovering the extent and unconditional nature of God's faithfulness and forgiveness, however, can and does!

In stark contrast to legal repentance, *evangelical repentance* describes transformation of a profoundly different kind. Whereas the former tends to focus sinners on their own self-interest, appealing to fear and the desire to escape God's wrath, the latter directs sinners right away from themselves in a manner which serves to generate the love for God and our fellow human beings which the *Torah* prescribes. The discovery that God loved and forgave them while they were yet sinners transforms people by directing their gaze to the unconditional love of the Father and the forgiveness and acceptance manifest as a free gift in the incarnate Son. Here *metanoia* (our transformation or repentance) is not seen as a condition of forgiveness but as the consequence of a forgiveness that generates it – a response to it! This is the transforming dynamic which John Wesley appreciated with such clarity when he referred to the Lord's Supper as a 'converting ordinance'. When we are presented with the bread and the wine and given the eyes to hear what our Lord is saying to us in and through it, the effect is transformative and reconciliatory. Consequently, we are motivated to repent and confess. It is only then, moreover, that we see our sin for what it *really* is – and are enabled, therefore, to repent *in truth.*

As JBT would regularly point out, the story of Zacchaeus (Lk. 19:1–10) exemplifies this evangelical *metanoia*. Zacchaeus is presented as an exploitative white-collar criminal whose desire to see Jesus is motivated by nothing more than idle curiosity – this latter element in the narrative obviates any suggestion that he might have been driven by a preparatory sense of guilt or the beginnings of repentance. Surrounded by victims of Zacchaeus's exploitative use of the tax laws, Jesus offers an unambiguous, public endorsement of his dignity reflected in the desire to come to his home. In the light of this act of unconditioned and unconditional affirmation, Zacchaeus finds himself loved and accepted. Precisely by virtue of that, however, he also sees his sin for what it is. This generates a radical *metanoia* in his whole orientation, not least towards others and the spontaneous recognition and affirmation of the dignity of those whom he has used and abused. Precisely because his repentance is not grounded in a self-interested concern for his future well-being or in the cold application of the condemnation of the law, we are presented with a selfless and self-giving desire to make amends to an extent that transcends anything that legal repentance could require. In short, his response is profoundly different from anything that could have been generated by Jesus presenting him with the condemnation of law or any desire to satisfy legal conditions for contractually conceived ends.

The so-called parable of the 'prodigal son' (Lk. 15:11–32) similarly illustrates the point. It is commonplace to misconstrue the story as concerning a son who takes his father's money, squanders it in sinful living but then 'comes to his senses', that is, repents. *Because he repents*, it is then assumed, he is forgiven by his father and accepted back into his father's home. The actual account is significantly different, however. A wealthy father loves his rogue son unconditionally and vulnerably – so much so that he allows himself to be humiliated by his son before his household by giving in to his son's insulting request, namely, that he receive his inheritance in advance of his father's death. Having insulted his father[10] and wasted his funds, he finds himself in abject poverty. Comparing the quality of food enjoyed by his father's servants with the pig food he is obliged to consider eating, he 'comes to his senses' deciding that the rational thing to do is to return home and seek his father's pity – in an attempt to redress the unhappy consequences of his cash-flow problem. In short, not only is his decision to return home driven by self-interest, it is even hinted that the account of his contrition, which he determines to tell his father, may suggest a cynical desire to manipulate his father still further for his own ends. In short, far from describing any *metanoia* on the part of the son, the story is quite candid in its description of the son's motives in returning home. Clearly, Jesus's concern is to illustrate quite specifically that the Father's love is unconditional and unconditioned by any repentance or transformed motivation on our part. The father does not look for any new-found respect for him on the part of his son – nor, indeed, in the eyes of others.

In *Poet and Peasant*, Kenneth Bailey comments on the implications of the reference to the father's running to meet his son. 'An Oriental

---

10 Kenneth Bailey, *Poet and Peasant* (Grand Rapids, MI: William B. Eerdmans, 1976). See Chapter 6 for an extended analysis of the cultural implications of Lk. 15.

nobleman with flowing robes never runs anywhere.'[11] Running required the father to lift his long robes above his knees before a household who saw a foolish old man first throwing away money and now his pride out of unrestrained love for a wanton son. The concern of the parable is not the nature or adequacy of any *metanoia* on the part of the prodigal – the focus is on the father. At the same time, however, it is significant to notice that the contractual arrangement that the son had conceived in advance out of his desire to secure the privileges of his father's servants is thrown to the wind when he finds himself in his father's embrace. He simply confesses that he has sinned. The implication is that any transformation or real repentance that took place occurred in the arms of his father – a father who did not hold back awaiting words of explanation or evidence of contrition or repentance, but ran to embrace his son loving, forgiving and accepting him unconditionally. The father's embrace, like the Eucharist, constituted a converting ordinance. The story then goes on to relate the love of the father for another son who is also using him, precisely through playing by the rules (laws) – but thereby, of course, turning the *Torah* on its head. As I argued earlier, the *Torah* simply articulates the form of the response to God's covenant faithfulness which is to love God and to love our neighbours as ourselves.

It is worth considering how the Gospel narratives to which I have referred would have run if the transformative dynamic were indeed to be characterized as legal repentance. Jesus and the father of the prodigal would have weighed up evidences of repentance or penitence or contrition and *only then*, if the conditions had been met to a sufficient degree, would they have forgiven and accepted the respective sinners. In the case of Zacchaeus, prior satisfaction of the legal demands of justice would have been required for forgiveness to be contemplated and in the second parable, the attitude of the elder son would have been commendable. Further illustrations of the same points are found in the narratives of the woman at the well (Jn 4) and the woman caught in adultery (Jn 8).

---

11 Ibid., 181.

CHRIST IN OUR PLACE[12]

By way of introducing JBT's next theme, it is worth noticing the difference between the God revealed in Christ and the father in the parable of the prodigal son. In the parable, the father remains at home while the son is in the far country, waiting and hoping that he will return home. In the Gospel, however, we find God travelling to the far country in pursuit of the prodigal and, in an act of inconceivable solidarity, establishing his home with him there.

Central to JBT's understanding of communion with the Father, of prayer and of worship, is a radically Trinitarian and incarnational doctrine of reconciliation.[13] The central focus and outworking of his understanding of grace is the eternal Son's taking our alienated humanity to himself, transforming and healing it within his person and presenting our humanity to the Father as cleansed and reconciled in his own person. Jesus Christ takes the condemnation of the *Torah* to himself and fulfils its righteous obligations in his life of union and communion with the Father. Given that the *Torah*, as we have seen, simply articulates the character and form of our appropriate response to God's faithfulness – to God and to our neighbour – Christ's act of reconciliation takes the form of the incarnate Son's presenting, by the Spirit, that perfect response ('Amen') to the Father's will that we cannot offer.

The very heart of the gospel of reconciliation requires to be understood, as the Greek Fathers interpreted it; namely, as an exchange (John Calvin would advocate it as the 'wondrous exchange' – the *mirifica commutatio*) whereby the eternal Son takes what is ours that we might have what is his. What becomes immediately apparent here is first, the integral connection between reconciliation, atonement and worship, and second, the fact that the very logic of worship and prayer requires to be interpreted in the light of the continuing Priesthood of Christ. Just as, for Paul, the righteous requirements of the law (*dikaiōmata tou nomou*) are fulfilled in Christ, so, for the author of the Epistle to the Hebrews, the righteous requirements of worship (*dikaiōmata tēs latreias*) are fulfilled in

---

12 See James B. Torrance, 'The Vicarious Humanity of Christ' in *The Incarnation*, ed. T. F. Torrance (Edinburgh: The Handsel Press, 1981), 127–47. Also, 'The Vicarious Humanity and Priesthood of Christ in the Theology of John Calvin' in *Calvinus Ecclesiae Doctor*, ed. W. H. Neuser (Kampen, Netherlands: J. H. Koh, 1980), 69–84. For a perceptive analysis and discussion of J. B. Torrance's theology of prayer and the priesthood of Christ, see Graham Redding, *Prayer and the Priesthood of Christ in the Reformed Tradition* (Edinburgh: T&T Clark, 2003), 1–4, 149–57, 178–81, 195–7 and 296–7.
13 See James B. Torrance, 'The Ministry of Reconciliation Today: The Realism of Grace' in *Incarnational Ministry: The Presence of Christ in Church, Society, and Family*, ed. C. D. Kettler and T. H. Speidell (Colorado Springs: Helmers and Howard, 1990), 130–9.

and through the sole Priesthood of Christ. In short, all parts of our salvation are completed by God for us and in our place in Christ the head.

What this means is that every act of worship, of thanksgiving and intercession requires to be seen as the gift of sharing by the Spirit in the incarnate Son's communion with the Father.[14] Every facet of our response is both cleansed and actualized *en Christō* (in Christ). The ramifications for how we understand every facet of our lives requires to be interpreted on this basis. Worship, ethics, prayer and even Christian social action require to be seen as the gift of participating by the Spirit in the incarnate Son's communion with the Father and his mission from the Father to the world. On this model, worship and prayer are no longer to be defined as something *we* do, as a work or task that we struggle to perform, but as a gift – the gift of participating by the Spirit in Christ's ongoing prayer, worship and praise. Whereas worship is so often seen as a legal requirement or obligation, a 'work' to be done, JBT argued for an evangelical (as opposed to a legal) understanding of worship which sees it as the gift of participating in the response Christ offers the Father in our place and on our behalf. This is not a response, however, that displaces or replaces ours but one in which we are not only invited to participate but which liberates us to respond and which affirms that response. Worship becomes, for JBT therefore, the supreme gift of grace – the gift of participating by the Spirit in the worship and praise and one true response offered by the One in whom we find ourselves belonging for all eternity within the love of the Father – a reconciled belonging which sets us free for worship which is an authentic and joyful response and not a burden.

Belonging

To seek to distil a conceptual key or idea which drove JBT's theology would be inappropriate. For him, the task of the theologian was to seek to articulate reverently and obediently the testimony of Scripture and emphatically not to submit it to a conceptual system. At the same time, however, the biblical emphases on covenant, the character of the *Torah* and the all-inclusive headship and vicarious Priesthood of Christ constitute an unambiguous endorsement of our *belonging* – not as the static possessions or 'belongings' of a creator, but as belonging to the one Father as his beloved children. For JBT, our very fulfilment as persons lies in our discovery of that belonging by means of the same Spirit who facilitates our active participation, as adopted children, in Christ's Sonship.

---

14   James B. Torrance, 'The Place of Jesus Christ in Worship' in *Theological Foundations for Ministry: Selected Readings for a Theology of the Church in Ministry*, ed. R. S. Anderson (Grand Rapids: William B. Eerdmans, 1979), 348–69.

Covenant denotes God's unconditional faithfulness to a people whom he has delivered from slavery as his own. The *Torah* articulates the implications of that belonging with respect to our response to God and to each other. The imperatives of law repose in the indicatives of grace – indicatives which express, quite simply, to whom we belong. As one of my students, Cindy Burris, continually reminds us, 'We do not understand *who* we are until we recognize *whose* we are!' It is a Trinitarian doctrine of belonging that underpins theological anthropology.

Worship is the expression and outworking of this belonging in and through which we participate, as adopted sons and daughters, in the Triune embrace. JBT would regularly refer to Irenaeus's doctrine of the Son and the Spirit as the two hands of the Father through which he embraces humanity in an all-inclusive act of love and forgiveness.

This brings me to a final facet of his theology. For JBT, this biblical understanding of belonging must inform every aspect of our approach to those outside the Church – be they Jew or Gentile, black or white, women or men, rich or poor. As such it must inform, mould and motivate our political commitments. To understand our belonging, to *be* the Body of Christ in truth is to see all those outside its bounds, not least our enemies, as belonging to the Father by right of creation and by right of redemption. Throughout the entirety of his theological career – from his student days, indeed – JBT sought to oppose and repudiate every form of 'limited atonement' in that it betrayed not only the Bible but also the Reformed doctrine of grace and the all-inclusive headship of Christ. From his perspective, to the extent that people determine to reject Christ, they are 'rejecting the Lord who bought them' (2 Pet. 2:1). They are rejecting the one to whom they continue to belong as children of God the Father and for whom Christ lived and died and was raised. Apart from the tragic consequences of limited atonement for Christian mission and outreach, its consequences for the Church's political witness are distressing. How is God related to those who are not elect from the perspective of limited atonement? The answer can only be, 'As Creator and Judge', – that is, by law! Thus, if the one who is their creator and judge neither loves nor forgives these nonelect, what can ultimately motivate Christians to be concerned for those whom God does not love, or to forgive meaningfully those whom God does not forgive. In short, such a theology undermines the very underpinning that theology should give to humanitarian concern and the concern for reconciliation in an alienated and divided world. JBT's theology has precisely the opposite effect of such an undermining.

For JBT, to see the other as belonging is to be radically concerned for the welfare not only of the poor, marginalized and culturally despised but those who are guilty, not least our enemies. It was this which characterized his radical commitment to opposing apartheid which for him was

118   An Introduction to Torrance Theology

driven by the nature-grace model of federal Calvinism with its resulting failure to interpret creation Christologically in the light of the one in whom there is neither Jew nor Gentile, black nor white. But his opposition to apartheid was always attended by a profound concern to witness constructively and graciously to its Afrikaner advocates. If the gospel was to transform their worldviews, it was to be evangelical not legal repentance!

JBT's Personal Witness to Our Belonging

Too often the message of theologians is falsified by the way they live their lives. By way of conclusion, it is perhaps appropriate to mention that JBT's vision of belonging shaped every facet of his life – not only his commitment to bringing an end to the theological advocacy of apartheid in South Africa and to seeking reconciliation in Northern Ireland but in his family commitments. Two brief anecdotes are illustrative of this. On one occasion, he was referring to Jesus's instruction in Mt. 23 that we are to 'Call no man "father"!' He explained, 'For all that I am your biological father, in Christ you and I are brothers and should regard each other as such.' Throughout our teenage years, my sisters and I enjoyed the immense privilege of being treated, respected and, indeed, consulted accordingly. A further glimpse of his vision of belonging was reflected in a particular incident one Christmas holiday. Whereas Christmas Day was invariably a fairly hectic affair, the day after was the day when we really relaxed as a family and invariably enjoyed the most spectacular dinner. One such Boxing Day, all the food had been served and distributed on the plates and we were just sitting down to eat when the doorbell rang. Our hearts sank! On opening the front door we found a cold, hungry and desperately apologetic tramp wondering if we could possibly spare a sandwich. My father welcomed him into our home with indescribable warmth, sat him down at his place and, insisting that there was plenty of food, urged him to start eating. He then discreetly slipped away to prepare himself bacon and eggs in the kitchen. It would have been unthinkable for my father to have treated the tramp as if he didn't belong.

In the small village of Roslin to the south of Edinburgh, there are two pieces of granite. The first is the sculpture located in the grounds of the Community of the Transfiguration and to which JBT referred in the concluding chapter of his book.[15] This was a gift to the community by a sculptor who had belonged to an exclusive Christian denomination but

---

15   James B. Torrance, *Worship, Community and the Triune God of Grace*.

who had decided to confess that he feared he might be gay. Rejected and banished by family and church alike, he turned up at the Community in Roslin where he found himself welcomed and given a home within this ecumenical community while he sought to rebuild his life. On departing he gave the Community a sculpture of two men locked in an embrace. The only difference between them were the holes to be seen in the hands of one. It portrayed, he explained, the second Adam embracing the first Adam. Within that community, he had glimpsed the belonging at the heart of the gospel.

The second piece of granite is my father's rugged headstone located in the small graveyard in the grounds of Roslin Chapel. On it are inscribed words chosen by my mother: 'He died as he lived, filled with gratitude for the unconditional love and forgiveness of the Triune God of grace.' His life and theology were characterized by a joy borne of knowing the welcoming hospitality of God in Christ and the overwhelming and liberating sense of belonging which that generated. His overwhelming desire in life was that all might know that it applied to them too.[16]

---

16 I am indebted to Robert T. Walker both for his helpful suggestions and also for the corrections he made to the final draft of this article.

Chapter 6

CALVIN AND THE CAFÉ CHURCH: REFLECTIONS AT THE INTERFACE BETWEEN REFORMED THEOLOGY AND CURRENT TRENDS IN WORSHIP

Graham Redding

It is not unusual to hear graduates from seminaries and theological colleges talk about one or two lecturers who had a dramatic and lasting impact on their thinking. Many people who had the privilege of hearing James Torrance deliver a lecture, including myself, speak of him precisely in that kind of way.

In the late 1980s, Professor Torrance was an occasional guest lecturer at the Theological Hall at Knox College in Dunedin, New Zealand, where his son, Alan, was the lecturer in Systematic Theology. Almost invariably, the subject of Professor Torrance's lectures would be the nature of worship: 'What is the right way to worship God?' he would ask the class, to which the reply would be, 'Through Jesus Christ'.[1]

Such a simple answer, but one with profound implications. It has stayed with me throughout my subsequent years of parish ministry, and become an occasion for further study and reflection.[2] In an age of institutional decline, when so much talk seems to be focused on the 'emerging Church' and the need for 'experiential worship',[3] Professor Torrance's prompt to think about what we are doing when we worship is especially relevant.

When James Torrance talked about worship he spoke not only as a Professor of Theology, but also as a Minister of Word and Sacraments in the Church of Scotland. Academic rigour was joined to pastoral insight

---

1   James B. Torrance, 'Christ in our Place' in Thomas Torrance, James Torrance and David Torrance, *A Passion for Christ: The Vision that Ignites Ministry*, ed. Gerrit Dawson and Jock Stein (Edinburgh: Handsel Press, and Lenoir, NC: PLC Publications, 1999), 35.
2   cf., my book, *Prayer and the Priesthood of Christ in the Reformed Tradition* (London and New York: T&T Clark, 2003).
3   For example, Thomas G. Bandy, in his book *Mission Mover: Beyond Education for Church Leadership* (Nashville: Abingdon Press, 2004, p. 106), presents a contrast between 'informational worship' that seeks to glorify God through liturgy and expository preaching, and 'experiential worship' that seeks to motivate God's mission through the use of technology and motivational speaking. He advocates the latter.

and a commitment to the life and mission of the Church that had ordained him. Just as Professor Torrance always represented something of his own church tradition in his discussion about worship, so too with each of us. In my case, it is the Presbyterian Church of Aotearoa New Zealand, a church that was transplanted from Scotland in the nineteenth century but which, over the course of time, has quite naturally moulded itself to the New Zealand social landscape. What follows will inevitably reflect something of that history and particularity. Far from limiting the chapter, though, it is my hope that much of what I talk about will resonate with observations and experiences further afield, and even serve as a catalyst for readers to think more critically about their own traditions.[4] In this way, the task of theology, understood in terms of faith seeking understanding, may be advanced.

Worship in a Fluid, Post-modern World

Imagine for a moment dropping in on four different worship services on any given Sunday.

The first worship service is what some might call traditional Presbyterian: a four-hymn sandwich led by organ and choir, written order of worship, minister in vestments, strong focus on the sermon. Starts and finishes on the hour.

The second has a more informal and contemporary feel to it: brackets of songs led by a band and an energetic and personable worship leader, extempore prayer, testimonies, a message instead of a sermon, PowerPoint.

The third is in a church hall converted into a café for the occasion: cappuccinos and homemade baking, jazz background music, sitting around tables, theme introduced by a kind of master of ceremonies through poetry and DVD clip and opened up for discussion, interactive.

The fourth is contemplative: candles, lots of silence, guided meditation.

If this is a sample of the variety of styles of corporate worship that exist today, a number of questions begin to present themselves. Amidst the variety, is there a common thread to these acts of worship that we can identify as being distinctively Presbyterian or Reformed or even Christian for that matter? And if not, does the absence of a common thread matter, or is it simply a reflection of the post-denominational age in which we live? Similarly, are there any criteria that we can use to help us discern

---

4   An earlier draft of this chapter was delivered to the Presbyterian Church of Aotearoa New Zealand's School of Ministry in 2005, and subsequently published in *The Record*, which is produced by the Church Service Society in Scotland (vol. 41, Winter 2005/6, 36–47).

what valid developments are in corporate worship, or are we compelled to adopt a relativistic and pragmatic attitude – anything is valid provided it's done with integrity and succeeds in meeting a perceived need?

Leonard Sweet, American author of the widely acclaimed book *Aquachurch*,[5] would likely see contemporary developments and experiments in worship as a valid part of the Church's process of making new maps to guide itself in a fluid, post-modern world. They would be expressions of what he calls the AncientFuture Church, telling the old story in new ways, taking the content of the gospel (which, he says, is timeless and unchanging) and putting it in new containers.[6]

MINISTERS AND PASTORS: CURATORS OF WORSHIP OR AMBASSADORS OF CHRIST?

Writing in a slightly more radical vein from within our own New Zealand context, Mike Riddell, Mark Pierson and Cathy Kirkpatrick, who five years ago published a book called *The Prodigal Project: Journey into the Emerging Church*, say that the content of worship will inevitably change as it is repackaged, but that's okay. They compare the task of preparing worship today to that of a curator of an art gallery.[7] A curator, they say, serves art by providing the context for others to engage and participate, giving attention to such things as juxtaposition, style, distance, light and shade. In worship, a curator is a maker of context rather than a presenter of content, a provider of a frame inside which the elements are arranged and rearranged to convey a message.

For these Baptist authors, AncientFuture worship is a way of describing the task of re-appropriating the traditional into the contemporary, and providing new contexts and new content for some of the old rituals, patterns and words. It's all about contextualization, and giving people an opportunity to experience God, not just to hear about someone else's experience of God.

If there is something our four expressions of worship have in common, then, it does not appear to be a common liturgical tradition, but rather a shared reference point, Jesus Christ, whom Leonard Sweet refers to as the North Star, a navigational point transcending our personal and cultural coordinates, yet relating to us all through the particularities of our cultures and personal experiences.[8]

---

5   Leonard Sweet, *Aquachurch: Essential Leadership Arts for Piloting Your Church in Today's Fluid Culture* (Loveland, Colorado: Group Publishing, 1999).
6   Ibid., 30.
7   Mike Riddell, Mark Pierson and Cathy Kirkpatrick, *The Prodigal Project: Journey into the Emerging Church* (London: SPCK, 2000), 63.
8   Sweet, *Aquachurch*, 40.

According to this logic, there is nothing intrinsic to Presbyterian or Reformed worship that might distinguish it from, say, worship in Baptist, Roman Catholic or for that matter Greek Orthodox churches. Moreover, one assumes, provided Jesus is the reference point, there is nothing that invalidates an act of worship from a Christian perspective.

In *Fractuals*, a follow-up CD to *The Prodigal Project*, Mark Pierson identifies six qualities of worship in a post-modern culture: authenticity, community, abandonment of dogma, focus on the arts, diversity and participation. Authenticity, he says, is the most important and the most difficult to achieve. It's about honesty and integrity, and not being driven by the worship leader to express beliefs we don't believe. Presumably, worship loses its authenticity when form is followed for the sake of form and fails to express or connect with people's personal experience. Inauthentic worship, says Pierson, becomes whoreship, a form of prostitution.

At this point, though, my question would be, authentic to whom? Authentic to the people that gather for worship (in which case, who decides if the bar of authenticity has been reached?), or authentic to the Triune God revealed in Jesus Christ?

When, in his letter to the Corinthians, the Apostle Paul describes the institution of the Lord's Supper, he says that he passed on to them the tradition that he had received.[9] Any notion of authenticity at work here has nothing to do with Paul's personal intentions, or with the intentions of the Corinthian congregation. It's about faithful transmission.

This notion of faithfulness to what has been given in and through Christ is inherent in the Presbyterian understanding of ordained ministry, which itself is an expression of the ancient notion of apostolic tradition. As the Westminster documents teach, ministry is a gift of Christ to the Church and is signified through the laying on of hands by those already ordained to the ministry. Similarly, the tradition of ministers robing for ordination and/or induction arose from the recognition of the corporate nature of the ministry rather than an opportunity for an earnest individual to do his or her own thing for God.

Of course, that's often not how it's perceived. What was intended as a symbol of the corporate nature of ministry is often interpreted as a symbol of hierarchy. But the main point here is that the Minister of Word and Sacraments, according to the Reformed tradition, is not so much a curator of worship, or the facilitator of a God-experience, as an *ambassador for Christ*, appointed to make the mystery of Christ known.[10]

---

9   1 Cor. 11:23. Earlier in that chapter Paul commends the Corinthians for maintaining the traditions just as he handed them on to them (cf. 1 Cor. 11:2).
10 c.f., Eph. 3:1–13.

Accordingly, for all the diversity of worship styles that exist, we are bound to ask if there are constant norms for Christian worship that transcend cultures and keep us faithful to the gospel of Christ. Without such norms there is a danger that, as we focus on contextualization and the individual experience of the worshipper, and become ever more pluralistic, we will lose sight of the fact that Christian worship is ultimately bound up with honouring who God is and how God acts, as we understand these things to have been disclosed in the person of Christ.

Changing Patterns of Worship

Clearly there is something of a tension here between the theology of worship and the reality of religious pluralism. The tension is more acute than it was 40 or so years ago, when Presbyterian worship pretty well had a standard template.

So what's changed? Thinking about the situation in New Zealand, I'd include in my list the following six things, most of which, I suspect, will be evident throughout the Western world:

1. *The changing nature of church membership*: Forty years ago, denominational boundaries were more distinct and denominational loyalties more pronounced than they are today. Baby boomer and subsequent generations do not place a great weight on denominational allegiance. Younger people tend to worship where they feel most comfortable, and don't care whether that's in a Presbyterian church, an Anglican church, a Baptist church, or an Assembly of God. Choices are often made on very practical grounds, such as the strength or otherwise of the children and youth programmes, the warmth of fellowship, as well as the style of worship and music. The denominational brand is less important than whether personal needs are being met and preferences catered for. An increasing proportion of our church membership base has neither an exclusively Presbyterian background nor an accompanying knowledge of and commitment to a Reformed approach to worship.
2. *A spirit of experimentation*: It has almost become something of a cliché to say that people today are into spirituality more than organized religion. An *NZ Herald* poll in January 2005 indicated that more than two-thirds of New Zealanders say they believe in God but fewer than half of them attend a religious worship service.[11] Spirituality is deemed to be less institutional and more personal, less prescribed

---

11   *NZ Herald*, Friday 7 January 2005, A4.

and more experimental. Recent developments in contemporary and alternative styles of worship, including such innovations as café church, are mindful of such perceptions and the need to make the Church more accessible, relevant and relational. As a consequence, there is an increasing leaning towards the experimental and the edgy, a working out of an ecclesiology from the margins of the Church rather than traditionally defined centres. I would further suggest that this spirit of experimentation in worship is a product not just of recently articulated notions of spirituality but also of the charismatic movement in the 1970s, which placed a high value on the freedom of the Spirit, and which in many ways was a kind of renewal movement even if, at times, it had the effect of dividing many 'traditional' congregations.

3. *The impact of technology*: In the 1970s it was the overhead projector. Today it's PowerPoint: from new songs projected on to a screen to video clips, DVD and CD tracks and visual images downloaded from the net and scanned into the laptop. It's about visual effect and multi-sensory engagement.

4. *The availability of resources*: Gone are the days when a single hymn book like the *Church Hymnary* provided the basis for congregational singing. Copyright licences enable congregations to access a huge range of musical material. It's an eclectic mix, in which no value judgement is made between material from, say, Hillsong and material from the Royal School of Church Music. And what is so in relation to music is also the case in relation to other liturgical resources. Lacking a *Book of Common Order* of our own or the equivalent of the *Anglican Prayer Book*, people use a wide variety of resources, including a plethora of lectionary-based material on the web, much of which offers sermon outlines, prayers, music selections and entire orders of worship. They opt for what works, not for what their tradition prescribes or recommends.

5. *Multiculturalism*: Corresponding to patterns of immigration in recent decades has been the growth of ethnic congregations and the provision of worship that caters for those who wish to worship in their native tongue. The growth of Pacific Island and Asian congregations has added considerably to the pluralism of the Church in New Zealand. We are increasingly a multicultural church.

6. *From ordained ministry to worship leader*: There has been a determined attempt in recent years to make worship more participatory, and to share the task of conducting worship. The modern worship leader may or may not be ordained, may or may not have any formal training in the theology and conduct of worship, and is not infrequently the leader of the music group.

Of course, there is nothing new or radical about pluralism. As Emily Brink and John Witvliet point out in *The Worship Sourcebook*, 'each week throughout the world Christians gather for worship in mud huts and Gothic cathedrals, in prisons and nursing homes, in storefront buildings and village squares, in megachurches and old country chapels. In these diverse contexts the style of worship varies greatly'.[12]

But the point I'm developing here is that when we fail to give adequate attention to the importance of a unifying tradition and enduring liturgical principles that flow from a Trinitarian doctrine of worship, the flip side to pluralism and contextualization is confusion. So, when *The Prodigal Project* offers a definition of worship as 'a person or persons responding to God',[13] it seems to me that worship has been reduced to an act of individual and collective self-expression, and the door is opened for everyone to do what is right in their own eyes.

This is where, following Professor Torrance's lead, we have much to gain from revisiting the liturgical theology of John Calvin and John Knox and allowing it to inform our understanding of worship as new styles of worship continue to evolve.

FROM SELF-EXPRESSION TO A TRINITARIAN EVENT

For Calvin and Knox, worship was a Trinitarian event. It has a Trinitarian structure. We worship the Father through the Son and in the Spirit. Worship is not something that *we* do in the first instance. It involves us, and is intensely dialogical, but it does not originate with us. Nor does it depend on our creativity and strength. Through the activity of the Spirit we are brought to share in the Son's worship of the Father, which is rendered through the Spirit in our place and on our behalf.

According to this understanding, Christ is not merely the *reference point* of Christian worship as Leonard Sweet would have us believe. He is the *leader and mediator* of worship. As Calvin himself declared, it is *Christ* who leads our songs, and it is Christ who is the chief composer of our hymns.[14] Christ is our great High Priest, the One True *leitourgos* of the heavenly sanctuary (cf. Heb. 8:2). As such the *leitourgia* of Jesus is contrasted with the *leitourgia* of humankind. This is the worship which God has provided for humanity, and which alone is acceptable to God. The worship that

---

12 Emily Brink and John Witvliet, *The Worship Sourcebook* (Grand Rapids: Calvin Institute of Christian Worship and Baker Books, 2004), 15.
13 Riddell, Pierson and Kirkpatrick, *The Prodigal Project*, 64.
14 John Calvin, *Institutes of the Christian Religion*, Geneva, 1559, ed. J. T. McNeill, trans. F. L. Battles (Philadelphia: Westminster Press, 1960), 2.15.6.

Jesus offers gathers up the worship of ancient Israel and completes it, and becomes the substance of all Christian worship.[15]

In emphasizing the mediatorial role of Christ in worship Calvin was being consistent with the understanding of the early church, at least until the fourth century or so. From that time onwards, however, as the Church countered the threat posed by the Arian denial of the deity of Christ, liturgical prayers and doxologies were increasingly directed to the Son as well as to the Father (to eliminate any possible doubt about the Son's divine status). While a Trinitarian formula was thus retained in public prayer it had in fact undergone a subtle yet profound change. For as the Son was worshipped and adored along with the Father, his mediatorial role in relation to prayer and worship was obscured, and substitute figures were found, including the medieval priesthood, the communion of saints and the Virgin Mary. Calvin was fiercely critical of these substitute figures, which he felt had displaced Christ from his mediatorial role, with catastrophic effects on the Church's worship. Hence his strong emphasis on the priesthood of Christ.

An important consequence of Christ's priesthood, as Calvin put it, is that 'we who are defiled in ourselves, *yet are priests in him*', and on these grounds alone are we able to 'offer ourselves and our all to God, and freely enter the heavenly sanctuary that the sacrifices of prayer and praise that we bring may be acceptable and sweet-smelling before God'.[16]

In other words, the concept of the *priesthood of all believers,* so often appealed to today in promoting a participatory approach to the preparation and conduct of worship, only has meaning, as far as Calvin is concerned, when it flows from a prior recognition of the *sole priesthood of Christ*. When the priesthood of all believers is cut adrift from its Christological mooring the entire focus of worship begins to shift from what is happening in and through Christ to what we do: *we* connect with God, *we* sing our songs and offer our prayers, *we* express ourselves.[17] Worship becomes human-centred rather than God-centred.

I would further suggest that as this shift in focus occurs there is an attendant pressure on us to get it right, to come up with ever new creative and innovative ways of generating God-experiences for the punters, and the more we come to rely on the personality, charisma and creativity of the minister or worship leader to deliver the goods. Forty years ago James Torrance's brother, Tom, coined the phrase 'Protestant sacerdotalism' to describe the displacement of the humanity of Christ by the personality of the minister. 'How frequently', he said:

---

15 c.f., James B. Torrance, 'The Place of Jesus Christ in Worship' in *Theological Foundations for Ministry*, ed. Ray S. Anderson (Grand Rapids: William B. Eerdmans, 1979), 350.
16 Calvin, *Institutes*, 2.15.6 (italics mine).
17 c.f., Torrance, *A Passion for Christ*, 36.

the minister's prayers are so crammed with his own personality (with all its boring idiosyncrasies!) that the worshipper cannot get past him in order to worship God in the name of Christ – but is forced to worship God in the name of the minister! . . . And how frequently the whole life of the congregation is so built up on the personality of the minister that when he goes the congregation all but collapses or dwindles away.[18]

Might I suggest the following exercise? The next time you attend a worship service take note of those aspects of the service that give expression to the mediatorial role of Christ and those aspects that obscure it. You might notice, for example, that prayers are concluded with, '. . . through Christ our Lord', or '. . . in Jesus's name' – a sure sign that the mediatorial role of Christ is being recognized. Conversely, you might notice that the worship seems largely directed to Jesus, especially in the music, and that as he is made the object of the church's worship so other mediatorial figures assert themselves, such as the music group or the worship leader.

Eucharistic Worship

For Calvin, one of the consequences of a commitment to the priestly and mediatorial role of Christ in worship is a strongly Eucharistic theology. This is often overlooked when we talk about the Reformed emphasis upon the Word, but for Calvin (and for Knox) the preaching of the Word should always be accompanied by the administration of the Lord's Supper. Christian worship is both kerygmatic and sacramental. The Word should lead us to the Table.

The fact that Calvin was unable to practise what he preached in terms of weekly communion did not alter the strength of his conviction. It is at the Table that the priesthood of Christ comes into sharpest focus. Again taking his lead from the book of Hebrews, Calvin argued that the priestly work of Christ refers not only to what he *accomplished* once and for all at Calvary, but also to what he *continues to do* as the One in whom our sanctified humanity has been lifted into the presence of the Father, and who intercedes for all humankind, including those for whom no one else intercedes.[19] The One in whom all humanity is represented in his incarnation, death and resurrection, continues to represent all humanity in his ascension. The vicarious (or representative) humanity of Jesus the

---

18 Thomas F. Torrance, *Theology in Reconstruction* (London: SCM Press, 1965), 167–8.
19 Calvin, *Institutes*, 3.20.20.

High Priest is just as important to his intercessory role (in the heavenly sanctuary) as it was to his sacrificial role (on the cross).

This insight concerning the priesthood of Christ at the Table has traditionally been given expression in the order by which the elements are served. In partaking of the elements before serving the elders and congregation, the officiating Minister is indicating that the true Host of this sacramental meal is none other than Christ himself. The Minister must first partake of that which the host gives before serving others in his name, thereby fulfilling the ambassadorial function which is implicit in the act of ordination. The increasingly common practice of the Minister being served last, after the congregation has partaken of the elements, might be based on an ethic of service, but it inadvertently displaces Christ by the person of the officiating Minister, who effectively becomes the de facto host whose actions are determined by the dictates of table manners and the convention of serving one's guests before oneself.

John Knox, who was deeply influenced by Calvin's liturgical theology, saw more clearly than any other Reformer what the Priesthood of Christ meant in relation to worship in general and the Eucharist in particular. He believed that the Eucharist should be regarded not merely as the event through which one receives Christ and his benefits, but also as the event at which, in union with him who continues to intercede for sinners, one engages in prayer. The Eucharist, thus understood, is not only a meal of thanksgiving; through the act of intercession it becomes a means of sharing in the saving ministry of Christ in the world. It has a missiological dimension.

Moreover, in the Eucharist, Christ, through the Holy Spirit, not only brings his once and for all earthly ministry to our remembrance. He also lifts up our hearts and minds in the *Sursum Corda* into his communion with the Father, to make us participants of the new humanity in him. This was why Calvin took issue with Zwingli who, by reducing the sacrament to a meal of remembrance and the elements of bread and wine to mere symbols, failed to acknowledge the real presence of Christ in the sacrament.

Even though the Presbyterian tradition has been no more successful than Calvin in celebrating weekly the Lord's Supper, it has endeavoured at various times to establish a Eucharistic pattern to its worship. As the introduction to the third edition of *The Church Hymnary* (1973) stated: 'The Committee in determining the order in which the hymns are arranged, has borne in mind that the Order of Holy Communion is normative for worship in the Reformed Church and that, where there is no regular weekly celebration of Holy Communion, the service should still follow the Eucharistic pattern.'[20]

---

20 *The Church Hymnary, Third Edition* (London: Oxford University Press, 1973), viii.

BRAVELY NAVIGATING UNCHARTED WATERS OR LOST ON A SEA OF CONFUSION?

Comparing Calvin and Knox's theology of worship with the reality of worship in our time, James Torrance has observed that most worship today 'is in practice Unitarian, has no doctrine of the mediator or the sole priesthood of Christ, is human-centred, has no proper doctrine of the Holy Spirit, is too often non-sacramental, and can engender weariness'.[21]

If this is indeed so, the question is, does it matter? Should we be concerned?

Yes. It seems to me that many developments and experiments in worship that accompany talk about the emerging church are taking place in a theological vacuum. Ignorance of the classic liturgies and what they have meant to the Church down the centuries, ignorance of the liturgical theology of Calvin and Knox, ignorance of the role of ordained ministry, will lead ultimately to an impoverishment of Reformed worship and a detachment of corporate worship from its Reformed, early church and indeed Jewish roots. Some would argue that that is happening already. Marva Dawn, for example, talks about the dumbing down of worship right across the Church.[22] That which we regard at one time as bravely navigating uncharted waters could with the benefit of hindsight turn out to be symptomatic of us having lost our way.

The gap between those who favour traditional or liturgical approaches to worship and those who favour non-liturgical approaches appears to be widening. There is a need to engage constructively with both ends of the liturgical and theological spectrum. In this regard, I would recommend *The Worship Sourcebook*. The editors, Emily Brink and John Witvliet, refer to their book as something of a unique experiment:

> It is designed to be used by Christians, who value free-church, low-church, nonliturgical, evangelical approaches to worship but who also want to learn from and draw on historic patterns of worship. At the same time, the book aims to be useful and instructive to congregations who practice traditional or liturgical worship and who may be looking for ways to adapt it or to rethink its meaning.[23]

---

21 James B. Torrance, *Worship, Community and the Triune God of Grace* (Carlisle: Paternoster Press and Downers Grove, IL: InterVarsity Press, 1996), 20.
22 c.f., Marva Dawn, *Reaching Out Without Dumbing Down: A Theology of Worship for the Turn-of-the-Century Culture* (Grand Rapids: William B. Eerdmans, 1995).
23 Brink and Witvliet, *The Worship Sourcebook*, intro.

I am not advocating here a slavish use of set liturgies, or suggesting that worship should be locked in a time warp, although I agree with Brink and Witvliet that a well-conceived order of worship is one of the most important things a congregation can have to ensure that the norms of Christian worship are faithfully practised.

Calvin's views on this matter were emphatic:

> Concerning a form of prayer and ecclesiastical rites, I highly approve of it that there should be a certain form from which ministers be not allowed to vary. That first, some provision be made to help the unskilfullness and simplicity of some; secondly, that the consent and harmony of the Churches one with another may appear; and lastly, that the capricious giddiness and levity of such as affect innovations may be prevented. . . . Therefore, there ought to be a stated form of prayer and administration of the sacraments.[24]

Brink and Witvliet acknowledge that 'for some, an order of worship might feel like a straitjacket, limiting creativity. But', they suggest, 'consider jazz music. Jazz features spontaneous improvisation. But it works only because the musicians are following a regular, predictable, repeated chord structure. Without this structure, the music would be chaos. Meaningful spontaneity and creativity happen within structure.'[25]

Of course, in the missional context in which the post-Christendom Church finds itself, some people will inevitably ask whether spontaneity and creativity within a given structure go far enough. How much latitude do we have to change the structure itself for the sake of engaging with an unchurched generation?

I'm not sure there is a clear-cut answer to this question, but I would argue that perceived missional needs do not absolve us from testing the theo-logic of our worship. In practical terms, I would want to ask of any proposed development in worship whether, in addition to connecting with people in ways to which they can relate, this will help in forming them for a deeper experience of the Triune God. I would further ask the extent to which the marks of Christian worship, as are found in Scripture, observed in the earliest forms of Christian worship and given such clear expression by Calvin and Knox, are present.

The practice of corporate worship in the Church is at a critical juncture. The diversity we may think worthy of celebration could equally

---

24 Cited in William D. Maxwell, 'Reformed', *Ways of Worship: The Report of a Theological Commission of Faith and Order*, ed. P. Edwall, E. Hayman and W. D. Maxwell (London: SCM, 1951), 121.
25 Brink and Witvliet, *The Worship Sourcebook*, 24.

overwhelm us. There is a pressing need for some theological reflection in relation to worship. In the nineteenth century the formation of the Church Service Society and Scottish Church Society responded to a similarly pressing need in Scotland. The concluding question thus becomes: while always maintaining the priority of the mediatorial role of Christ, what comparable forums and opportunities might we create for our day in our respective contexts?

Chapter 7

THE CHRISTIAN LIFE AND OUR PARTICIPATION IN CHRIST'S CONTINUING MINISTRY

Gary W. Deddo

INTRODUCTION

There has been in recent years here in North America a rising emphasis on the nature and obligations of the Christian life, especially within the evangelical branches of the Church, whether within mainline denominations, historically evangelical denominations or even independent Churches. This emphasis in itself is not problematic and could be an indicator of a growing awareness that being Christian requires a living coherence of piety and practice, faith and obedience, private devotion and public witness, personal holiness and social righteousness. In these days when there seems to be a significant moral decline, a call within the Christian Church to obedience and faithfulness is understandable. This focus on the Christian life is registered in the vast sales of books like *The Purpose-Driven Life*. A certain hunger for more integrity and depth in the Christian life can also be seen in the ongoing interest in Henry Blackaby's *Experiencing God* materials and the growing interest in spiritual formation and the accompanying proliferation of books, seminars and retreats on this theme.

There are also those in the Church who see the great social needs of our society and world especially apparent and magnified by events such as the tsunami of Indonesia and the devastation of Hurricane Katrina along the Gulf Coast. The issue of global justice has grabbed the attention of many in the Church who are wrought up over terrorism, war, child slavery, starvation and the devastating AIDS epidemic especially witnessed on the continent of Africa. There is an acute awareness that the Christian Church ought to be more involved in bearing faithful witness to the justice and compassion of God in these situations.

On yet another front are those who long for a transformed and emerging church in which we would find 'A New Kind of Christian'. In such emerging churches Christian witness would attempt to address our post-modern society more by deeds than by words, more by community than individuals. Among the youth we saw a brief and not unrelated revival of concern for faithful Christian living embodied in the motto that was printed on thousands of armbands worn by teenagers and admired by adults: *WWJD?* What Would Jesus Do?

Moreover, in light of the seeming ineffectiveness and apparent irrelevance of the Christian faith in our secularized culture, various other voices are now calling for the establishment of a *missional church*. Such a church would be one captivated by a vision that saw its very reason for being the engagement of the world through service, evangelism and outreach. All of what the Church is and does would gain its impetus and justification by virtue of its contributing to the *missio Dei*, the mission of God, to take the gospel to our post-modern culture.

I mention these interests, trends and themes of our contemporary Church not to disparage them. Clearly there is a genuine hunger for Christian faithfulness in all of these. There is much to affirm, admire and commend in each of these movements that no doubt reflect something of the heart of the God of our Lord Jesus Christ. But further, I have no intention to commend to you yet another emphasis, programme, theme or movement as a superior alternative to those just mentioned.

THE QUESTION OF A PROPER FOUNDATION

Taking as my cue the theological vision of the Torrance brothers,[1] I do want to raise a question about the foundations upon which these various approaches to the Christian life are built – about the theological foundations which undergird them. Further, I would like to offer a theological foundation for any or every one of these movements. First, so that they might remain faithful to the gospel and its Lord, Jesus Christ. Second, so they do not lead to burnout and disillusionment in the Christian life and ministry.

The theological insight of the Torrances bears witness that if these genuine impulses of the Spirit regarding the Christian life are not properly grounded, if they do not begin with a proper theological starting point, they will be open to subversion, even co-option by alien spirits and sooner or later take their adherents into spiritual exhaustion. As the former student of Thomas F. Torrance, Ray Anderson, has repeatedly stated throughout his 35 years of seminary teaching, 'Burnout in the Christian life and ministry is essentially a theological problem.' Unfortunately, but to the glory of God, I can attest to this truth, hidden from me

---

1 Having studied with Professor James Torrance at King's College, Aberdeen for three years as my PhD adviser, I am pleased to take this opportunity to acknowledge my debt of gratitude to him. I offer these words in memory of him.

until well into my 20 years of university campus ministry. It turns out that theology, when properly grasped at its centre, is the most practical aspect of the Christian life. It must undergird and direct all other Christian practice: whether prayer or the practice of spiritual disciplines, social justice, racial reconciliation, worship, evangelism, compassion for the poor, church renewal or the *missio Dei*, God's mission. But it was not until I had a profound grasp of the Torrances' theology that I could clearly see this. The Christian life itself requires a properly grasped theological foundation that directs us to the living source of our Christian work, witness and worship.

The legacy of the Torrance theological vision guards against faulty and false foundations for the Christian life and the worship and witness of the Church by grounding the whole of the Christian life in its true source. For the life of the Church has but one foundation. There is only one thing that makes the Church Christian. That foundation is Jesus Christ himself. And it is not first the faithfulness of Christians or the richness of their experience or the dedication of their service or even the acumen of their theological pronouncements. Theological reflection that honours this foundation takes as its sole starting point the question: who is Jesus Christ? After addressing that enquiry, and only after, can we take up the secondary theological question: who are we in relationship to Jesus Christ? Following that theological trajectory, the Torrances provide the essential answer to who we are in Jesus Christ. They hold forth the reality and actuality of (a) our union with the risen and ascended Lord Jesus Christ and (b) our participation in his continuing mediation and ministry for us and on our behalf.[2] James Torrance often referred to them as the twin doctrines of our union with Christ and our participation in the gift of the life of Christ. The Torrance tradition identifies this as the core reality of the Christian life.

For some, the words that follow may be a welcome review. For others I trust this word concerning our union with Christ and the Christian life as participation may, God willing, renew your faith, as it did mine years ago. So let me try now to unpack the astounding reality to which these twin doctrines point.

---

2 The material on these themes is especially concentrated in Thomas F. Torrance, *The Mediation of Christ* (Edinburgh: T&T Clark, 1984) and James B. Torrance, *Worship, Community and the Triune God of Grace* (Carlisle: Paternoster Press and Downers Grove, IL: InterVarsity Press, 1996). Essays by all three Torrances which touch on this theme can be found in their book, *A Passion for Christ* (Edinburgh: Handsel Press and Lenoir, NC: PLC Publications, 1999). We should keep in mind that the Torrance vision first reaches all the way back to the teachings of Scripture and then takes cues from the writings of the Church Fathers, especially Irenaeus and Athanasius. Also prominent in this connection is the teaching of both Luther and Calvin.

THE REALITY TO WHICH THE DOCTRINE OF UNION WITH CHRIST POINTS

A case easily can be made from the New Testament that essential to the very meaning of being a follower of Christ is that one is *united* to Christ. If you asked someone in the early church whether they were followers of Jesus, they would likely answer, 'Yes, I am united to Christ.' And centuries later this was also true of the magisterial Reformers. Being a Christian meant for each: *I am united to Christ*.

Now think of how we most often identify ourselves as Christians. Is one of the *first* things you think of, 'Well, yes, I'm united to Christ?' Or would you begin, 'Yes, I made a decision for Christ.' 'I follow the teachings of Jesus.' 'I believe that Jesus Christ is the Son of God.' 'I attend church regularly. I was baptized and confirmed.' 'I'm committed to Jesus Christ.' 'I am born again.' Now there's nothing wrong with these answers in themselves. They contain part of the truth. We notice, however, that they all refer to something *we* do or have done. The emphasis is on our response and action. But does this get to the root of who we really are as Christians?

By leaving union with Christ unacknowledged, all these other definitions and declarations actually leave us on a precarious perch. As James Torrance used to say, we can easily be thrown back on ourselves when we concentrate on our response apart from grasping the truth, reality and actuality of our union with Christ.[3] Jesus Christ, when viewed from within an emphasis on our making a response, can appear to be at a great distance from us. The work Christ does can be regarded as largely in the past and relatively external. The grace of God can begin to seem merely as if it provided us with a new potential. We can end up thinking: 'By grace God made the Christian life possible by forgiving our sins and giving us a new status of being in right relationship with him. Now all *we* have to do is appropriate, apply or actualize that new potential life that God has graciously given us.' And so we turn with enthusiasm (or perhaps in desperation) to one of those emphases, visions, tasks or goals I noted earlier. We attempt by our efforts to make the Christian life practical, relevant and vital. That, at any rate, is how I went about my Christian life for many years even in ministry – as if God in Christ had given me a potentially new life. It was up to me to make it real and actual.

What I have observed so often in the Christian Church is that whether conservative or liberal, traditional or contemporary, emergent or megachurch, Christians basically live as if saved by grace but sanctified by

---

3   See, for example, James Torrance, *Worship, Community*, 29.

works. We depend on our own efforts, choices, accomplishments or zeal. Grace is where we start the Christian life but often we somehow end up 'thrown back upon our own resources' and feeling under a great burden. Then we become first unimpressed, then perhaps depressed, and finally even coldly cynical about the whole Christian life itself. A great part of the problem is that we often have not grasped and we often have not been taught, either in our churches or in our seminaries, about the full extent of the grace of God extended to us in Jesus Christ. We have failed to hear what union with Christ means and of our participation in the continuing mediatorial ministry of Christ.

Scriptural Teaching on Union with Christ

So what do the Scriptures teach? What did the early church and the Reformers at least begin to grasp? And finally, what legacy have the Torrances passed on to us regarding our union with Christ? Let me say first what it is not. (1) Union with Christ is not essentially a *moral* union with the result that I agree and am committed to doing what God regards as right and righteous. That may be a moral fruit of our union, but that is not what it is. (2) Nor is it essentially a *psychological* union where Jesus has positive regard for me and I feel warmly connected and desirous of his approval and presence. Again that may be a fruit, but not the source. (3) Union with Christ is not a *volitional* union where I am willing to do the practical work of God, accomplishing all that he sets out for me to do, so that my will is a mirror image of God's will. (4) It is not even a union of purposes, a *telic* union, where my goals, aspirations, dreams, ideals and hopes match God's. Even at that level we are not to the bottom of union with Christ. Our union with Christ is much deeper, more enduring and far more effective in our lives than these other aspects of the Christian life.

The New Testament message is that we are so united to Christ that the core of our very being is changed because it has become spiritually joined to the perfected humanity of Jesus. The Apostle Paul writes that we are one in Spirit with Christ (1 Cor. 6:17). In the letter to the Ephesians we read that we are so connected that we are, presently – right now – seated with Christ in the heavenlies (Eph. 2:6). We are so joined that what has happened to Christ 2,000 years ago has actually included us. So in the letter to the Colossians we hear that we have 'co-died' with Christ and we have been 'co-raised' with Christ (Col. 2:12–13; 3:1). Paul announces this fact as a completed action which is actually true of all the members of the body of Christ.

Of course Jesus himself indicated his purpose to so unite himself with us. He teaches that our oneness with him is comparable to his oneness with the Father. He declares 'On that day you will know that I am in my Father, and you in me, and I in you' (Jn 14:20). He prays 'I in them and you in me, that they may become perfectly one . . . that the love with which you have loved me may be in them, and I in them' (Jn 17:23, 26). Jesus teaches that eternal life, salvation, involves an incredible communion so that 'Whoever feeds on my flesh and drinks my blood abides in me, and I in him' (Jn 6:56).

In 1 Corinthians Paul announces that everything that Jesus has is actually and really ours. He declares that Jesus himself is our wisdom, our righteousness and our sanctification (1 Cor. 1:30). The New Testament is filled with language that points to a profound reality that we belong in an astounding way to Jesus Christ. We can be said to indwell him and he us. We are often depicted as being *in* Christ, not just with or alongside him. The book of Ephesians is full of this kind of description that frankly blows our minds and fries our rational mental circuits. We have become new creatures in Christ (2 Cor. 5:17), because he has made us his own (Phil. 3:12) in such a way that there is what Calvin called a 'wonderful exchange' at the deepest level of who we are, so that Christ takes our fallen and broken natures and gives us a share in his sanctified and perfected human nature.[4] The truth is that who we are is no longer who we are alone. For we are not alone. We are who we are by virtue of being united to Christ. As James Torrance tirelessly reminded us, by his grace we are given the gift of sharing in the Son's union and communion with the Father in the power of the Spirit.[5] As the early church expressed it: He who was the Son of God by nature, became a son of man so that we who are the sons of men by nature might, by grace, become the sons and daughters of God.

When Calvin and Luther commented on Eph. 5:21–32, following the early church teachings, they did not exposit on the nature of human marriage, but marvelled that we are far more united to Christ than a man and woman are in matrimony! Marriage is a dim and distant reflection of the deeper truth about our real communion with Christ. The ultimate companion we are made for is Jesus Christ who is truly bone of our bone and flesh of our flesh and to whom we are united by the Holy Spirit.

In the New Testament, especially in the book of Hebrews,[6] we see that such a union had its beginning in the incarnation, in Christ's assuming a complete humanity reaching from conception to his death. What qualifies Jesus to accomplish this exchange with us is his assumption of our

---

4 John Calvin, *Institutes of the Christian Religion*, ed. John T. McNeill, trans. Ford Lewis Battles (Philadelphia: Westminster Press, 1960), 3.2.24.
5 See James Torrance, *Worship, Community*, 30–1.
6 See, for example, Heb. 2:11–18 and 4:14–16.

humanity along with its fallen condition. The early church recognized the depths of the incarnation when it declared not only that Jesus was one in being (*homoousios*) with the Father, but also one in being (*homoousios*) with humanity. His divinity, by virtue of his union with the Father, is no more true of him than his humanity, by virtue of his union with us. The Apostle Paul, of course, laid the ground for this doctrinal explication of the Council of Chalcedon (AD 451) when he identified Jesus with the new Adam (Rom. 5:14; 1 Cor. 15:45). Jesus Christ is united to us even more than we are united to the Adam of the Garden in Genesis. Thus our relationship with Christ puts our very existence on a whole new basis.

Our redemption does not just depend upon what Christ did, but upon who he is in the depths of his being – one with God and one with us. For our salvation, our life in Christ, was not only accomplished *by* Christ but *in* Christ as Calvin used to say and James Torrance used regularly to remind us.[7] Our new life is not external to us and layered on over us, but is worked out first in the humanity of Jesus and then given to us through his Spirit.

LUTHER, CALVIN AND STEWART ON UNION WITH CHRIST

One older book that James Torrance often referred to was James Stewart's *A Man in Christ*. Stewart concluded after his careful study of the New Testament that our union with Christ was the central element in the message of the gospel. That is, without union with Christ, there would be no gospel. For God's grace reaches that deep into who we are. We are no longer ourselves alone. But we are who we are only in and through our union with Christ. We really and truly belong to God in Christ.

Calvin used to warn that we ought never to consider Christ at a distance. We are, to the root of our being, who we are in relationship to him who made himself one with us.[8] This is why both Luther and Calvin recognized that our whole salvation was complete in Christ: not just our

---

7 See James Torrance, *Worship, Community*, 28.
8 See Calvin, *Institutes*, 3.11.10:

> Therefore, that joining together of Head and members, that indwelling of Christ in our hearts – in short, that mystical union – are accorded by us the highest degree of importance, so that Christ, having been made ours, makes us sharers with him in the gifts with which he has been endowed. We do not, therefore, contemplate him outside ourselves from afar in order that his righteousness may be imputed to us but because we put on Christ and are engrafted into his body – in short, because he deigns to make us one with him. For this reason, we glory that we have fellowship of righteousness with him.

justification, but our sanctification and glorification as well.[9] To have Christ was to have the whole Christ. Christ could not be divided up into pieces, so neither could our salvation. What is complete and actual in Christ is truly and really ours even if it does not yet appear to be so. Our lives *are* hidden in Christ (Col. 3:3). Our life *in him* is being worked out *in us* by the Spirit. But this new being wrought in us comes through the sheer gift of our union with Christ. It does not come through our working out a potential that might be true if we properly apply ourselves. Rather the Christian life is living out and manifesting the present reality of our union with Christ.

OBSTACLES TO GRASPING THE REALITY OF OUR UNION WITH CHRIST

Now we must acknowledge that there are significant obstacles to our even beginning to grasp the truth of our union with Christ. I'd like to give some consideration to those concerns that often have blunted if not obliterated any concerted effort to grasp this profound theological truth.

Too Good to be True?

First is the sheer wonder of the profound depths of such a grace. Would God really go to such lengths, heights and depths for us? It sounds too good to be true. But when it comes to God, shouldn't we expect the good news to sound like it is too good to be true? Is not God's grace beyond all we can ask or imagine? Certainly this response is no reason to rule out its gracious reality.

Confusion of Ourselves with Christ

Also union with Christ has often been avoided because of fear that if we say we are united to him at the ontological depths of our being we will collapse ourselves into him and confuse ourselves with him. That particular misunderstanding of our union with Christ is a possibility expressed not just in what we think, but reinforced by how we *are taught* to think. We learn that what things really are is what they are all by themselves. They are individual substances, all one stuff. So, if two things are truly united, the difference between them as well as the distinction of each must be lost. Either one thing would turn into another, or both would turn into a third thing. Following this pattern of thinking, union with

---

9   Calvin, *Institutes*, 2.16.19.

Christ would mean we turn into Christ or he would turn into us, each ceasing to be what we were. Now the Torrances were quick to warn that it is this way of thinking about ourselves as individual substances (a way that can be traced back to Aristotle) that leads to such confusion. If we assume that we are what we are independent of anything else, then of course a relationship, such as union, cannot contribute in any essential way to what things actually and really are.

But what if Aristotle was wrong? What if what we human beings are is what we are by virtue of our being in some kind of relationship with God? What if relationship is essential to human being and not optional or accidental, but constitutive such that we would not be what we are except by virtue of the relationships in which we exist, especially in relationship to God? If that is the case, then the Triune God who has his being as Father, Son and Holy Spirit reconstitutes our humanity by forging a new relationship with fallen humanity through his incarnation and indeed his entire life, death, resurrection and ascension as the New Adam. In that case, Jesus Christ has become our Lord from the inside of our humanity. It was the truth of our union with Christ that led the Torrances to rethink our Aristotelian *ontology* (the study of the nature of being itself), and conclude that being itself, divine and human is 'onto-relational'.[10] If relationship is essential to who we are, then in union with Christ, we are really united, but remain distinctly ourselves without confusion with Christ. We are most truly ourselves just when we are really united to our Lord and Saviour Jesus Christ. Union, then, is a continual relationship with Christ at the deepest levels of our being, not a confusion of ourselves with Christ.

Grasping the truth of our relationship to Christ really calls for the renewing of our minds so that we begin to think differently about what makes us who we are. In the end, we even have to approach reading Scripture differently. The challenge becomes not so much taking the Bible literally, but taking it *realistically*. When Paul declares that we are seated with Christ in the heavenlies (Eph. 2:6) we have warrant, despite our Aristotelian philosophical training, to grasp this realistically. The good news is that who we are as Christians is those who are united to Christ in such a way that all that is ours is his and all that is his is ours. So that Paul says, 'though he was rich, yet for your sakes he became poor, so that by his poverty you might become rich' (2 Cor. 8:9).

---

10 See, Torrance, *Mediation*, 47 and *The Ground and Grammar of Theology* (Charlottesville, VA: The University of Virginia Press and Belfast: Christian Journals, 1980), 173–8.

No Place for Us: Antinomianism?

Now the temptation to worry that any real union must confuse us with Christ, the second obstacle, can be reinforced if we feel somehow compelled to trace out a false logic, a third obstacle, which goes something like this: if who we are is who we are in Christ and if our whole salvation is complete in Christ, then there's no place for me and no significance to what I do. This is the antinomian objection: if we are really united to Christ then there is no reason or purpose for my choices or obedience. I can do what I like. Of course this might be one logical implication of our union with Christ. But first, theology is not the result of logical implications. Secondly, everything depends upon what we mean by union. Of course we can see that the New Testament affirms a profound union with Christ, the completed work of Christ, and the wonderful exchange, and yet it calls for our involvement, our activity, our participation. So can we make any progress in understanding how these two elements fit together? I think the answer is yes. And the Torrances lead the way. Union with Christ in this realist way does not eliminate the trusting obedience of the Christian life, but actually strengthens it!

A Personal Union

First, we should remember that the biblical picture points to the union of persons who remain persons. The union is a personal union, not a mechanical or functional or impersonal one. Such a personal unity calls for interaction, for inter-relationship. A personal unity means that neither person is lost, but the distinction of persons is maintained while the personal exchange takes place. Unity in this frame means the establishment and fulfilment of the creature in relationship to God through the humanity of Jesus Christ, bone of our bone and flesh of our flesh. This of course is a reflection of the Triune relationships but now mirrored in God's relationship to us in Christ and through the Spirit. Jesus can pray to the Father in a meaningful way even though he is one in being with the Father in the Spirit. From all eternity the Son can glorify the Father and the Father glorify the Son and yet be one. It turns out that the oneness of God is a unity where relationship is intrinsic to the being of God so that if God were not Father, Son and Spirit, God would not be God. Aristotle's presuppositions about what things can be and how they exist are apparently incorrect. Relationship can be essential to who, at least, God is – and who we are.

A Saving Relationship

And within those relationships there is real interaction, personal activity. So the saving relationship of exchange into which we are taken by grace actually calls for interaction, inter-relationship and responsiveness. Salvation, rather than being an impersonal steady state of being, like a statue, is a relational reality. This is what makes salvation personal and alive. Being united to Christ is not being formed into a perfect, inert statue, but more being in a dynamic relationship where there is intimate giving and receiving in a wonderful communion. That relationship determines the essence of who we are and who we are becoming.

Perhaps we can draw a distant comparison with marriage in answer to the question, 'Why should we do anything if we are united to Christ and our whole salvation is complete in him?' Raising the question that way about our union with Christ would be like asking why two people who are married should live together, since after all they have entered into the state of matrimony. But isn't marriage by definition a sharing of life together? It would make no sense and be a violation of the logic of relationship to say, 'Well, since we're already married there's no point in living together.' So too in our union with Christ. As James Torrance used to exhort us, following Calvin, union with Christ and communion or participation in Christ are twin doctrines that can never be separated and never collapsed.[11] Our unity with Christ in a relationship of wonderful exchange is a completed gift in which we personally participate so that the truth and reality of who we are in Christ becomes more and more manifest in our lives as we grow up into him.

We live out our life in union with Christ because we live and move and have our being by being in communion with Christ. It is a personal reality in which we are meant to participate. Neglecting our active participation is neglecting our present salvation established in Christ. What does it mean to be a Christian? It means living by the grace that we are united to Christ as his actual, true brothers and sisters. Nothing less. That is who we are *in* him.

The Christian Life as Participation in Christ's Continuing Ministry

So then what light does our union with Christ shed on the Christian life of obedience, or our calling to ministry? I have found that the word

---

11 See James Torrance, *Worship, Community*, 84 and *Passion for Christ*, 51.

participation, which is a translation of the Greek word *koinonia,*[12] is indispensable. Our obedience and our ministry can only be properly grasped as a sharing in or participating in the obedience and ministry of Jesus Christ.

But if Christian life and ministry is somehow participation, what is it that we actually get involved in? Christ has completed his once for all ministry. How can we get involved in that? Certainly we can't attempt to redo what he has done. How exactly can we participate? This line of questioning indicates that we often forget or perhaps never fully grasped the fact that the risen Christ ascended in his bodily form with his humanity, a humanity not only intact but now glorified. James Torrance used to put these questions to his classes:

> When do we really see the true humanity of Christ? Was it when he was hungry? Was it when he was asleep in the boat? Or was it when he was angry in the temple? No. We see Christ's true humanity and so ours, in his *ascension.* There we see our humanity sanctified and glorified in him as he takes us with him as our substitute and representative into the very presence of the Father.

The humanity Christ assumed at conception was not cast off like the empty external fuel tank of the space shuttle, only to fall back to earth some minutes after its blast-off for outer space. No, the incarnation is permanent because, as Paul put it, the man Jesus Christ is and remains to this day our mediator (1 Tim. 2:5). And his perfected humanity remains the only meeting place for God and humanity to meet.

But not only does his humanity abide, his ministry also continues.[13] His gracious service did not end at the cross. Yes, the reconciling work was finished, but that reconciling work was for the sake of our living out of that recreated relationship now securely re-established. As we see throughout the book of Hebrews, we serve a living Lord who continually intercedes for us. He remains the one true apostle, the one true leader of our worship, the one true pioneer and perfecter of our faith.[14] Our Lord Jesus Christ remains ever vigilant, ever active. He is no retired saviour who is now unemployed.

So all our responses to Christ are nothing more than following Christ

---

12 See, for example, 1 Cor. 10:16 in which *koinonia* is translated as 'participation', or John 1:3 in which it is rendered as 'fellowship'. *Koinonia* can also be considered as 'partnership' or 'communion'.

13 See James Torrance, *Worship, Community,* 84–7 and David Torrance in *Passion for Christ,* 71–5. Also, Torrance, *Mediation,* 73

14 See Heb. 7: 25, 3:1; 8:2 and 12:2 respectively.

in his present activity and engaging in the ministry that he is actively doing now through the Holy Spirit. When we preach the gospel we participate in the apostolic ministry of Jesus, by the Holy Spirit, for the Spirit continues to bear witness to Christ and to our need for Christ. When we love a neighbour, or love an enemy for the sake of Christ and his kingdom, we are merely catching up with God. We're merely going to work with God. When we pray, we're joining Christ in his faithful prayers of intercessions for us and for the world. When we worship we are joining in with all the faithful, including those who have gone before us who are continually worshipping following the leadership of Jesus Christ, our great *leitourgos*, or worship leader (Heb. 8:2). Even when we confess our sins we join with Jesus himself who really is the only one who truly knows the depth of sin, who is truly and perfectly repentant and so for us received the baptism of John the Baptist. But as our great mediator who knows our weaknesses, he takes our weak faith and meagre repentance and graciously makes it his own, perfects it and passes it on to the Father. On the basis of the work of Christ to save us, rescue us *from* sin, we are saved *for* participation in an ongoing relationship of wonderful exchange.

When we see our whole lives this way we join with the Apostle Paul who proclaimed, 'I live, yet not I but Christ who lives in me.'[15] But that is not just a general platitude that sounds nice. The whole of the Christian life is actually a participation in the life and ministry of Christ. So that we can say, I pray, yet not I but Christ prays in me. I obey, yet not I but Christ in me. I have faith, yet not I but Christ in me. I hunger and thirst for righteousness and reconciliation, yet not I but Christ in me. The joy, peace and love that Christ wants for us is not a joy, peace and love that is *like* Christ's, that *we* somehow achieve with God's help. No, by *his* Spirit, Christ intends to share with us *his* joy, *his* peace, *his* love, *his* righteousness.[16] And, from the foundations of the earth, he never thought otherwise! Never view yourself apart from Christ for that is not who you are.

GOING AGAINST THE GRAIN

Yes, we can live in denial and hide the truth when we attempt to depart from Christ. But that cannot undo the truth of who we are in Christ. We may indeed get splinters but we cannot change the grain of the wood when we go against it. The only choice we really have is (1) to affirm the reality with our minds and in our actions or (2) to deny the reality of

---

15   Gal. 2: 20, author's translation.
16   See Jn 14:27, 15:11 and 17:13.

who Christ is and who we are in relationship to him. We never need to ask the speculative question, '*WWJD?* What would Jesus Do?' but rather should ask the practical question, '*WIJD?* What is Jesus Doing?' We seek to discover what Christ is doing in this present situation and how we can get involved with his activity. For once we see the depth of the grace of God in uniting us to Christ to share with us his communion with the Father, what else can we possibly do with our lives except go where he goes, do what he does, and live for the glory of the Father as he always has?

WHAT DOES PARTICIPATION LOOK LIKE? JESUS AND FEEDING THE FIVE THOUSAND

A familiar Gospel story from Mk 6:30–44 illustrates how our union with Christ and our participation in his ministry are held together. As this story begins, Jesus took some unanticipated initiative. He told the disciples that *they* should feed these five thousand people. They'd been listening to the teachings of Jesus until very late that afternoon. There was, perhaps, just enough time to get home by nightfall to prepare supper. So the disciples were astounded at Jesus's suggestion. How could they possibly feed so many? They didn't have two years' worth of daily wages in their wallets to buy bread and they certainly didn't have a chain of bakeries ready to deliver truckloads of it. Jesus had asked them to do the impossible. But Jesus was not stymied by their incredulity. He had another word for them. 'How many loaves do you have? Go and see.' I'm sure the disciples must have wondered at the relevance of such a request. But it got worse. The results of their count yielded only five loaves and just two fish. The disciples did not know what to do next.

Jesus took over. He directed the disciples to get all the people to sit down in groups on the green grass. Amazingly the people actually did what the disciples asked though it would not have been clear what would follow. Some must have muttered, 'It's getting a little late isn't it? I thought he was finished.' Next, Jesus took from them the loaves and fish. He then looked up to heaven, directing his gaze and his words of thanksgiving for the food to his heavenly Father. For what was going to take place not only would involve Jesus and his disciples but also Jesus with his Father. He broke the fish and loaves in pieces to distribute to the 12 standing around him. Then the disciples were called back into action. Jesus directed them to hand out the food to the people. I suspect that the people followed the example of the disciples and broke off pieces to give to those next to them. Almost without realizing (Mark here is so understated!) 'they all ate and were filled'. Not only that, but from those five loaves and two fish there were 12 baskets full of broken pieces of bread and fish left over! Twelve baskets – one for each of the disciples: can you imagine their reaction as each one lugged back a full basket after handing out just a few scraps?

How did this happen? Well, we could simply say Jesus performed a miracle. Of course, but how did he go about it? Was it with great fanfare, a spectacular Hollywood magic show complete with light, mirrors and smoke by which the amazing Jesus impressed us again with his phenomenal powers? Not at all. It is crucial to realize that Jesus did not multiply the loaves and fish by himself. In fact, he drew very little attention to himself. In lifting the food to heaven and saying a blessing, Jesus understood himself as dependent upon his Father. This situation was like all the others he encountered in his earthly life: Jesus only *did* what he *saw* his Father doing (Jn 5:19). Jesus participated in the actions of his Father. Further, Jesus had said to the disciples, 'You feed them.' And they did. Now I suppose that Jesus (with his Father) not only could have provided the loaves and fishes, but he could have had the disciples stand back, saying 'Watch this, boys!' and sent those loaves and fishes flying instantly right into the laps of all five thousand. What an amazing magical moment that would have been. But he didn't go about it that way at all. He involved his disciples. They participated with him in feeding the hungry.

I am not suggesting that Jesus needed the disciples – or even their fish and loaves. That would be a gross misrepresentation of the truth. But rather, Jesus delighted to find ways for his disciples to get involved in the very things he and his Father were doing. Did these disciples have the understanding or the resources needed for the task? Not at all. But Jesus found a wonderful way for them to participate in his humble exhibition of the divine compassion of his Heavenly Father. The disciples got to be involved in the very thing Jesus (and his Father) was doing. I'm sure they were astounded – not just that all the people got fed but that he took what was theirs, made it his own, and then gave it back to them to serve the people in his name. Can you imagine the joy and wonder of being involved in God's feeding of five thousand?

PARTNERSHIP WITH CHRIST

This story illustrates Christian life and ministry. What is needed, good and right, is always overwhelming, even seemingly impossible. We hear a word from Jesus which sounds like 'You feed them', and we quickly become aware that we have so little. It's humiliating, at least to our pride, to admit how meagre our resources are compared to the compassionate aims of God. At that point the question becomes: will we act in faith, trusting in the character of the one calling for our action and obedience? Will we give him what we have so we can see what *he* will do with what little we really offer to him? We may offer to him our failures and our sin in confession, or offer our resources, action plans and obedience with thanksgiving. Will we trust him to do with our meagre action just as he did with those disciples? Will we marvel at the miracle of participating in Christ's own obedience to the Father in his continuing ministry to his neighbours and his world? That's the wonder of Christ's Lordship; he always makes room for our participation though we never really have what it takes. It is only in partnership with him, in fellowship and communion, in union with him, that we reflect the glory of God as his children.

Preaching, Teaching and Counselling In Participation with Christ

As energizing as this story may be, there is a further crucial question. How then do we motivate Christians to participate as the disciples did? Ironically, having understood something of our participation, in turning to teaching and counselling we can easily enough revert to addressing people in ways that ignore altogether the reality of our union and participation! When we focus on our own obedience we are in the habit of thinking that our individual will is the key to our behaviour and actions. If something is going to get done then we tend to depend upon one of two things: (1) the strength of our own wills, or (2) the effectiveness of our native or learned skills, and their deployment in the programmes, plans, techniques or formulas available. But if we lack both these, we may simply conclude that we have no responsibility at all. It must be someone else's calling. How do we properly call people to join us in the Christian life as communion, fellowship and partnership with Christ?

First, let's consider how all of Scripture is structured as it invites us to participate. As the Torrances reminded us so often, all the commands of God are built on the premise of the unconditional covenant promises of God. All obedience is moved by faith in the character of God. 'I will be their God, and they shall be my people' (Jer. 33:33; Gen. 17:8; Exod. 6:7) is the foundational refrain throughout the whole Old Testament. God made a unilateral covenant with Abraham: 'I will bless you . . . in you all the families of the earth shall be blessed' (Gen 12:2–3). That covenant is renewed throughout Israel's history. It was not, Paul reminds us, until 433 years after God made his covenant with the people who were to be a light to all the nations that God provided them with the law (Gal. 3:17). The law falls within the circle of the unconditional promise of blessing.

And notice how even the Ten Commandments unfold. They were given *after* the great Exodus of Israel from slavery under the Egyptians. Then, in Exod. 20:2, we find a theological preface to those holy obligations. 'I am the LORD your God who brought you out of the land of

Egypt!' Then the commands follow as a result of this saving work. We could insert a 'so' or 'therefore' before each one. So, 'you shall have no other gods before me.' So 'you shall not take the name of the LORD your God in vain'. So, 'remember the Sabbath day, to keep it holy'. So, 'you shall not murder . . . commit adultery . . . steal . . . covet'. That preamble calls all Israel, and us, first to remember who God is and who we are in relationship to him. It does not first address our wills or set up conditions. It announces the unconditioned, good, gracious and faithful character of God. The stipulations of obedience are built upon that foundation. From our New Testament vantage point, God's own faithfulness is further demonstrated in the fulfilment of that promise. In Jesus Christ God has become our God and we have become his people in an unimaginably intimate way. We became united to Christ who lived, died, was raised and ascended for us that we might share in his divine life. All our obedience, then, is meant to follow the same pattern. Trusting in God to be true to his character provides the foundation for all obedience. For behind the promises made to us stands the Great Promise Maker and Promise Keeper. It is this God who then subsequently calls us to a life of obedience in relationship to him.

James Torrance, in full harmony with his older brother, used to point out that all the imperatives of Scripture are founded upon the unconditional indicatives of grace. Obedience then is not a means to condition God to be gracious to us. No. God's unconditional grace brings with it a call for our unconditional obedience. The imperatives point out obligations of grace, not the conditions for grace. The imperatives of our obedience describe the shape of our participation in the covenant relations in which we live and move and have our being.[17] They show us the direction of the grain of relationship so that we don't get splinters.

But are there not consequences for disobedience? Yes there are. When we move against the grain of our relationship with God, we won't enjoy the relationship and its benefits. In fact we experience the negative consequences of it. We cannot receive them when we fail to trust in God and participate in the life he has provided for us. This failure, however, does not amount to the negation of the unconditioned grace of God. Our disobedience has no power to undo what Christ has done. We cannot change the grain of God's character and decision for us in Jesus Christ. We can live in denial, we can close our eyes and cover our faces at noonday and say the sun is not shining, but our denial has no power to create a counter-truth and counter-reality. But, yes, if you kick against the goad, you'll get a broken toe.

---

17 See James Torrance, *Worship, Community*, 53–4; *Passion for Christ*, 57; and T. F. Torrance, *Mediation*, 83, 98.

The Pressure to Preach Sanctification by Works

If faith in our gracious union with Christ is the foundation for all our obedience, then how do we build upon it? Do we merely yell more loudly what God wants his people to do? Do we give endless advice? Do we perpetually offer as the key to effective Christian life new programmes, new methods, new understandings, improved seminars and conferences? Do we change from plan A of preaching the unconditioned grace of God, to plan B and threaten people with a subsequent *conditional* grace of God? Do we preach as if God were finished with his work so now it's all up to us, as if he had no further plans – so that, if we fail, then God's plans fail? Do we preach grace for salvation but works for a life of obedience?

I'm afraid we often do resort to these tactics. Despite the pattern of biblical teaching which begins with God and his faithfulness, we feel the pressure to preach and teach and motivate folks to obedience by addressing the naked will with raw commandments. We speak as if we were God's slaves and as if God was dependent upon us, as if God was at a distance, and ministry was really up to us, as if God's grace merely established a potential which we, if we are able, realize and actualize and make true.

But this is not how Jesus or the Apostle Paul addressed the 'problem of the Christian life'. For if all the imperatives of Scripture are founded upon the unconditioned indicatives of grace and the very character of God represented by them, then when obedience is not forthcoming, we must go back and build the foundations up and not attempt to find another one. We must go back to preaching and teaching and discovering the character and heart and promises of God. For everything that we are called to do mirrors what God is always and continually doing for us and in us on the basis of the vicarious ascended humanity of Christ and our union with him. Obedience is built on trust – not trying.

Preaching the Indicatives of Grace as the Basis for the Imperatives of Grace

If we are intent on seeing people more faithful to Christ, we must first show the faithfulness of Christ to them. For their own faithfulness can only be a participation in the faithfulness of Christ. If we want folks to be forgiving, then the basis for that is the announcement of God's forgiveness for us. If we see that we need to be generous, then we need to hear of God's great generosity to us and even to the unjust. If we are concerned that people do not seem to care for the lost, then we need to be reminded that Jesus is the one true Apostle sent to seek and to save the lost (Lk. 19:10). He is still drawing people to himself, and still sending us to participate in his mission to the lost. If we announce we should be more compassionate towards the poor then at the same time we need to hear of God's own heart towards the poor. We require seeing his provision for the orphan, widow and foreigner and even ourselves as we recognize our own spiritual poverty. If we are concerned for racial reconciliation, then we require being continually reminded that God in Christ has already recreated us into one new humanity (Eph. 2:15). We are reconciled to God and to each other in Christ. We can count on that work having already taken place, rather than see ourselves as given the task of realizing an ideal that God has put before us and is waiting for us to make it happen. Then, all of our efforts in this direction will be moved by faith in the completed work of Christ and his ongoing ministry to make the fruits of that reconciliation visible. All our activity will be generated by our faith in God.

Legalism

For every act of desired obedience we must present and focus on the character of God manifest in Christ that corresponds to that imperative. For all obedience that gives glory to God must arise out of faith, hope and love for who God really is, both in himself and towards us. The Apostle Paul says, both at the beginning and the ending of Romans, that his whole ministry is to bring about the obedience of faith (Rom. 1:5 and 16:26). He explains that any obedience that does not proceed from faith is sin (Rom. 14:23). We often think that legalism is the problem of someone committed to consistent obedience and so who needs to be corrected by allowing for, well, *inconsistent* obedience! But really legalism is obedience that does not arise out of faith, hope and love in the character of the Gracious Law-giver. Legalism is obedience without faith. James Torrance often reminded us of Calvin's concern to avoid especially any kind of legal repentance, that is repentance without trust in the gospel of grace.[18] Thus, it is a grave mistake merely to preach the commandments by addressing the will of the Christian and calling for volitional conformity to the standards of God. Concentration on the requirements of God or even the ideals of God may even tempt hearers to a faithless obedience. It is even more dangerous to misrepresent the character of God by speaking as if God had two sides to his character, as if God was two-faced, or double-minded, first offering grace and then switching to a concern for moral and spiritual conformity to his will and threatening the withdrawal of his grace. Preaching this way communicates that although we are first saved by grace, we are really sanctified by works. The Christian life may have begun by grace but is essentially lived

---

18 See James Torrance, *Worship, Community*, 54–7.

out in a conditional and contractual relationship with God. Under such guidance many, I think, see their lives under a great impossible burden and sometimes even long to be non-believers again so they can become Christians all over, experiencing afresh the grace of God. But such admonishment, undoubtedly concerned for faithful and consistent lives, still obscures the truth and actuality of Christ's gracious and unconditioned continuing ministry and our union with him. It regards Christ as at a distance sending us out to do for him what he is unwilling or unable to do himself, somehow being dependent upon us. We end up communicating that God, at least subsequent to our conversion, can no longer be more faithful than we are!

Preaching the commandments apart from the promises of the unconditional grace of God is like putting people in a windowless room with the door shut and the lights off and telling them, 'On the count of three start enjoying the sunset!' Few have such imaginative powers. But if we could take someone to the top of Sentinel Dome on the 3,000-foot-high western-facing ridge of Yosemite Valley, just at sunset, all we would need do is declare, 'Watch!' and their joy would be irrepressible. So in preaching, only the glory and the character of God can draw out of us a faith that leads to a faithful obedience. Otherwise, our sacrificial endeavours are most often driven not by faith, hope and love, but by guilt, fear and anxiety as we are thrown back upon ourselves and our own five loaves and two fishes while standing in front of five thousand hungry souls. Only the presentation of the heart and character of God fully revealed in Jesus Christ can bring us to the point of faithful obedience. And this is why all our preaching and teaching must take as its starting point the question of who this God is, not the question of what should we do, or how should we do it. I find this is often not the starting point for preaching, teaching and counselling in connection with living the Christian life. And I think that fact contributes to the weaknesses of our Churches and burnout in the Christian life and ministry. It will also erode any of the many new initiatives intended to renew the Church mentioned at the beginning of this essay.

Too Much Grace?

There is one further concern that I have seen James Torrance respond to on numerous occasions. There are those professional theologians, pastors and laypersons who fear that we can preach too much grace. They would counsel that we have somehow to counterbalance grace so as to prevent people from taking advantage of grace. But what are we going to preach and teach to substitute for and counterbalance this overgenerous grace? Will we offer some new means for us to condition God into being gracious? Or preach a stingy God or a God dependent upon us? A God who cannot be more faithful than we are? If so, we will end up misrepresenting the true God of the Bible for all our good intentions to get people 'doing stuff' for God.

Grace Means No Exceptions

Further, if it were somehow possible to preach too much grace, then it isn't really grace that's being preached! I think that our understanding of grace is unfortunately often quite insufficient. This is in large part due to the general, cultural understanding of grace. Grace is often taken to mean making an exception to the rule. So we have 'grace periods', and we say someone is gracious when they let us off the hook of responsibility. The grace of forgiveness can be taken to mean diminishing the seriousness of sin or pretending it never happened. But we cannot take our cues from these misguided understandings. Following in the Torrance tradition, I suggest that real grace makes absolutely no exceptions. In fact, if it did make exceptions it would not be gracious! God is eternally and implacably opposed to sin, whether in the world or in us. In his divine providence sin and evil have no future. The sanctifying work of Christ brought to completion in us by the Spirit's glorification will leave no trace of sin in us. It will, one day, all be done away with. What exactly would it be like in heaven if it were full of people for whom God had made a few little exceptions here and there? Wouldn't it be fairly much like the condition we find ourselves in today? The only difference is that we'd be in that condition of injustice eternally! Where would be the grace in that? Grace certainly is God's forbearance, God's patience, God's long-suffering. But in the end there will be no exceptions for sin. God accepts us where we are unconditionally, in order to take us where he's going, just as unconditionally. No exceptions! Grace means that God is for us and will not give up on us, no matter how long it takes or how far we have to go, or how many times we fall. He'll pick us up because our whole salvation is complete for us in Christ and we belong to him. Grace is God's faithfulness to see us through to his perfect end even if we sometimes resist or are ungrateful, or only want his blessings because we prefer it to hell! The gracious love of God is implacably committed to perfecting us with Christ's own glorified humanity. For true love longs for the perfection of the beloved.

Can we preach too much of this kind of grace? We preach the inexorable God of love who will not give up on us and has pledged himself to see us to the glorious end of being his children through Jesus Christ. Isn't this the way to lead people to a faith, hope and love that believes that he who began a good work in you will bring it completion (Phil. 1:6)? We have a hope that knows God wills our sanctification, and believes that, as Paul tells us, 'He who calls you is faithful; he will surely do it' (1 Thess. 5:24). Can we believe this too much? Can we count on God too much to provide us even our sanctification in Christ? No. God is gracious because he makes no exceptions. On that we rely.

THE OBEDIENCE OF FAITH, HOPE AND LOVE

The Christian life must be one moved by faith, hope and love for God's Word spoken and living that presents a God who out of his own graciousness promises to be faithful and to give us an inheritance as his children united to Christ, who invites unswerving confidence in Christ's continuing work of ministry and the power and joy to enable us to participate in it. All our endeavours built on this foundation will reflect in word and deed the very character of God and exude a joyful trust in his continuing work. Putting our trust in ourselves, our programmes, our commitments, convictions, our techniques, our skills, our training or our sophistication and formulas, no matter how ideal, morally ambitious, or spiritually sincere, can only lead to lives that indicate a God who wants slaves not children, a God who depends upon us and who cannot be more faithful than we are, a God who begins with grace but who somehow ends with conditional blessings. The Good News is that this is not the God of the Bible, nor the God we worship today. Rather, God has united himself with us and us with himself so that all that we think or do we do as his children, participating with him in all that he is doing in our world now through the continuing ministry of Christ by the power of the Spirit.

The Christian life is nothing but the gracious gift of daily thanksgiving for our real union with Christ in his glorified humanity and participating by faith in his faithful and continuing ministry to us and all those around us. This is the theological legacy left by the Torrances. On this we may surely build our lives in Christ's name.

Chapter 8

THE HERMENEUTICAL NIGHTMARE AND THE RECONCILING WORK OF JESUS CHRIST[1]

C. Baxter Kruger

All things have been handed over to me by my Father, and no one knows the Son except the Father, and no one knows the Father except the Son and anyone to whom the Son wills to reveal him.

Jesus (Mt. 11:27)

Lord Jesus Christ, beloved, eternal and faithful Son of the Father incarnate, thank you for your gentle mercy on me in my darkness. Grant to me that which I do not have in myself – faith, hope and love. Bind all forms of darkness and evil that influence me. Continue to share with me your own knowledge of the Father's heart, that I may know your confidence, your passion, your joy and peace. Continue to pour out your Spirit upon me, that I may be of service to you in your liberation of the human race.

Jesus wants his Father known. He is passionate about it. He cannot bear for us to live without knowing his Father, without knowing his heart, his lavish embrace, his endless love – and the sheer freedom *to be* that works within us as we see his Father's face. Jesus knows the Father from all eternity. He sits at his right hand and sees him face to face, and shares life and all things with him in the fellowship of the Spirit. How could he be content to leave us in the dark with no vision of his Father's heart? How could the Father's Son be indifferent when we are so lost and afraid and bound in our mythology? Burning with the Father's love for us, inspired with the Spirit's fire, the Son ran to embrace our broken existence, baptizing himself into our blindness. He braved the seas of our darkness to come to us. Why? So that he could share with us his own communion with his Father in the Spirit, and we could know the Father with him, and taste and feel and experience life in his embrace.

---

[1] This essay summarizes parts of my book, *Across All Worlds: Jesus Christ Inside Our Darkness* (Vancouver: Regent College Publishers, 2007).

BLIND AS BATS

> The natural person does not accept the things of the Spirit of God, for they are folly to him, and he is not able to understand them, because they are spiritually discerned.
>
> St Paul (1 Cor. 2:14)

I will come back to the stunning truth that Jesus Christ shares himself and all he is and has with us, and to what such a gift means to us in our lives, but we cannot get there until we think hard on something else. When Jesus says, 'No one knows the Father but the Son', he is making a penetrating statement about the problem of sin and reconciliation. Most of us have been trained to think of sin in legal terms as breaking the Ten Commandments. But when Jesus declares 'no one knows the Father but the Son', he is confronting us with a far more devastating notion of sin than that of breaking the law. Let me put it this way: if eternal life is knowing the Father, as Jesus teaches us (Jn 17:3), then eternal death is not knowing the Father, and sin is the cause of our not knowing. Sin has to do with being blind, with being so profoundly wrong-headed that it is *impossible* for us to know the Father.[2]

The biblical story is driven by the love of the Triune God and in this love, by the *relationship* between God on the one side and Adam, Israel, and humanity on the other. In this relationship, the Father speaks. He reveals. He gives. Humanity is thereby summoned to hear, to know and to receive the Father's love. And in hearing the Father's voice, in knowing his affirmation and receiving his love, humanity is quickened with an unearthly assurance that frees us to live and relate, to know and be known, to love and be loved. The life that comes as we know the Father's heart overflows from us into our relationships with one another and with the whole creation.

---

2 My discussion of the fallen mind and the inevitable pain involved in reconciliation grows out of my intense study of the works of Professor T. F. Torrance. One of his greatest contributions to Christian thought, in my opinion, is his steadfast refusal to separate revelation and reconciliation – knowing God and conversion. In holding together the unveiling of God and our need for conversion to perceive the truth, Professor Torrance – along with his brother James – has generated a fresh theological vision and a new series of far-reaching questions. It is not accidental that as we try to think through these issues we find kindred souls in the great leaders of the early church. Of particular importance here are T. F. Torrance's books, *The Mediation of Christ* (Grand Rapids: William B. Eerdmans, 1982), *Space, Time and Resurrection* (Edinburgh: The Handsel Press, 1976), *The Trinitarian Faith* (Edinburgh: T&T Clark, 1988), and his essay 'The Atoning Obedience of Christ' (*Moravian Theological Seminary Bulletin*, 1959, 65–81). For further reading see the writings of Irenaeus and Athanasius and my book, *The Great Dance* (Jackson, MS: Perichoresis Press, 2000 and Vancouver: Regent College Publishers, 2005).

But what happens to us if we cannot hear the Father's voice? What happens to Adam, to Israel, to the human race at large, what happens to the relationships between us and creation if we cannot see his face? What happens if we become so wrong-headed and blind that we cannot possibly know the Father's heart, and thus cannot receive his endless love and believe he will never forsake us?

The great disaster of Adam and Eve was not simply that they sinned or were disobedient to a divine rule. The disaster was that in believing the lie of the evil one they became blind. And by 'blind', I do not mean that they could not see physically. I mean that their perception of reality became skewed, so skewed that they could no longer perceive the real truth about God or about themselves.

Now if we are designed to experience life in knowing the Father's heart, in hearing his voice of affirmation and joy, and in perceiving his lavish embrace, then becoming blind to the Father is the single greatest disaster that could possibly happen to us.

Adam and Eve moved from hearing and knowing and receiving the Father's love to hiding in fear in the bushes. The obvious question is why? Why were they hiding? Clearly they were afraid, but afraid of what? Of course, their hiding comes on the heels of their outright disobedience, and most people would assume that they were afraid of God's punishment. But then again, how could Adam and Eve stand *in the garden*, the recipients of such astonishing blessing, and be afraid of *the Lord*? Had God changed? Had the Lord who created Adam and Eve out of sheer grace and love and poured such astounding blessing upon them, suddenly done an about-turn? Had he ceased to love? Did the Lord transform himself from an eager and lavish philanthropist into a quick-tempered judge? Adam and Eve had no history of disappointment or hurt. There is no record of divine indifference or neglect, and certainly not of rejection and abuse. There is only astonishing and lavish blessing. So why would they suspect that the Lord would hurt them?

Surely Adam's disobedience did not alter the being of God. *Or perhaps it did.* Perhaps God did change, abruptly and radically so, not in reality of course, but in Adam's mind. Could it be that Adam's pain – the pain of his own unfaithfulness – altered his mind? Could it be that Adam's infidelity reconfigured his default settings? Could it be that his failure changed his understanding, his inner vision, his perception of himself, his world and others, but most importantly, did it alter the way he saw the face of God? Could it be that Adam projected his own brokenness on to God's face? Could it be that he tarred the Father's face with the brush of his own angst? Perhaps Adam took a paintbrush, dipped it into the cesspool of his own double-mindedness and guilt, and painted an entirely new picture of god with it. And perhaps it was this god, created by his own darkened imagination – not the Lord – that he feared, and from whom he hid.

How could Adam change God? How could human action of any kind change the being of God? Is the character of God so fickle, so unstable, as to be dependent upon us, or upon what we do or do not do? As my friend, Gary Arinder, says, 'God does not walk around with a thermometer in his hands taking our temperature to see how he feels about himself or about us.' God is God, the same now as always, steadfast in love, unbending in faithfulness, eager and determined to bless and share life, overflowing in grace and mercy and fellowship as Father, Son and Spirit. What changed in the relationship was not God, but Adam, and he now projected his pain on to God, thereby creating an entirely mythological deity, a figment of his own baggage. But this figment was nevertheless frighteningly real *to Adam.*

Standing before this mythological god, this projection, Adam was scared to death. How could he not be? He believed himself to be standing guilty before a divine being who was as unstable as he. Sheer terror struck his soul. For in his fallen mind, he was staring down the gun barrel of utter rejection. In his mythology, he stood a hair's breadth from abandonment and the abyss of non-being.[3]

This is the problem of sin. The impossible has happened: the truth about the Father is eclipsed. The unforgettable love of the Triune God is now forgotten, so forgotten that it is now *inconceivable*. A profound blindness has taken over Adam's mind. His inner vision is now so terribly alienated – *so fallen* – that he no longer has a clear perception of the Father's heart at all. He cannot see the Father's face. And worse, in the place of the Father's heart, his fallen mind invented a new god, a nightmarish mythological deity. There is now a terrible incongruence between the being and character of God as Father, Son and Spirit and the divine being Adam *perceives* and *believes* God to be. And for Adam, and indeed for all of us, the god of our imaginations is the only way God can be. Any other god makes no sense to us.

From this moment, the Father's face will be forever tarred with an alien brush, and his heart, his beauty, his goodness, will be misunderstood. Our darkened imagination will recreate the Father's character in its own image. Our shame will disfigure the Father's heart. The projections of our fear will rewrite the rules of his care.

The human race is lost in the most terrible darkness – the darkness of its own fallen mind, the darkness of wrong belief and unfaithfulness, of anxiety and projection and misperception. Tragically, the fallen mind is

---

3 The phrase 'the abyss of non-being' is from Dr Bruce Wauchope's lecture: 'The Gospel and Mental Health'. This lecture is available at www.perichoresis.org.

consistent. It never fails. Its dark and anxious imagination creates a false deity, the proof of which it sees everywhere it looks. And this god is very, very real to us, so real that it has become quite 'natural' to us, the most obvious thing in the world; it has become the unquestionable truth about divinity, through which we misperceive the heart of the Father without even knowing it.

It would be far easier if sin were indeed a legal matter, for then God could arrange a legal sacrifice to cover our sins and all would be well. But such a view, while quite consistent with the mythology of the fallen mind and its projections, fails to answer the fundamental problem: what kind of forgiving God could be satisfied with having the guilty legally clean, yet so trapped in their wrong-headedness and anxiety that they cannot possibly receive his forgiveness and live in its joy? What kind of reconciliation leaves us in our darkness, hiding in the fear of our mythological deity – utterly blind to the Father's heart and lost to the freedom of his embrace? What kind of reconciliation leaves us at the mercy of generational, cultural and ecclesiastical darkness, with no way to perceive the love of the Father?

I saw an interview once with a man whose daughter had been murdered. The murderer had been caught and tried, and the court had issued the death sentence. The interviewer, scurrying to be first in line to speak with the father, stuck the microphone in his face, and asked, 'Do you feel that justice is at last being served?' Staring a hole straight through the poor interviewer, the father shot back, 'There can never be justice until I get *my daughter back.*'

Jesus's Father is not and never will be satisfied with mere forgiveness or legal reconciliation. How could he be? Such a 'forgiveness' and 'reconciliation' would leave us lost to his heart and hiding from him in our fear. The truth is, however, that Jesus's Father will not rest until his forgiveness has cut a swathe into our pain, until his forgiveness is known in our darkness, received and believed, and issues forth in the restoration of *our* fellowship with him and our forgiveness of others.

Jesus Knows the Father

> For you know the grace of our Lord Jesus, that though he was rich, yet for your sake he became poor, so that you by his poverty you might become rich.
>
> St Paul (2 Cor. 8:9)

Reconciliation is not about Jesus suffering punishment so that the invisible, faceless and nameless god up there somewhere can wipe the legal slate clean. It is about the Father's forgiveness in action, entering into our estrangement and its hell, and penetrating the fundamental problem of sin. As James Torrance would say, 'The Father does not have to be conditioned into being gracious.' There is no sense in which he needs coercing to forgive. Forgiveness is first, overflowing out of the way the Father, Son and Spirit love one another. With this forgiveness rises passion for it to be known and received.

Reconciliation began when the Father saw that his children could not see his heart, and when the Son realized that we could not receive his Father's love, and when the Spirit saw the joy of fellowship with the Father vanish from our lives. Reconciliation is about the Father sending his own Son into our darkness. It is about the Son identifying with us, seeing our god, feeling our fear, experiencing our brokenness. Reconciliation is about the Spirit bridging the horrible gap between the Father's heart and our blindness, as Jesus embraced it in his own being. It is the suffering of the Triune God, righting the doomed ship of our fallen minds, until we know the Father with Jesus in the fellowship of the Spirit.

Reconciliation is the Father's forgiveness determined to become flesh, determined to incarnate itself into our fallen existence to undo our alienation. It is the relationship, the fellowship and communion of the Father, Son and Spirit stepping into our blindness and mythology, into the cesspool of our trauma and wounds so that human perception can be thoroughly converted and the Father's love can be truly known and experienced. The purpose, the aim, the object of reconciliation is not to change God, but to bring *us* into communion with the Father, so that we can know him and his lavish heart, and live life in the baptism of his unearthly assurance.

But how do you penetrate human wrong-headedness? How can the forgiving Father even begin to reach *us* in our darkness? How can he possibly cross the frontiers of our alienation and baggage and bring us to know his heart? Revelation is the obvious answer, but what good is revelation without the healing of our minds? What good is a beautiful painting if we have wrong eyes? Without the conversion of the fallen mind, our 'internal processor' remains broken. So we do not have the capacity to receive the revelation and know the Father. What the Father *says* is one thing, what we *hear* is quite another. The revelation of the Father to us, irrespective of how powerful and clear and inerrant it is from his side, is always perceived through our mental baggage, through our alien and alienating vision, and that revelation is therefore always skewed by our minds.

The fallen mind is a misreading machine. But it is really worse than that. We not only misread the communication of the Father; we take our misreading and build our own vision of god with it. It is inescapable. Out of the very truth revealed to us, our projections manufacture an utterly foreign god. And then, we misuse the word of God itself to prove our own darkened notions of divine being. Revelation itself thus becomes more grist for our mythological mill – divinely sanctioned proof that our conception of god is the truth. We are caught in a hermeneutical nightmare and don't even know it. And the nightmare is so 'natural' to us, we could never entertain even a doubt about its vision of god. Any other vision of god is inconceivable. For the one unquestionable absolute in the universe of our minds is that our notion of god could not possibly be wrong.

How will we ever escape the quagmire of our own fallen minds? How will humanity ever break out of the nightmare and come to know the true Father? How will we ever see the Father as he truly is, and thus begin to live in the assurance and freedom and joy of his embrace? Who can know the Father?

The human plight is truly hopeless. We have only one mind, and it is thoroughly alien to the truth. There is therefore no escape from our own twisted self-referential incoherence. Unable to step out of our own fallen minds we cannot push our mythological projection to the side and get a true vision of the Father's heart. And even if we could, we would never believe it. It would be too incredible, too foreign, too strange, too good to accept. Face to face with the outright impossibility of our knowing the Father and the misery-producing doom of living life in the absence of his unearthly assurance, we are poised to appreciate the blessed Trinity and the shocking reality of the incarnation of the Father's eternal Son.

The reality of the Trinitarian life of God means there is hope for the human race trapped in its alien and alienating vision. The hermeneutical nightmare is not the end of the story. For there is one who truly knows the Father and shares all things with him in the fellowship of the Spirit. There is one whose default settings are not alien to the Father's heart, one who knows the Father as he is, one who sees his face and experiences his lavish love. There is one who believes. *Imagine:* what if this one entered into our darkness? What if this Son became human? What if this Son stepped into the gnarled and twisted world of the fallen Adamic mind?

I do not mean, 'What if the Son became human in order to reveal the Father to us?' Such revelation is, of course, absolutely critical, but in itself revelation alone does not solve the problem. For we are blind and cannot receive it. And worse, as we have seen, our twisted minds turn the revelation of the Father into proof of our false god. But what if the Father's Son stepped into Adam's skin, put on Adam's fallen eyes and *received* the revelation of the Father for us? And what if he used our twisted darkness to do so?

The Shocker

The child who played with the moon and stars, waves a snatch of hay in a common barn.
In the lonely house of Adam's fall, lies a child, just a child that's all.

(Pierce Pettis)

This, of course, is exactly what happened in the shocking reality of the incarnation. The eternal Son of the Father became flesh. He entered into our human existence, into the far country of our profound blindness. Jesus Christ did not come to change God. He came to identify with us, to stand on our side of the mess, to see what we see in our blindness and shame. He did not come to camp out on the frontiers of our great darkness and shout across the chasm. He came to experience the hell of Adam's alien vision, and thus to establish a bridgehead between his communion with his Father and the human race in its tragic mythology.

The miracle of the incarnation is that the Son of the Father stepped not only into human existence, in some abstract sense, but into the quagmire of Adam's fallen mind, into his skewed vision, and into the traumatic existence of his mythology. As the Gospel teaches, the Word became not only human, but *flesh* (Jn 1:14). Jesus stood in our place, in our pitiful darkness, and feeling our shame, found his way inside our damaged, projecting, mythological deity-creating self-image. Whatever it was that Adam painted on to the Father's face, and whatever it was that he felt when he did so, Jesus Christ saw and felt, and he saw it and felt it with the same intensity and reality as Adam.[4]

The eternal Son of the Father truly entered the fallen world – and he did not come with a cloaking device to shield him from our suffering. He came to experience our tragedy for himself. So he embraced the world where his Father's face has been tarred with the brush of human pain, the mythological world where the Father's eyes have been painted with indifference and disgust, judgement and rejection. Refusing to watch from a safe distance, the Father's Son invaded our darkness and alienation, where our fallen minds have created a pagan god so real to us that it would never cross our minds to question its character, and where we sabotage our lives in living out of this vision in self-protecting fear, hiding and brokenness.

'My God, my God, why have you forsaken me?'[5] Who has cried this cry?

---

4 For a fuller treatment of the work of Christ, see my *Jesus and the Undoing of Adam* (Jackson: Perichoresis Press, 2003) as well as *The Great Dance*.
5 Ps. 22:1; Mt. 27:46. For a more extended discussion of this cry from Jesus on the cross, see Thomas F. Torrance, *Theology in Reconstruction* (London: SCM Press, 1965), 123–6, Torrance, *Mediation of Christ*, 42–5, and my *Jesus and the Undoing of Adam*, 58ff.

Is this not the cry of Adam, blind and trembling in the bushes? Is this not the unspeakable fear of every human heart trapped in the great darkness, with no true vision of the Father? And is this not the terrifying hell that Jesus embraced, the withering, appalling, gut-wrenching pain of our perceived rejection by god?

Jesus saw Adam's god, the unstable, quick-tempered judge, eagerly watching every move from the infinite distance of a disapproving heart. He saw this god with Adam's eyes. Under the shame of our angst-ridden imaginations, mocked by the endless misperception of the self-righteous and the ridicule of the all-seeing religious eye, Jesus met Adam's god, our god, the god of the fallen mind. He identified with us. He heard the haunting, harassing whisper, 'I am not acceptable, not good enough, not important', and felt the bitter curse of its judgement. With the leaves of the garden rustling with the rumour of our failure, he stared into the terrifying shadows of rejection and abandonment. Clothed in Adamic humanity, pierced with the brutal loneliness of universal rejection, he stood speechless before the refrain of the lie: *'I am not acceptable. I am not good enough. I am separated from God – the proof is everywhere.'*

From the cradle to the grave, Jesus Christ was one of us, seeing what we see, feeling what we feel, knowing what we know, and even more. Baptized in the terrible insecurity of our cloud of unknowing, afflicted with our conscience, pestered by the whisper of evil – and damned by his own people – Jesus experienced what we never dare allow ourselves to face. Standing alone before absolute rejection, he squared off against the invisible arms of non-being as they snatched for his untethered soul.

HE FOUND THE FATHER

But – and the existence and destiny of the universe hang on this *but* – Jesus Christ refused to believe a word of it. Face to face with Adam's god, feeling the hair rise on the back of Adam's neck, crushed under the weight of the crowd's rejection, Jesus steadfastly refused to acknowledge this god or this world and its verdict, or this future, as real at all. Stepping into the fallen world of Adam, he absolutely refused to be 'fallen' in it. The one who knows the Father embraced the gnarled and twisted world of our darkness and pain, where the whisper of evil and the fear of rejection, the threat of abandonment and cosmic loneliness, self-serving betrayal and the blindness of the crowd utterly rule and dominate the human scene. There, Jesus – the good shepherd, accused of leading the sheep astray; the anointed one, accused of being possessed by evil; the Father's true Son mocked as a bastard and rejected – there, Jesus took his stand. Against the whole world, he fought his way through the trenches of our delusion, through the terrorizing jungles of our tragic nightmare, through the sneering, hostile judgement of his own people, to find his Father's face. Inside Adam's skin, peering through our wrong eyes, seeing the unstable watcher, feeling the trauma of the world's insanity, Jesus found his Father and his lavish embrace in the fellowship of the Spirit.

Reconciliation is not about changing God. It is about the Father's Son entering the darkness and so suffering its pain that a personal relationship, a living union is formed between our tragic blindness and the Father's heart.

The revelation of the Father's heart, so disfigured by the projections of anxious humanity, found a reconciling foothold in the fallen mind assumed by the incarnate Son. He refused to believe in the god of Adam. In the teeth of our wrong belief and projections, restless with our anxiety and hopelessness, baptized with our insecurity, bearing the pain of our panic-stricken souls, he incarnated his own knowledge of the Father. Inside the hell of our fallen mind and the hell it makes of the world and relationships, the Son was steadfastly faithful to himself as the Father's Son. He believed. Standing alone and condemned, feeling the affliction of the whisper, experiencing the shame of the system's sneer, he fought through the darkness, the pain, the rejection, the veil of unknowing, the mythology and its trauma, and experienced his Father's love.

At every point, through fire and trial and tribulation, through condemnation and shame, through fears without and within, he broke through the great darkness into the knowledge of the Father. At every level of human despair, Jesus found his Father and the healing fellowship of his embrace in the Spirit. He loved the Father with all his heart, soul, mind and strength. This is the miracle of the reconciling love of the Father in the incarnate life, death, resurrection and ascension of his beloved Son. The one who knows the Father embraced our darkness, using our own bitter rejection of himself as the way to penetrate deeper and deeper into our estrangement.

How could this be? How could the eternally beloved Son of the Father truly enter into our blindness and fear and insecurity? How could *he* step into Adam's mythological world and take on our baggage and skewed vision? How could the Father's Son, who lives face to face with the Father himself, assume Adam's fallen mind, riddled with its pagan god, its insecurities and pain, its fear of rejection, its self-centredness and endless hiding? How could this Son suffer the condemnation of the world? Herein lies the paradox of the incarnation and the very meaning of reconciliation.

The incarnation of the Son of God means nothing short of the incarnation of the communion of the Father, Son and Spirit, and it means the incarnation of the Trinitarian fellowship precisely in the mythological world where our communion has been shattered with impossibility. The beloved Son lived out his own sonship, his own unbroken fellowship with his Father, inside our hell. The sheer beauty of his relationship with his Father exposed us all as empty, sad and broken. His life in the Spirit revealed our religion to be dead. His goodness stripped away our pretence. We hated him for it. We rejected him and ridiculed his heart. We made him the scapegoat for all our ills.

'Crucify him! Crucify him!' (Mk 15:13–14; Jn 19:6). This is the universal verdict of the 'natural' mind. For 33 years Jesus experienced our abuse. He experienced the venomous pain of our hostile indifference and our rejection. He used this experience as the way of incarnation. He used it to 'hammer out', as J. B. Torrance would say, his own knowledge of the Father, 'on the anvil' of our terrible brokenness. Clinging to his Father's love and to the witness of the Spirit, Jesus *suffered* the incarnation of the Trinitarian communion into the hell of our alienated human existence. Instead of retaliating, instead of returning our anger and rejection with his own anger and rejection, Jesus embraced our enmity. He faced, endured and accepted our anger, and in doing so he established a real relationship between the Trinitarian life he lives and the human race at its absolute worst.

Reconciliation is not a theoretical doctrine; it is not even news. Reconciliation is the relationship established between the Triune God and the human race in Jesus through his own painful incarnation. In this impossible union between the Son who knows the Father and the human race so violently lost in the darkness, lies the mystery of the incarnation and of reconciliation – and the hope of the human race.

There is one who knows the Father. There is one from our broken and twisted world of wrong belief and projecting fear who sees the Father's face and believes. There is one from our terrifying nightmare, one from the cold silence of the great darkness, one from the hell of human betrayal who knows the unearthly assurance of the Father's heart. The dark and traumatic and fallen world of Adam's mythology has been invaded and experienced, exposed and shattered in Jesus Christ. He knows the Father in the deepest recesses of our hell.

What If?

> I am the light of the world. Whoever follows me will not walk in darkness, but will have the light of life.
>
> Jesus (Jn 8:12)

There was no rest in the Father's heart until one inside the pain of Adam's tragic darkness came to know the truth about him, and to taste and feel and experience his passionate, unflinching love. This is why the Son of God became human. He came to know his Father and life in his embrace, as he has always known him and experienced that life, but now from inside our pain and wounds and fear.

At this very hour, one from the hell of Adam's traumatizing mythology sits at the Father's right hand. He sees not through brokenness and baggage, he sees clearly, face to face with the Father himself. And what does Jesus Christ see in the Father's eyes? What does he know? What does he feel? What does he experience?

Is it hopelessness? Is it fear? Is Jesus scared? Does Jesus feel that he sits beside a father who is cold, detached and indifferent, whose disapproving heart watches every move he makes? Is the fundamental truth of the Father's heart toward his Son that of a judge? Does Jesus hear 'I am not acceptable, not important, not of any value', whispering through the halls of heaven? Does he struggle, hoping against hope that the Ogre will have a good hair day and overlook his failures? Does he see the world's scoffing verdict reflected in the Father's face?

Think about it. Think about it long and hard. What does Jesus Christ experience at the Father's right hand? Are his knuckles white, grasping the spider's web as he dangles over the flames of hell? Is Jesus exhausted from hiding, from pretending, from keeping appearances up? Is he weary with the fear of it all, wondering if today the faceless, all-powerful potentate will finally leave him on the edge of the abyss, banished from his presence and abandoned forever?

Think of the incarnate Son right now, sitting at the Father's side. Can you not see *how* the Father *loves* his Son? Can you not see his sheer delight? Think of the Father's heart. Think of how he looks at his Son. What do you see in the Father's eyes? Think of how his words, his touch, his embrace, are filled with pride. 'Thou art *my beloved Son*, in whom *my soul delights.*'[6] What does Jesus know? What does Jesus experience in the Father's presence? Does the condemnation of the world carry weight at the Father's right hand? How could Jesus be afraid?

There is no whispering at the Father's side. There the shame of the blind is silenced and the darkness has no voice. Jesus is the apple of the Father's eye, and he knows it. In his Father's eyes he sees no hesitance or neutrality or indifference. His Father loves. Jesus knows no fear for today or tomorrow. Unearthly assurance baptizes every nook and cranny of Jesus's soul as he sees the Father's face in the fellowship of the Spirit. At his Father's right hand, looking into eyes filled with ancient love, the

---

6 Mk 1:11, Lk. 3:22, author's translation.

beloved Son knows the sheer hope and freedom of the Father's passionate embrace.

Now, what if this Son turned and shared himself and his mind with you? What if Jesus reached into his own soul, as it were, and took his own spiritual knowledge of the Father's heart and gave it to you, put it in your soul? What if he were able to penetrate our projections and share his own perception with us in our fallenness? This is where the gift Jesus gives to the human race is far greater than any religion. This is the stunning turn in the history of human existence.

The good news of Jesus Christ is not that at last we have an accurate religious manual to follow and a master leader to show us the way. And it is not that we finally have perfect information about God to learn. The gospel is about Jesus himself. He *knows* the Father. And the gospel is about the stunning fact that the Father's Son has established a real relationship with us in our darkness. And in this relationship, he is sharing with us – with the world – his own mind and knowing, his own communion with his Father, forever. What a gracious, merciful brother. He bears our sneers, suffers our hostility, and returns for them his own knowledge of the Father's heart.

Remember, we are wired to experience life in fellowship with the Father and in soul knowledge of his delight. But we have only one mind, and it is utterly blind to the Father. We cannot push the weeds of our fallenness to the side and see the Father's heart. Left to ourselves, we have no option but to live in our own broken notions of god and the hell they create. We are imprisoned in the dungeon of our mythology where our god cannot be trusted, and the one thing we know for sure is that we are not good enough, not acceptable, not important. But what if Jesus Christ has found his way into our world? What if he could step into our hurt, our anger and rejection? What if he could penetrate our denial and share his own knowledge of the Father's heart with us? What if Jesus could steal behind the watchful dragons[7] of our mythology and share himself with us?

Herein lies the very heart of the gospel of Jesus Christ, and of reconciliation itself. He has known the Father from all eternity, and he also knows the Father from inside our tragic nightmare. The gospel is the news that this Jesus is now sharing *himself* with you and me, and indeed with the world – *inside our darkness.* That is the only reason there is any sanity in our world at all.

---

7 The imagery of 'watchful dragons' comes from C. S. Lewis' essay, 'Sometimes Fairy Stories Say Best What's to be Said', in his *On Stories and Other Essays on Literature*, ed. Walter Hooper (New York: Harcourt Brace & Company, 1982), 47. I am grateful to Cary Stockett for sharing the image with me.

Jesus knows the trauma of being human in a fallen world. He walked into the darkness, where we cower, where we fight to pretend all is right, where we busy ourselves to avoid hearing, where we frantically grasp at anything to find relief – and where we condemn any hint of our exposure. In the place where we can find no hope, no solace, where we see no possibility of tomorrow, he faced the sleepless demons and their accusing shadows. Staring into the lifeless eyes of the abyss, Jesus threw himself headlong into the jaws of our greatest fear. Free-falling in the darkness of Adam's mind, Jesus found the unfailing arms of his Father.

Is there a place in our darkness that does not bear his footprints? Where could we go that he has not been? What pain could we suffer that he has not known, and learned the hope of his Father's love within? Think this through. Is there a wound so deep that it cannot be reached by Jesus with his knowledge of the Father? Is there an abuse so traumatic, a betrayal so brutal, a rejection so personal, as to be beyond the experience of Jesus Christ himself and his healing light?

Are we unreachable in our brokenness? Is our darkness impenetrable? Is there a corner of the abyss of non-being that Jesus overlooked? What is there about our hell that is beyond Jesus Christ? What whisper has he not heard? What shame, what injustice, what rejection, what condemnation has he not felt? Is there a single leaf in our broken and mythological world that Jesus Christ has left unturned? Through living, through fire and trial, through hands-on experience of the great darkness, through suffering the abusive condemnation of the human race, through finding his Father in the hell of the human plight, Jesus has received the love of the Father into the fallen Adamic mind. He has received the anointing of the Spirit into every form of human brokenness. Is Jesus not now the most seasoned prophet in the universe? Does he not know how to minister the Father's heart to us where we are? Is he not able to share his Spirit with us in the darkest corners of our fear?

The gospel is the news that Jesus became what we are, and within our fear-twisted world of whispers, of darkness and rejection, he fought his way forward into the vision of the Father's heart. *He knows the Father.* With Adam's eyes, he sees the Father's face and knows the unearthly assurance of his embrace, and the sheer joy of his heart. The unspeakable communion of the Father, Son and Spirit has pitched its tent inside our hell itself – forever. But that is only the beginning of the gospel. For this Jesus, in his stunning grace, is now sharing what he knows with us. He is not huddling in the corner of the tent with his Father. Our hell has become his heaven. The darkness has become his light. He is free to be himself as the Father's Son and the anointed one in our world of illusion. 'The light shines in the darkness' (Jn 1:5). 'Take courage; I have overcome the cosmos' (Jn 16:33).

Is this a polite theological dream? Is this another chapter of our religious romanticism? Could God be this good? Could we be so wrong? What if it is so? What if Jesus is this good? What if he is already out of the tent? What if he has already stolen behind the watchful dragons? What if he is not waiting for us to clean up our acts and invite him into our world? What if he has already accepted us as we are, already met us in our shattered lives? What if he is already walking through our fallen minds, already sharing himself with us? Could it be that there is far more going on in our lives than we ever dared dream? Could it be that we are now included in his knowledge of the Father?

The gospel is not the news that you can be involved with Jesus, if only you get your religion right. The gospel is not news of what *can be* at all. It is news of what *is*. It is the news that you *are* involved. It is not a dream. Through bearing our rejection, Jesus has access to us in our darkness. Indeed, he used our rejection to establish a relationship with us at our very worst. The stunning truth is that Jesus exists in union with his Father and the Spirit, *and with us in our darkness.* He has included us in his world, in his life and communion with his Father, in his anointing with the Spirit. He is sharing his own heart, his own knowledge of the Father, his own assurance and hope and joy with us all. He is putting his communion with his Father inside our own endarkened souls.

It is not a question of whether or not we are worthy of such a gift or whether or not we have earned his grace. It is a question of his abounding love and of his prophetic skill – born in the crucible of our blindness and abuse – to reach us in our darkness. He is an expert at knowing his Father in our hell. He accepts us and meets us where we are, and he is sharing himself with us in our brokenness and sin.

Do you know who you are and what is going on in your life? Do you know that you are the one Jesus loves, you are the one the Father has determined to come to know his heart? It is not about you inviting Jesus into your life; it is about Jesus already including you in his. Through his suffering he has forged a living union between his communion with his Father and you in your darkness. Jesus dwells in your darkness. He is sharing himself with you now. He always has been and always will. He will never stop giving himself, his mind and heart and soul, to you. He is passionate about your coming to know his Father with him and living life in the freedom of the Spirit of adoption. This is the non-negotiable of the grace of the Triune God.

THE COMMAND OF RECONCILIATION

We belong to the Father, Son and Spirit. We always have, and always will. It is this blessed fact, this truth that in Jesus Christ the Father has established an abiding relationship with us in the Spirit, that tells us who we are and why we are here. We have a beautiful life to live. We are included in the Trinitarian life of God. It is ours for ever, as much our life as it is the life of the Father, Son and Spirit. Our place at the Father's table is eternal, as eternal as Jesus's own relationship with his Father. This is the truth, the real world, the ways things are and forever will be.

Written into the truth, and into the knowledge of the Father's love that Jesus himself is sharing with you, is the command of faith: 'Trust me. Dare to doubt your vision of god. Believe in my Father and his love.' And with the command of faith is the summons of freedom: 'Get up, stand on your feet, and live in the joy of my knowledge of the Father's heart.'

Implicit in the truth, its command to faith and its summons to freedom is a serious warning. For at every point we are free to deny the truth and cling to our own way of seeing. We are free to live in our own worlds and to impose our illusions upon others – or try. Such a non-relational world is utterly foreign to who we are, but we can live in this world, dooming ourselves to suffer the consequences of hanging on to our projecting fear and the god of our imaginations. But why? Why choose such a broken existence? Why choose the tragic and miserable hell of belonging to the Trinitarian world and yet insisting on living in our own? Why oppose such a Father? Why resist Jesus?

The great irony is that it is Jesus Christ alone who enters into our dark worlds and walks with us in them. No other person truly can or will. He meets us in our fallen minds. I hear his words this way:

> I, Jesus, the one who has been there, the one who understands your darkness, the one who has cried your cries, tasted your shame, felt your fears, the one who has seen your god and his rejection, I embrace you and take responsibility for finding a reconciling foothold in your fallen mind. As I walk into your alienation and share myself with you, my knowledge of the Father's heart commands you to rise and live. I will walk with you in your world of darkness. I will bear your scorn. I will jump with you into the abyss of non-being, so that you can know that it is not, and never has been, and never will be real at all, so that you can know that there is only the Father's embrace.

You can see now why the New Testament is so full of the summons to repent and believe in Jesus. We are so confused and lost in the darkness.

But Jesus is sharing himself with us, and in so doing he commands us to a vast reinterpretation of our own existence. We are not rejected. We are not separated from God. The Father loves us with an endless love, and he has found us in his Son. This is what repentance is all about; it is a radical change of mind, a thoroughgoing reorientation of the way *we perceive* God himself and his heart, of the way we perceive ourselves and others. Jesus shares his mind with us and commands us to put aside our own judgement. He is not asking us to be brainless or to give up our own minds; he is telling us that our default settings are dead wrong, and that they are killing us. In staggering grace, Jesus has made us part of his world and his life with his Father and Spirit. He is commanding us to see what he sees, to believe with him, to participate in his way of seeing his Father. He gives us his own faith and summons us to accept it and live in it. He shares his own unearthly assurance with us and commands us to rest.

What will happen to us when our fallen minds are restructured by the faith and knowledge of Jesus Christ – when, as Paul says, 'we all come to the unity of the faith and of the knowledge of the Son of God' (Eph. 4:13)? What will happen to us when we know as we are known (1 Cor. 13:12)? What will happen to our relationships with one another, and with the whole creation, when Jesus's knowledge of the Father's heart has free reign in our souls? What will happen when he teaches us to be seasoned veterans in finding his Father's love in every twisted form of darkness?

Jesus crosses all the worlds of our unknowing and meets us in our mythology. He is not afraid of our darkness. He dwells there in the freedom of the Spirit. He shares his light and life and love with us. What will happen to you when Jesus proves himself the seasoned prophet, the true and faithful witness, when he finds his reconciling foothold in your darkness? What will happen to you when you say, 'Amen, come, Lord Jesus'? What will happen to you as you give him permission to walk through the corridors of your soul with his peace and to restructure your default settings in his light?

Consider this prayer:

Lord Jesus Christ, beloved, eternal, and faithful Son of the Father incarnate, thank you for sharing your knowledge of the Father's heart with me. Come into my darkness with your light. Search out my blindness and share your unearthly assurance with me in the place of my deepest fears. Find all my broken parts and bathe them with your Father's love. Send your Spirit to baptize my soul with your peace.

What will happen to us as we pray this prayer? What will happen to our god, to the mythological deity we fear? What will happen to our fear and our terrible insecurity, to our hiding, our hesitant spirit, to our greed and lust and lethargy? What will happen to our self-centredness and broken relationships? Will chaos abound? Will we be destroyed? Of course not. We will have, we will taste, we will know, we will feel the unearthly assurance of Jesus Christ himself as he sits at the Father's right hand. In the place of our unspeakable fear and its debilitating fruit, we will know the unutterable love of the Father, Son and Spirit. And such soul knowledge will set us free to live life in the Father's embrace, and the life and relationship of the Father, Son and Spirit will overflow into our relationships with one another and with all creation. The Son's knowledge of his Father in the Spirit will cover the earth as the waters cover the sea (Isa. 11:9; Hab. 2:14).

ABOUT THE AUTHORS

David Torrance is a retired minister in the Church of Scotland. With his brother, Tom, he edited *Calvin's New Testament Commentaries* and with his brothers Tom and James, co-authored *A Passion for Christ: The Vision that Ignites Ministry*.

Andrew Purves is the Hugh Thompson Kerr Professor of Pastoral Theology at Pittsburgh Theological Seminary. He is the author of *Reconstructing Pastoral Theology: A Christological Foundation*.

Elmer Colyer is Professor of Historical Theology and Stanley Professor of Wesley Studies at the University of Dubuque Theological Seminary. He is the author of *How To Read T. F. Torrance*.

Gerrit Dawson is pastor of the First Presbyterian Church of Baton Rouge, Louisiana. He is the author of *Jesus Ascended: The Meaning of Christ's Continuing Incarnation*.

Douglas Kelly is the Jordan Professor of Systematic Theology at Reformed Theological Seminary in Charlotte, NC. He is the author of the forthcoming *The God Who Is: The Holy Trinity*.

Alan Torrance is Professor of Systematic Theology at St Mary's College of the University of St Andrews, and the author of *Persons in Communion: Trinitarian Description and Human Participation*.

Graham Redding is the Principal of the School of Ministry at Knox College in Dunedin, New Zealand and author of *Prayer and the Priesthood of Christ*.

Gary Deddo is Associate Editor for Academic Books at InterVarsity Press and author of *Karl Barth's Theology of Relations: Trinitarian, Christological, and Human.*

C. Baxter Kruger is the Director of Perichoresis Ministries, an international ministry sharing the good news of our adoption in Christ with the world, based in Jackson, MS. He is the author of *Across All Worlds: Jesus Christ Inside Our Darkness.*

INDEX

Adam 86, 158–60, 163
  Adamic humanity 56, 165
  Second Adam 119
Alienation 4, 7, 40, 53, 67, 162
Anderson, Ray 136
Antinomianism 144
Arian Denial of Christ 128
Aristotelian ontology 143
Assurance 11, 19–20, 80, 163, 167–71
Athanasius 30, 53, 76, 83, 85, 158
Atonement 4, 30–2
  Atonement, external or juridical 31, 40–3, 70
  Atonement, incarnational 34–8, 50–3
  Atonement, Limited 12, 32, 53–4, 109, 117
  Atoning exchange 50–3, 71, 147
Augustine 65
autotheos 85

Bailey, Kenneth 113
Barth, Karl 1, 3, 28, 88
Basil 66, 69, 84
Belonging 105, 116–18
Boettner, Lorraine 64
Bonhoeffer, Dietrich 23–5
Boston, Thomas 111
Brink, Emily 127, 131
Bruce, Robert 2, 30
Bultmann, Rudolph 6, 88, 94

Calvin, John 3, 16, 62, 111, 127, 141
  and Christ as the scope of the Bible 3
  form of prayer 132
  internal testimony of the Holy Spirit 89
  whole course of his obedience 56
  wonderful exchange 7, 51–3, 62, 115, 147
Campbell, John McLeod 31
Contextualization 123, 125, 127
Contract 103–7
Covenant 12, 103–7
Cross 45, 60–3, 72, 81, 130, 146

Dawn, Marvin 131
Default settings 159, 163, 173

Einstein, Albert 11, 95, 99
Epistemology 10, 75, 78
Erskine, Thomas 56

Father, Son and Holy Spirit
  blindness to 157, 162
  communion of 157, 162, 166
  eternal joy of 100
  mutual knowing 87
Father, the 20, 28, 109–10
  Heart 157–9, 160, 163, 166, 168–70
  Love of 112, 116
  Son's worship of 127, 175
Filioque controversy 85

Grace
  Imperatives and Indicatives   106, 151–2,
  Unconditional   12
Gregory of Nazianzus   33, 68, 84

Hermeneutical nightmare   20, 157, 163
Hilary of Poitiers   70, 81
Holy Spirit   6, 18, 56
  Participation   7, 16, 116, 148
  Union with Christ   11, 44, 57, 87, 99, 138–43, 173
homoousios   49, 83, 141
Human freedom   32
Hypostatic union   3, 10–11, 38, 78, 81–3, 99

Idealism   96–9
Incarnation   3, 6, 25–7, 28–31, 35–9, 42, 44, 50n, 53, 56–7, 61, 65, 71–2, 87, 91, 95, 98, 140–1, 143, 146, 163–7
Incarnational Redemption   33, 51–4, 61n
Irenaeus   52, 60n, 86, 117, 137n, 158n

Jesus Christ
  Ascension   9–10, 41, 43, 45, 50–1, 56–7, 61n, 129, 146, 166
  Assumed fallen humanity   7, 39–45, 56, 63, 71–4, 141, 164–7
  Continuing ministry   17–18, 145–7, 156
  Cry of Dereliction   9, 37, 43–4, 48–9, 69, 72–4, 164–5
  leitourgos   127, 147
  Priesthood   9, 16–18, 37, 42–3, 50, 61, 63, 66, 72, 115–17, 127–34
  Resurrection   9, 42, 46, 55, 57, 61n, 78, 94
  Temptation   8, 37, 43, 52, 64–5, 67, 106
  Union with us   7, 50, 61–2, 141

Vicarious humanity, sacrifice, or worship   4, 5–6, 8n, 18, 30–1, 37, 45–6, 85–6, 115, 129–30, 153
Word became flesh   26–7, 29, 45, 164
Justice   17, 41, 70, 110, 135
Justification   40, 44, 71, 102, 136, 141–2

Kirkpatrick, Cathy   123
Knox, John   10, 16, 30, 127, 130

Legalism   153
Lord's Supper   45, 129–30
  Converting ordinance   112, 114
  Faithful transmission   124
Luther, Martin   2, 76, 137, 140–1

Mackintosh, H. R.   29, 34n, 85
MacMurray, John   14
Maxwell, James Clerk   11, 95, 99
Missional Church   136
Mythological world   164, 166, 170

Nominalism   96–9

Old Testament Sacrificial system   45–8

Participation in Christ   44, 53, 106, 116, 135–7, 139, 144–5, 146n, 147–8, 150–2
Pierson, Mark   123–4
Polanyi, Michael   11, 93, 101
Priesthood of all believers   *see* Jesus Christ
Priesthood of Christ   *see* Jesus Christ
Priestly aspect of redemption   47

Reconciliation   11, 79–83, 115–16, 153, 158, 161–2, 166–7, 172
  Atoning   5, 33, 40, 43–8, 50–3, 72, 82
  In Christ's person   8, 43

Real, The 100
Realism, Christian 75, 97
Repentance 13–14, 52, 106, 118, 147, 153, 173
  Evangelical vs. Legal, 111–14
  Summons to 172
Revelation 10–11, 14, 16, 21, 34, 76–7, 79–82, 87, 89, 98, 158n, 162–3
Riddell, Mike 123

Science 75–8
  How we know from science 89–93
  Methodology 92
Service 17–20, 145–50
Sin 4, 8, 36–8, 58–9, 64–6, 79–83, 161
  Mystery of 4, 32
Soteriological reserve 32
Stewart, James 141
Suffering Servant 45, 49–50, 60–2, 107–8
Sweet, Leonard 123, 127

theopoiesis 51
Trinity
  Doctrine of 11, 83–5
  Perichoretic relations 84, 87
  Trinitarian Formula 110

Trinitarian Self-Revelation 33
Triune God revealed in Jesus Christ 124

Unassumed is the unhealed 68
Union with Christ 6–7, 16–18, 32, 44, 61, 65, 86–8, 138–45
  Sharing in the Son's union with the Father in
  The Spirit 140
Universal range of atonement 53, 61n
Universalism 54

Walker, Robert 78
Watts, Issac 58
Wesley, John 40, 112
Westminster Standards 28, 88, 124
Who?, The Question 3, 23–6, 137, 154
WIJD? What is Jesus Doing? 18, 148
Witvliet, John 127, 131–2
Worship 15, 121–34
  Ambassador for Christ 124
  Christ as leader 127
  Curator of 123
  Participation in Christ's worship 115–16
  Trinitarian 16, 115, 127–9

copy
3/4 up ↑
→ half